URBANIZATION OF THE EARTH
URBANISIERUNG DER ERDE

5

Urbanization of the Earth 5
Urbanisierung der Erde

Edited by Dr. Wolf Tietze, Helmstedt

Frank J. Costa, Ashok K. Dutt,
Laurence J. C. Ma and Allen G. Noble

Asian Urbanization:
Problems and Processes

GEBRÜDER BORNTRAEGER · BERLIN · STUTTGART · 1988

Asian Urbanization
Problems and Processes

by

Prof. Frank J. Costa, Prof. Ashok K. Dutt,
Prof. Laurence J. C. Ma, and Prof. Dr. Allen G. Noble

With 53 figures and 21 tables in the text

GEBRÜDER BORNTRAEGER · BERLIN · STUTTGART · 1988

Front cover: Varanasi (Benares), the Ghats on River Ganga
Photo by Wolf Tietze

Authors' Addresses:
Prof. Frank J. Costa, Center for Urban Studies,
Prof. Ashok K. Dutt,
Prof. Laurence J. C. Ma,
Prof. Dr. Allen G. Noble, Department of Geography,
University of Akron,
Akron, Ohio 44325, USA

ISBN 3-443-37007-1

Preface

The studies which are presented in this volume are outgrowths of papers presented at the First International Conference on Asian Urbanization held at The University of Akron, Akron, Ohio in April, 1985. The editors of the volume were the co-chairmen of that conference. Each of the authors of the chapters presented in this volume are recognized scholars and authorities on the urbanization of parts of Asia. Most have resided for varying periods of time in Asia and bring to this work an intimate familiarity with Asian urban conditions.

With the population of the world now in excess of five billion, with three-fifths of the world's population in Asia, and with the cities usually offering the best opportunities for economic support of this burgeoning population, it seems timely to offer a collection of expert views and analyses of the processes, results and implications of Asian urbanization.

The editors have been fortunate to have had the benefit of the assistance of several highly skilled and efficient persons in producing this volume. Judy Sherman produced the typeset copy, Barbara Hajek created the tables, Arlene Lane and Hildra Kendron typed many of the original manuscripts, M. Margaret Geib redrafted several illustrations, Sonna James did the layout for the volume in The University of Akron Laboratory for Cartographic and Spatial Analysis under the general supervision of Deborah King. None of these competent individuals complained about the burdens of working with no less than four editors. We are also most grateful to Dr. Wolf Tietze, Editor-in-Chief of the internationally known journal, *GeoJournal*, for recognizing the worth of this volume at an early stage of the project.

Table of Contents

List of Contributors

Bilkis Banu
University of Akron
Akron, Ohio, USA

John E. Brush
Rutgers University
New Brunswick, New Jersey, USA

Kenneth E. Corey
University of Maryland
College Park, Maryland, USA

Frank J. Costa
University of Akron
Akron, Ohio, USA

Ashok K. Dutt
University of Akron
Akron, Ohio, USA

Norton Ginsburg
East-West Center
Honolulu, Hawaii, USA

Jack Huddleston
University of Wisconsin
Madison, Wisconsin, USA

Meera Kosambi
University of Stockholm
Stockholm, Sweden

Laurence J. C. Ma
University of Akron
Akron, Ohio, USA

Charles B. Monroe
University of Akron
Akron, Ohio, USA

Sudesh Nangia
Jawaharlal Nehru University
New Delhi, India

Allen G. Noble
University of Akron
Akron, Ohio, USA

Bernard L. Panditharatne
University of Peredeneya
Kandy, Sri Lanka

Ved Prakash
University of Wisconsin
Madison, Wisconsin, USA

Neil E. Sealey
College of the Bahamas
Nassau, Bahamas

Bruce Taylor
Chinese University of Hong Kong
Hong Kong

William A. Withington
University of Kentucky
Lexington, Kentucky, USA

List of Figures

List of Figures (Continued)

List of Tables

Divergent Paths and Policy Responses in Asian Urbanization and Planning

Frank J. Costa, Ashok K. Dutt, Laurence J.C. Ma, and Allen G. Noble

Asia is a vast continent containing an immense diversity of nations. All aspects of the human social, political and economic conditions are visible in Asian countries. Economic progress and opportunity co-exist with economic backwardness and despair. The living conditions of the people of Asia range from the internationally-envied affluence of the Japanese through the rapidly rising living standards enjoyed by the people of the Pacific Rim nations of South Korea, Taiwan, Hong Kong, Malaysia and Singapore to the abject and ever deepening poverty of the people of Bangladesh and Kampuchea. Political organization varies from pluralistic democracies to oppressive military dictatorships and ideologically driven single party states.

Everywhere in Asia, however, one factor is present and that is population expansion and its corollary of urban growth. Although Asia is the least urbanized of continents, its vast area and population have created the largest number of major urban agglomerations in the world. Asian nations have responded to the rapid growth of their cities and urban regions with a wide range of political and economic measures. In analyzing these divergent national responses two important factors are dominant. These are the political systems and related economic systems within each national society. The varying mixtures of political and economic institutions are schematically presented in Figure 1.1, *Dominant Political-Economic Systems in Asian Nations*. The range of institutional arrangements finds its parallel and, indeed, is the causal factor of a similarly varied set of policy responses to the critical issues of national economic planning and urbanization. In this introductory chapter we examine three widely divergent approaches to these issues in three important countries from different parts of the continent: China, India and Saudi Arabia.

People's Republic of China

In a Communist economic system where all the important means of production and transportation are state-owned, the progress of the nation depends to a great extent upon planning. China adopted national planning almost from the inception of the Communist regime in 1949 and embarked on its First Five-Year Plan in 1953 after a pre-planning and economic rehabilitation period of 4 years (1949-1952). In formulating a national development plan, and a planning process suitable for the country, China was limited both by time and lack of experience. This was reflected not only in China's imitation of the Soviet model, at least until the middle of the 1950s, but also in the recurring conflict between certain revolutionary goals on the one hand and the need for economic and political stability on the other. Principal among these conflicts were the "Great Leap Forward" (1958-1960) and the Cultural Revolution (1966-1976), about which much has been written.

Chinese National Planning (1949-1979)

Chinese economic planning underwent several major changes in direction during the period from 1949-1979. Initially the planning emphasis was upon the use of a central economic plan covering a 5-year period and prescribing rates of growth in output for major industrial and agricultural products. Eventually this Soviet-style approach was abandoned in favor of an ideologically-based effort of mass involvement and self-reliance. This was the period of the "Great Leap Forward." The failure of this

Dominant Political System — Dominant Economic System	Single Ideology		Pluralist Ideological Structure ·
	Socialist Based	Private-Sector Based	
Public Sector	VIETNAM CHINA NORTH KOREA LAOS KAMPUCHEA	ISRAEL	BURMA
Mixed		IRAN	SRI LANKA MALAYSIA INDIA THAILAND INDONESIA
Private Sector		HONG KONG SAUDI ARABIA TAIWAN SOUTH KOREA BRUNEI	JAPAN SINGAPORE

Fig. 1.1   Dominant political-economic systems in Asian nations.

poorly organized effort, however, resulted in a return to fixed planning objectives. As the resumption of the "traditional" approach began to take effect, ideological counter-pressures were unleashed through the efforts of Mao Zedong to push for non-routinized, non-hierarchical development. This recurrence of ideological conflict over national development processes was most evident during the Cultural Revolution. China recovered from the chaos and disruption of the Cultural Revolution and followed a more stable form of socialist planning. The development of agriculture remained a top priority, and many large- and small-scale industries were built to support agricultural growth.

Economic planning in China during the period 1949-1979 proceeded according to a shifting set of policies that reflect underlying conflict and subsequent synthesis. The period also witnessed a progressively greater emphasis upon rural development and a corresponding de-emphasis upon urban development. At least 12 million people moved from the cities to the countryside with a million people from Shanghai alone in the late 1960s and early 1970s.[1] For Mao the transfer of urban youth to the countryside was like remaking a man. Such a drastic shift, in his view, was the way to combat undesirable elitism and overcome the "three great differences" between town and village, worker and farmer, and intellectual and manual work.² The cities are depicted as the home of parasites and exploiters — evil forces which were to be eradicated through a de-urbanization policy emphasizing regional and local self-sufficiency both in food and industry.

During the latter phase of the 1949-1979 period the goal of Chinese national economic planning was a developed society with spatial equity, but contrary to Marxist thought, the incremental phases were to be classless as well. The attempt was an ambitious one of achieving development through the equal participation of all members of the society.

Chinese Planning Since 1980

The death of Mao in 1976 made it possible for the new leaders to experiment with an entirely different approach to national planning characterized by the employment of market forces as determinants of production and distribution and by the development of city-based industries and services. At the same time, foreign investment and advanced technology are eagerly sought after. Unlike earlier periods in which the gaps of urban and rural development were to be narrowed and eventually eliminated, China since 1979 has expected its cities to play an active role in stimulating regional economic development. Rural to urban migration has been significantly relaxed and, under such a policy, large cities can be expected to grow even larger. Although the state still pays lip service to the old urban policy of "controlling the size of the large cities, rationally develop the medium-sized cities and actively develop the small cities," the Seventh Five-Year Plan (1986-1990) makes it very clear that the more developed and urbanized regions of the nation will grow at a faster rate than less developed areas.

China's future development is difficult to predict, but the fluctuations of the past, with respect to economic and national planning, should continue into the future. China's growth into a major economic and political power, however, is assured because of the willingness of a cohesive and hardworking people to exploit the resources of this vast nation.

India

Immediately after Independence in 1947, India faced immense problems resulting from partition, the death of Mahatma Gandhi, language divisions, caste friction and declining economic conditions. Drastic political change and tenuous economic conditions dependent upon the vagaries of the climate impelled India's leaders to embark upon an institutionalization of national planning within the framework of a new government. Prime Minister Jawaharlal Nehru, calling attention to the profound economic difficulties of the country, advocated the establishment of a Planning Commission which would formulate a national plan for the most effective and balanced utilization of the country's resources.

In July, 1951 the Commission issued its draft outline for the First Five-Year Plan. The program called for expenditures by the central and state governments of the equivalent of more than 4 billion dollars with new expansion in the field of private enterprise of around 250 million dollars. The government's main effort in the plan was to increase the supply of food, hence the allocation of 45 percent of plan capital to agriculture and irrigation projects. Twenty percent was set aside for social services, health, and education, and eight percent for industry with two-hundred million dollars to be spent in the fields of shipbuilding, iron and steel, machine tools and fertilizers.

The most spectacular feature of the First Five-Year Plan was its provision for huge multi-purpose power projects.³ These were the Bhakra Nangal project for Punjab, Haryana and Rajasthan, the Kosi project for North Bihar, the Damodar Valley project for Bihar and West Bengal, and the Hirakud project for Orissa.

Gandhi believed that there could be no basic improvement in the Indian standard of living without emphasis upon the reconstruction of its villages. Village planning was given an important thrust as a development theme in the First Plan largely for this reason. In 1948 the pilot project for village improvement was started at Etawah in the state of Uttar Pradesh. On October 2, 1952, Gandhi's birthday, a nationwide campaign of village community development was initiated in several states.

The goals of the plan, as expressed in increases in national and per capita income, were largely achieved even though the plan itself was not a systematic document of interrelated goals and objectives but, rather, largely a compilation of projects which had been devised during the previous decade.[4]

The main objective of the Second Five-Year Plan (1956-1961)[5] was the establishment of a socialist society in India. In contrast to the First Plan, the Second Plan was an interrelated set of quantified goals in each of the essential sectors of the national economy. The Second Plan, in contrast to the First, emphasized basic and heavy industries. Some critics believe this emphasis resulted in a strategically unsound disinvestment in agriculture. Had the high level of investment in agriculture, which characterized the First Plan, been carried into the Second Plan, a more highly developed, labor-intensive agricultural economy would have been created. The Second Plan fell far short of its goals due in part to lack of financial capital and poor bureaucratic management.

The Third Five-Year Plan (1962-1966) was in large part a re-issue of the Second.[6] Emphasis continued to be placed on heavy industry. Labor-intensive economic activities were neglected because of the high proportion of total investment devoted to heavy industry. A border skirmish with China in 1962 and a full-scale, albeit short, war with Pakistan helped to throw planning objectives to the winds.

During the period 1966-1969, India devised a series of three annual plans. The annual plan period was a time for re-thinking and as a result some new strategies were devised. Annual plans were necessary because the economy had been severely damaged by the Pakistan war. The annual plans continued an emphasis on heavy industry. Two important new objectives were introduced during this period, i.e., a re-emphasis on agriculture and a new emphasis on family planning. The government of India embarked upon a serious nationwide effort to curb the growth of its population by setting up a network of family planning centers, by offering free birth control devices, by encouraging sterilization operations and by mounting a vigorous propaganda campaign.

The Fourth Five-Year Plan, covering the period from 1969 to 1974, demonstrated the renewed emphasis on agriculture.[7] Resources were allocated for the development of fertilizer plants, and new high-yielding seed varieties increased Indian grain production to its very highest levels during the early years of this planning period. The Fourth Plan also contained a strong basic industry commitment, as evidenced by the investments proposed for the expansion of the steel industry. On balance, the Fourth Plan can be considered more realistic and pragmatic in outlook than previous plans. The Fourth Plan returned, in part, to the early planning emphasis of village self-sufficiency and a labor-intensive agricultural economy.

The Fifth Five-Year Plan (1974-1979), which was revised in 1975 because of sky-rocketing inflation, partly the result of a second war with Pakistan, continued to emphasize a balance among heavy industry, fertilizer production and agriculture.[8] Two new strategic goals, however, were added to the plan: removal of poverty and the promotion of self-reliance. These goals were to be achieved by increasing employment opportunities, increasing productivity levels in both agriculture and industry and by providing state-supported stimulation to backward regions and deprived sectors of the population. The Fifth Plan eventually fell prey to political instability caused by the collapse of the National Congress Party government in 1977.

Indian Planning in Recent Years

The Sixth Plan (1980-1985) was designed to bring about a structural transformation of the economy with a development perspective extending through 1995. 'Removal of poverty, generation of gainful employment, and technological and economic self-reliance' were the main goals of the plan. The GDP was planned to rise at a rate of 5.2 percent annually, while the per capita GDP by 3.2 percent, and per capita consumption by 2.8 percent. Employment was to rise from 151 million standard person years to 185. Life expectancy was to increase from 53 to 55 years and people in poverty to drop from 38 percent to 30 percent. The public sector outlay, which emphasized irrigation and power, accounted for 40 percent of plan funds. Agricultural improvement was meant to combat poverty at the rural level. The food-grain production target of the Sixth Plan was met 99 percent, producing 151.5 million tons in 1985, 60 percent of which was rice and 40 percent wheat. Thus the Sixth Plan can be counted a success, although the percentage of people in poverty declined only to 37 percent in 1984-85. The performance of the plan provided a basis of optimism for the Seventh Five-Year Plan.

The guidelines of the Seventh Five-Year Plan (1985-1990), under the leadership of the new Prime Minister, Rajiv Gandhi, are 'growth, equity, social justice, self-reliance, improved efficiency and productivity.' Emphasis was given to acceleration of food grain production, increased employment and improved productivity. As energy was thought to be the most important component of development, 30 percent of the plan outlay was earmarked for power. The Seventh Plan has an ambitious target of reducing the poverty level to 26 percent of the country's population by 1990 and registering an annual growth rate of 5 percent (a 4% growth rate in agriculture and 8% in industry). The plan also aims at developing a 'high tech' and electronics industrial service base. Increased emphasis on industrialization during the plan periods raised the proportion of India's urban population between 1941-81 by two and one-half times.

Saudi Arabia

In recent years Saudi Arabia has evolved rapidly from a traditionally pastoral society to a highly urbanized, modernizing one. Wealth from oil exploitation was a principal impetus for this shift. Economic planning at the countrywide level began with a series of multi-year plans, the first of which was for 1970-1975. Subsequent ones were for 1975-80, 1980-85, and 1985-90.

Between 1970 and 1975 Saudi Arabia emerged from economic underdevelopment, although the important achievements of the period were chiefly "showcase" types of projects. They included construction of the Jizan Dam in the southwestern province of Asir, the completion of which marked the start of permanent water impoundment in the kingdom, the new airport at Jidda, and erection of primary and secondary schools as the foundation for comprehensive education.

Coordinated countrywide planning and development began with the initiation of the Second Five-Year Plan for 1975-80. Seven chief goals guided the development policies of the planners. These goals were: (1) to maintain the religious and moral values of Islam, (2) to assure the defense and internal security of the country, (3) to foster a high rate of economic growth by developing resources, maximizing earnings from oil over the long term, and conserving depletable resources, (4) to reduce dependence on export of crude oil, (5) to develop human resources through education, professional training, and improved health standards, (6) to increase well-being of the population and to foster social stability in the face of rapid societal change, and (7) to install an infrastructure to support and achieve the first six goals.[9]

Investments were made in many sectors, but especially in the communications infrastructure. For example, four seaports were constructed, including the huge port at Dammam that opened in 1979. The system of hard-surfaced roads was created during this period: approximately 15,000 miles of paved roads were built, augmenting all-weather roads, to link all large- and middle-sized urban centers in the country. The magnitude of the project is suggested by the fact that the country had no paved roads in the mid-1950s. By 1980 the paved highway network not only linked the principal cities, but also connected with the earthen-surface roads that serve the almost 7,000 villages in Saudi Arabia.[10]

Air transportation is particularly important in a vast country such as Saudi Arabia. Hence, investment in air transportation had a high priority in this planning period. International airports were built at Riyadh, Jidda and Dammam; and 22 domestic ones were constructed or improved to create a dense network of air transportation for the country.

A second principal investment priority for this period was creation of two industrial centers: Jubail on the eastern coast and Yanbu on the western coast. Together these projects represented the largest single investment undertaken by the Saudi government, or, for that matter, in the entire world. Lying approximately 325 miles northeast of Riyadh and 100 miles north of Dhahran, Jubail will eventually encompass an area as large as Greater London with a population of 350,000. Currently an oil refinery, a petrochemical plant, an industrial chemical plant, and an iron and steel complex as well as a fertilizer pellet plant are under construction at Jubail. The cost for Jubail may exceed US$60 billion.[11] Central to the industrial base of Jubail as well as Yanbu is the installation of the Master Gas System (MGS), in which gas formerly burned as a waste product will be used as a fuel for industries.

The 1975-80 and 1980-85 plans had the character of massive national investment activities. Approximately US$250 billion were spent on various elements of the two plans during the ten-year period. The total represents a per capita investment of almost US$35,000, a truly impressive figure. Qualitative improvements in the living standard of Saudi citizens were significant. Approximately 500,000 new dwelling units were completed between 1975 and 1985. Educational and health facilities are widely available throughout the kingdom. The highway system is one of the best in the world. In short, the Saudi people have shifted from a subsistent agricultural, pastoral economy to an advanced service economy in two or three decades.

A slower pace has been evident in the Saudi development process since 1982. The worldwide oil glut has had a tremendous effect on revenue, so that the objectives of both the 1980-85 and 1985-90 plans have been revised downward. Nevertheless, ongoing projects like Jubail and Yanbu will be completed. Saudi Arabia must move rapidly to meet a crucial developmental goal of lessened dependence on oil resources.

Comparisons and Conclusions

India, China and Saudi Arabia have each decided to employ some form of national planning to achieve development goals, but the content of planning and the role of the public and private sectors in plan implementation are very different in each.

China has experienced the greatest ideological conflict in planning goals and methods. Early Soviet-style, multi-year planning was disrupted and eventually replaced by ideologically-based mass involvement efforts which failed because of poor organization and a policy of radicalism which created broadly-based opposition. The rigid directive approach to planning has in recent years been modified by a decision to introduce free market incentives, initially in rural areas and more recently in cities. Conflicts concerning purposes for planning as well as methods of planning are still evident and unresolved.

India has created a much more stable national planning system which has not altered its institutional character since its inception. One reason for this stability may be because of the lesser stakes involved in Indian national planning. In a Communist society like China, national planning is the focus for most of the important political and economic decisions affecting the life of the nation. In an economically-mixed democracy like India, where at least two economic systems exist concurrently, national planning has not assumed the dominant position it has in a Communist or Marxist system.

The Indian five-year plans contained objectives which were seldom achieved, not so much because of internal ideological conflict, but more because of inability to mobilize human and natural resources. India has attempted to carry out national economic planning within the framework of a heterogeneous and democratic society. This attempt has contributed much to internal dialogue but has often resulted in an atmosphere uncongenial to the achievement of quantified national goals.

Nonetheless, national planning is important in India and has aided that nation in its economic and social development. National planning provided the infrastructural investments in communications, transportation and basic industries which are essential to the nation-building process. National planning investments in irrigation, fertilizer production and seed improvements paved the way for India's "green revolution" — one of the developing world's great success stories.

Saudi Arabia differs significantly from both India and China. National planning in Saudi Arabia has sought to create a national infrastructure in much the same way as in India and China. But in Saudi Arabia, national planning is viewed as a framework within which private capital can be introduced. Thus national planning becomes a partnership between the public and private sectors to a much greater extent than in either of the other two countries.

Saudi Arabia's underlying value framework for planning is traditional. The religious and social values of Islam are paramount reference points for all planning decisions. Saudi Arabia differs from China and India where national planning objectives have often sought to break the hold of traditional values and religion rather than to reinforce them.

Finally, Saudi Arabia has had the good fortune, until very recent times, to command the required fiscal resources for the achievement of national planning goals. The much more populous nations of China and India have never been able to finance a comprehensive national planning effort as has Saudi Arabia.

About This Book

Diversity in the goals and mechanisms employed in the national planning process is paralleled by the great diversities in the urban life and form of the Asian continent. This book is devoted to a wide-ranging discussion of these diversities. The chapter authors describe a range of urban phenomena from historical urbanism to current trends. Kosambi and Brush in Chapter 2 discuss the historical events leading to the separation of European and Indian populations in the cities of Bombay, Madras and Calcutta. Social and cultural differentiation of people within these cities and the spatial reflection of differentiation through the creation of separate living areas began to exert itself from the earliest days of European settlement in these towns.

Sealey in Chapter 3 surveys the historical evolution of three different Indian cities, which are unique because they originated as planned centers. Each of the cities is representative of particular epochs in the long history of India. Jaipur represents urban planning and design according to traditional Indian values. New Delhi, of course, represents the power of the British presence while Chandigarh tells us something of the optimistic nation-building efforts of the first years of Indian independence.

Several chapters describe current urbanization trends in a number of Asian countries. Ginsburg in Chapter 4 reviews the development of the primate city concept and its application to Asian countries. His analysis confirms the relative stability of Asian urban system hierarchies. The issue of primacy varies from country to country with two prevalent patterns easily discernible. These are the lack of primate cities in the larger Asian nations of China and India and the dominance of primate cities in the smaller Asian nations, Thailand being an extreme example. Ginsburg also voices an interesting development issue when he asserts that national planning efforts to create a "balanced hierarchy" are frequently "ill-founded" and may result in wasting scarce national resources.

Panditharatne and Noble in Chapter 5 provide a detailed analysis of urbanization and national development planning in Sri Lanka. They note that Sri Lanka as a producer of agricultural raw materials is dependent upon world markets. Development planning in that country is tied to the physical resource base. But as planning progresses and economic growth rates increase, a shift toward urban regions will be the most appropriate forum for planning.

Prakash and Huddleston in Chapter 6 discuss four strategic urban development trends in Asian countries. These concern: (a) demographic and urbanization processes, (b) planning approaches currently being applied in national development and urban development, (c) policy responses to rapid urban growth, and (d) the economic and fiscal aspects of development policies. An in-depth description of these general strategic policies is then provided for Sri Lanka. This case study of one nation helps the reader understand the nature as well as the specific impacts of these general processes.

Withington, in Chapter 7, discusses the urban hierarchy of Sumatra with a special focus on the roles played by intermediate-sized cities in the urban hierarchy and in the regional development process. He examines the urban hierarchy in Sumatra and draws conclusions about its impact on development.

Planning at various levels is the primary focus of three of the chapters of the book. In Chapter 8 Corey describes the use of the Program Planning Model (PPM) in two Asian settings — Seoul, South Korea and Sri Lanka. PPM is a qualitative planning method which utilizes a procedure of soliciting informed opinions and professional advice in the process of developing policy as the case in Seoul or in analyzing the content of policy in Sri Lanka.

Costa and Noble, Chapter 9, discuss an approach to city planning and design which recognizes the importance of the small-scale, intimate, neighborhood setting as well as the large-scale, impersonal, urban setting in which economic transactions are facilitated. The special problem of creating suitable urban environments for large numbers of recent migrants into the rapidly growing cities of Saudi Arabia is the focus of their chapter.

Taylor in Chapter 10 describes an interesting approach to urban and regional development currently underway in Hong Kong and nearby areas in the Peoples Republic of China. The limited territorial extent of Hong Kong and Macau make extensive new developments difficult at best. A process of negotiation with the authorities in the Peoples Republic is resulting in the use of nearby parts of China as "overflow" areas for new industrial development. It is an extremely interesting process which depends largely upon successful negotiation among the parties involved.

Finally, three chapters deal with urban social and spatial issues. Dutt, Monroe, and Banu, in Chapter 11, discuss the ratio between males and females in Indian cities. Several important distinctions exist in this ratio. These are explained by considering demographic and socio-economic variables for 216 class I cities. Their data source is the 1981 census. Among the significant findings are: an inverse relationship between the size of the city and the male-female ratio; the south and northeast regions of India have a greater percentage of Christians in cities compared to other regions; higher or lower literacy rates polarize the sex difference in the northeast, east and south regions; and the *purdah* system, widely practiced in north India and resulting from Moslem influence, is partly responsible for discouraging female migration.

Nangia in Chapter 12 describes the extent of, and physical conditions prevalent in, the slums of Indian cities. Nangia also discusses the various slum improvement programs initiated by the Indian government and gives reasons for the success of some and the failure of others.

Noble, Dutt and Monroe examine in Chapter 13 the effect which a major Hindu pilgrimage site has had upon the form and evolution of the Madurai town center. The study provides a detailed discussion of the locational patterns of different types of commercial activity and represents the first time such a specific investigation has been undertaken for an Indian city.

It is evident from the chapters included in the book that Asian nations have followed divergent paths of urbanization and adopted different ideologies and objectives in planning. Planners in Asian as well as Western nations have long realized that it would be unwise and counterproductive to copy without modification the approaches and methods of planning used in such advanced countries as the United States and the Soviet Union. As each nation is unique in its history, culture, ideology and resource base, different approaches to planning must be followed to suit the needs of each country. The planning approaches of China, India and Saudi Arabia not only differ from one another, but also from those of other Asian nations.

As we approach the 21st century, the emergence of Asia as a dominant political and economic area is evident. Increasingly, the destiny of the entire world is linked to phenomena happening and conditions existing somewhere in Asia. Rapid urban growth is one of the most significant features of modern Asian society. The diversity of social and political systems permits comparative analysis of the greatly varying attempts of Asian nations to deal with the problems associated with rapid urbanization. By observing these phenomena, planners and geographers may be able to offer additional solutions to the problems of Asian urbanization.

END NOTES

[1]*Mao Tse Tung Unrehearsed* (Harmondsworth, England: Penguin Books, 1974), p. 60.

[2]T. P. Bernstein, *Up to the Mountains and Down to the Villages: The Transfer of Youth from Urban to Rural China* (New Haven, Connecticut: Yale University Press, 1977), p. 11.

[3]Government of India, Planning Commission, *First Five-Year Plan* (New Delhi: Manager of Publications, 1952).

[4]Ashok K. Dutt (ed.), *India: Resources, Potentialities and Planning* (New Delhi: Oxford and IBH Publishing Company, 1975), p. 116.

[5]Government of India, Planning Commission, *Second Five-Year Plan* (New Delhi: Manager of Publications, 1956).

[6]Government of India, Planning Commission, *Third Five-Year Plan* (New Delhi: Manager of Publications, 1961).

[7]Government of India, Planning Commission, *Fourth Five-Year Plan*, 1969-74 (New Delhi: Manager of Publications, 1972).

[8]Government of India, Planning Commission, *Draft Fifth Five-Year Plan*, 1976-79, Vols. I and II (New Delhi: Manager of Publications, 1974).

[9]Francis Tibbalds, "Planning in Saudi Arabia," *RIBA Journal* 85 (May 1978), p. 165.

[10]John Lawton, "Foundations: A Decade of Development," *Aramco World Magazine* 33 (Nov.-Dec. 1982), pp. 8-10.

[11]"The Energy Upheaval," *New York Times*, October 5, 1983.

2

Early European Suburbanization in the Indo-British Port Cities

Meera Kosambi and John E. Brush

Suburbanization is usually considered a modern phenomenon, associated with the Industrial Revolution and use of mechanized mass transport in Europe, America and some other areas of overseas European settlement during the late 19th and early 20th centuries. Suburban development is not considered to have occurred in non-European cities until the late colonial period. However, there was a form of pre-industrial suburbanization which appeared in the leading British port cities of India, namely, Madras, Bombay and Calcutta, prior to the introduction of railways and before the main period of urban development in the Indian subcontinent. A description of the physical and social configurations of early European[1] suburbs in the Indo-European port cities forms the substance of this paper.

Fundamental parallels are discernible, although details differ in the foundation and evolution of the three cities. The three settlements began in the 16th and 17th centuries as planned towns[2] for the conduct of maritime commerce between Europe and India. The initial components were: first, the fortified factories or trading establishments, housing the offices of the European merchants, clerical staff, goods storage and military garrison; second, the European residential settlement, surrounding the factory and protected by a wall; and third, the separate Indian settlement, sometimes walled, accommodating the indigenous merchants and manufacturing or service workers.

During the 18th century British military conquests, increase of trade and acquisition of territory promoted growth and allowed spatial expansion. By the late 18th century some of the Europeans were beginning to live outside the original compact settlements, away from the crowded commercial areas. In the first decades of the 19th century distinct suburbs had been formed, although transport was still dependent on human or animal power. This early suburbanization resulted from the perceived need for protection of health and the increasing British desire to maintain social distance from Indians. It was also a matter of residential preferences; Indians choosing to live in closely-built housing, as near as possible to the center of town; while Europeans preferred to live in semi-rural surroundings in spacious housing. The cultural antecedents of this European preference can be traced to the taste of the elite in Europe for suburban mansions and country estates.[3] In the context of colonial rule this divergence from the Indian urban residential pattern became a conscious policy, implemented by clear separation of the European suburbs from the Indian settlement areas.

By the late 19th and early 20th centuries further population and mechanization of transport brought rapid spatial expansion and culmination of the colonial port city pattern.[4] Analysis of this final stage of development is not to be treated here. Attention is directed in each of the three places: first, to the selection of sites and establishment of permanent towns with municipal jurisdiction and then to the growth of early European suburbs. The common elements of life in the European suburbs in the three cities is described in the final section.

Madras

Madras was acquired in 1639 by the British, preceding the acquisition of Bombay by a quarter of a century and of Calcutta by half a century. The founding of Madras was the culmination of earlier British attempts to gain a foothold on the Coromandel coast of peninsular India at Pulicat, Armagaon and Masulipatam. The nucleas of Madras was Fort St. George, completed in 1641. This was a small square enclosure about 100 by 100 yards with earthen walls and bastions at the four corners. It was well protected by the rivers Cooum and Elambore on the inland side and accessible from the open sea on the other side.[5]

The Fort was soon surrounded by the houses of Europeans (mainly British and Portuguese) and this area on being enclosed by a rectangular wall came to be known as the Outer Fort or White Town. The Black Town of Madras, also called Chennapatnam, was separated from the White Town by "the Buzar" or the market place. The first settlers under the Company's regime were traders and "dubashes" (literally, interpreters of two languages) who acted as middlemen. They lived in the area closest to the Fort gates (refer to Fig. 2.1). Extensions of the Black Town started in the early 18th century when Muthialpet appeared immediately north of Chennapatnam and the much larger settlement of Comerpet, or Peddanaickenpet, grew to the west along the Elambore River. Residents of the two new *peths*, or divisions, of the non-European settlement area were mainly merchants and moneylenders or other occupational groups involved in the cloth business, clustered in their own enclaves within the divisions. Peddanaickenpet was occupied by weavers, washers, bleachers and "painters" who prepared printed cloth. In 1734 Chintadripetta, a weaving town, was built a short way upstream on the Cooum River on the opposite side.[6] Mylapore, some three miles south of the fort, was a small separate town which grew around the ancient Hindu Kapaleshwar Temple and the Portuguese Church honoring the missionary, Saint Thomas.

Madras was the most populous of the three British port cities during the 17th and 18th centuries. The tract of some three square miles covered by the initial lease north of the River Cooum is reported to have had 7,000 inhabitants by 1639.[7] The British presence proved so attractive that the population grew to 19,000 in 1646 and increased to 40,000 or 50,000 in the 1670's as the development of the city continued.[8] The population living within the much enlarged territory of Madras grew to 300,000 in 1791, despite the military conquest and occupation by French forces in the mid-19th century. However, until the 1800's the agricultural villages and outlying towns beyond the Fort, Black Town, Chintadripetta and Triplicane remained largely self-contained communities[9] and land uses remained overwhelmingly rural. Yet the process of suburbanization had begun which was to bring about the transformation of the settlement patterns in Madras during the 19th century.

Suburbanization of the English

By the end of the 18th century, when the whole peninsula of India had been brought under direct or indirect British military control and the vast southern territories under their direct rule were organized into the Madras Presidency governed from Madras city, political stability and the growing affluence of the British East India Company gave impetus to the suburbanization of the English. At the beginning of the 17th century there had been extensive gardens and a few European houses along the Elambore in Peddanaickenpet within half a mile of the Fort. In the early 18th century, "the Island" between the two rivers was landscaped for recreational activities of the Governor and other high-ranking persons."[10] Peddanaickenpet now had ceased to be the fashionable European quarter (because it had been encroached upon by the expansion of Black Town) and there were only two garden houses in this area. The map of land use in 1798 shows more than a dozen houses with large compounds in Vepery within a mile of the west wall of the Black Town and extending along the river frontage as far as two miles above Chintadripetta.

The growth of the European suburbs in Madras was clearly influenced by considerations of accessibility. The Madras country house, set in a garden, was originally used only on weekends and holidays; but during the 18th century it was transformed into a mansion for permanent residence. At this time good road connections became a necessity; and Mount Road, the principal thoroughfare from the Fort leading southwest, as well as Poonamallee High Road leading west, determined the main directions of suburban expansion which spread in a broad southwestern arc (see Fig. 2.2). The Choultry Plain, an open treeless expanse in the villages south of the Cooum on both sides of Mount Road, which had earlier served as a military encampment, was later available for the proliferation of country houses. By the end of the 18th century it is estimated that there were about 200 garden houses on the Choultry Plain.[11]

The suburbanization of the colonial European elite contrasted sharply with the more compact indigenous form of settlement, producing the distinctly dual pattern.[12] The detailed map of 1822 by Ravenshaw (see Fig. 2.1) gives an image of the then-existing suburban landscape of mansions set in the midst of compounds, made accessible by tree-lined avenues traversing the previously described Choultry

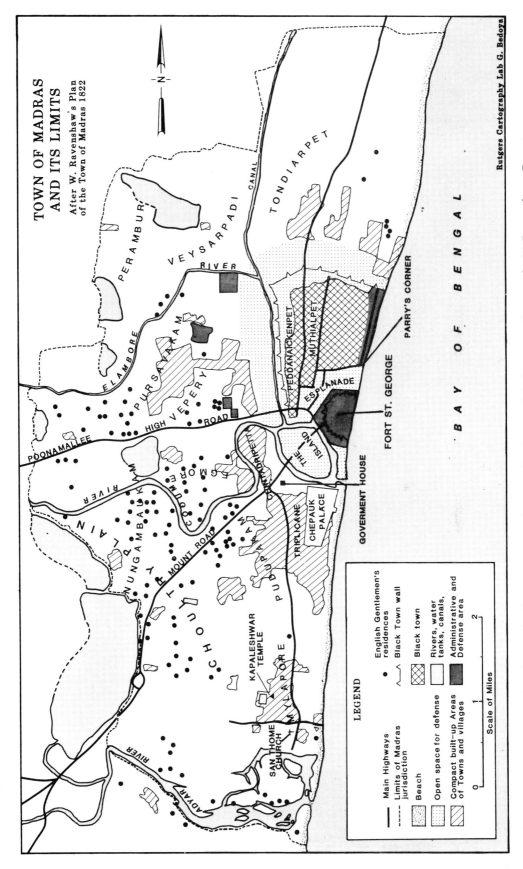

Fig. 2.1 Plan of the town of Madras and its limits as surveyed in 1822 for the use of the Justices in Sessions by W. Ravenshaw, Captain Civil Engineer. Approximate scale: 5.8 inches to 1 mile.

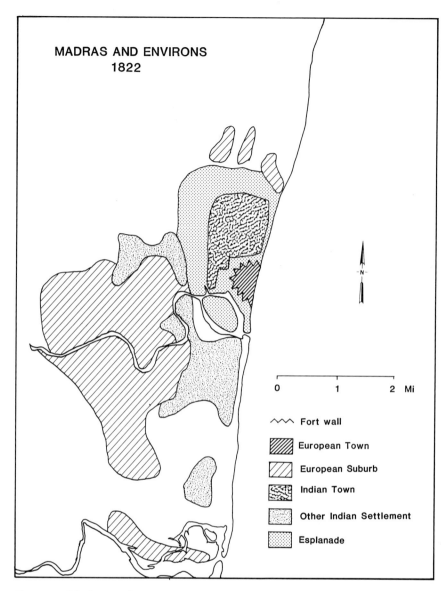

Fig. 2.2 Madras and environs — generalized settlement patterns, 1982.

Plain in the belt along Poonamallee High Road. Thus, in the early 19th century Madras presented a pattern of low-density European settlement, filling the interstices between pre-existing clustered villages and expanses of irrigation tanks, wet rice fields and palm groves, in contrast to the almost continuously built-up Black Town and nearby indigenous urban settlements of Triplicane, Chintadripetta, Vepery, Pursavakam and Tondiarpet, all situated within a mile of the Fort and the Black Town, but separated from the inner walled settlements by open space for defense.

Bombay

Bombay was built on some islands off the Konkan coast in the western side of peninsular India. Originally a group of seven separate islands, several of which were loosely joined by tidal marshes, Bombay was gradually welded into a single island through natural silting and land reclamation. The southern most island, known as Colaba, was a long and narrow strip adjoined in the north by the small triangular Old Woman's Island (a corrupted form of the Arabic 'Al Omani' meaning "deep-sea fishermen"). North of this was the main H-shaped Bombay Island, which derived its name from Mumbadevi or Mumbai, the patron goddess of the original inhabitants of the place. Two ridges of high

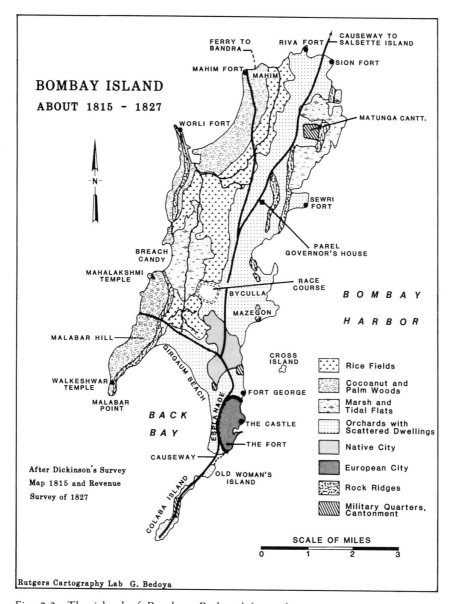

Fig. 2.3 The island of Bombay. Reduced from the original survey undertaken by order of government by Captain Thomas Dickinson, in the years 1812-1816. Scale of 1 inch to 1200 yards or 1:31:200. See *Gazette of Bombay City and Island*, 1909, vol. 2, p. 334.

ground formed rows of "islands," aligned north-south. The eastern ridge consisted of Mazagon Island, and the elongated Sewri-Wadala-Sion island. The western ridge comprised Malabar, Cumballa, Worli and Mahim (see Fig. 2.3).

When these islands were acquired by the Portuguese in 1532, Mahim had been the largest town and port in consequence of its earlier function as the seat of local administration. Under the Portuguese it continued to be a *cacabe* (from Arabic 'kasba' denoting the chief town of a district), and in 1639 Bombay town near the harbor was also promoted to the status of a *cacabe*. Mahim administered the villages of Parel, Sion, and Wadala; while the smaller town of Bombay claimed Masagon and Worli. The island groups came into British possession in 1661 as the dowry of the Portuguese Princess Catherine on her marriage to Charles II. The English king in turn transferred this poor and unproductive territory to the East India Company at an annual rent of 10 pounds in gold.[13]

The nucleus for urban growth in Bombay island was provided by the company's fortified factory, known as Bombay Castle, which was built around the manor house of the earlier Portuguese governor and adjoined the harbor. Accounts of Bombay in the early 18th century describe the castle as a well defended square structure with four bastions of unequal size built on the rocky shore where its eastern walls were constantly washed by the sea. The town was at this time divided into "two distinct limits, the English and Black." The straggling English town lay south of the castle, and most of its buildings were one-storied. The Indian section, which was larger and more densely built, lay north of the castle and was divided into several streets of thatched houses, and also contained a relatively large and well supplied bazaar. The custom house and the company's warehouses adjoined the harbor.

Bombay acquired definite contours with the construction of protective walls (Fig. 2.3) in 1716, which increased security and attracted immigration. Henceforth the town itself came to be known as the Fort, a name still in use long after the fortification walls have disappeared. The walls had three strong gates; Apollo Gate in the south (named after the locality of Polo or Polio which it bordered), Bazaar Gate in the north at the end of the Indian bazaar, and Church Gate in the west near St. Thomas' church (the first Protestant church in Bombay, completed in 1718).

The increased security of the Fort attracted an influx of settlers, and a conscious effort was made to separate the Europeans (mainly British and Portuguese, with a few Armenians) who inhabited the southern section of the Fort, from Indians (Gujaratis, Hindus, and Parsis) who occupied the northern section. An attempt was also made to remove the non-mercantile Indian population from the bounds of the Fort, priority being given to merchants, most of whom lived in separate enclaves for each of the several groups: Hindus, Jain, Muslims, and Parsis (Zoroastrians). As a result, another straggling settlement started to grow outside the Fort to the north.

By the mid-18th century, Bombay Fort contained a sizable town. The center of the roughly semi-circular area was Bombay Castle which contained the Governor's formal residence (Fig. 2.4). It was surrounded by a large open space of the Bombay Green. Northwest of the Fort, along the waterfront, are the soldiers' barracks and custom house with the mint adjoining them on the Green. The waterfront to the south of the Castle was lined with the Company's warehouses, the pier, the marine storehouse and yard, a hospital, and the docks. The major streets radiated from the Green to the three gates. The southern or European section showed loosely occupied plots with several empty spaces, while the northern section is densely built up and made accessible by a rough street grid.

The second phase in the spatial development of Bombay, and one which has left a permanent imprint, occurred in the early 19th century with the extension of the Native town. In 1803 a fire devastated a large section of the crowded Indian quarter inside the walls (the original Black Town) and as a result an Indian settlement was enlarged to the north of the fort and beyond the esplanade and was called the Native Town. The Company authorities deemed it "preferable to allot a space in the *oarts* (orchards) adjoining the forest and esplanade for the erection of a black town such as at Madras; or gradually to effect such a separation between the town and fortifications, as exists at Calcutta."[14]

The Native Town, and its later extension known as Kamathipura (after the Kamathis, immigrants from the region of modern Andhra Pradesh, employed chiefly as construction workers) replaced former rice fields. This residential area was separated from the Fort by the Esplanade, which was further widened to 800 yards. Of its inhabitants, the merchants and shopkeepers congregated in the area closest to the Fort, the rest being claimed by other occupational groups and workers.

European Suburbs

The earliest European settlement outside the Fort walls was at Colaba. The island was specially reserved for military purposes in the early years and European officers lived there in temporary tents. In 1784 it was decided that, in the interest of economy and efficiency, all European officers and troops should be cantoned at Colaba throughout the year and housing was accordingly built. Attempts to reserve all of Colaba Island for a military cantonment were restricted to only part of the island in 1802, and the rest of the island was let on long term leases to European civilians. On the adjoining Old Woman's Island a gunpowder mill and barracks were built in the late eighteenth century. These two islands were

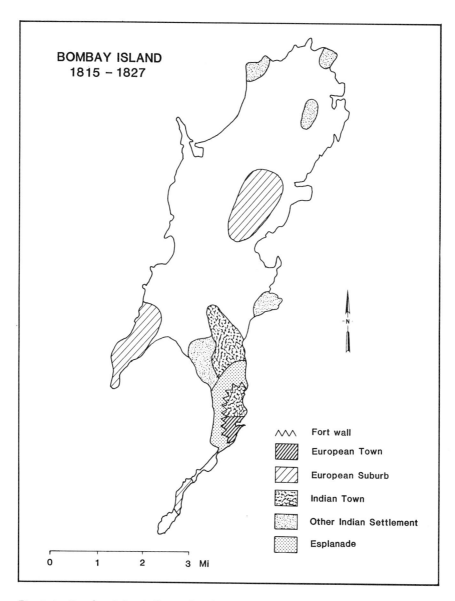

BOMBAY ISLAND
1815 – 1827

⋀⋀⋀ Fort wall
European Town
European Suburb
Indian Town
Other Indian Settlement
Esplanade

0   1   2   3 Mi

Fig. 2.4 Bombay Island. Generalized settlement patterns, 1815-1827.
Sketch of the islands of Bombay and Colabah, showing the positions of
all the principal military buildings, outposts, etc. Bombay: Revenue
Survey Office, 1826, scale of 200 feet to one inch. Also, Bombay and
Salsette: reduced from the revenue survey completed in the year 1827,
no scale.

linked to each other and to the Fort by ferry. As a European suburb Colaba was considered "a pretty,
retired spot, whose dullness is redeemed by the health-inspiring breezes;" and only those European
families lived there "who prefer such quiet to the gaieties of the sister island."[15]

The most popular European suburban residential area was located near the Governor's country
house at Parel, a few miles north of the Fort. It was originally a Portuguese Jesuit estate, confiscated by
the Company in the late 1690's. The sparsely inhabited wooded area here was favored by Europeans who
built houses surrounded by large gardens, so that "a constant succession of gentlemen's houses"
reminiscent of the "the neighbourhood of London" existed here. Most houses were one-story flanked by
roofed verandas, with a set of nearby buildings for offices and servants' quarters. The architecture was

plain but the interiors were often fitten up with elegance, creating a combination of "English comforts and oriental luxuries."[16] A garden house at Malabar Point was made into the new Government House about 1820, and became the nucleus of the large English suburb of Malabar Hill, which grew rapidly in the late 19th century, when encroachment of cotton mills and workers' quarters made Parel and its vicinity less desirable for residences of the European.

Another notable phenomenon was the seasonal European suburb on the Esplanade in the first half of the 19th century. The Esplanade was required to be kept free of permanent houses by defense regulations, but temporary structures were exempted. These were constructed in the hot summer months in the long belt along the Back Bay stretching from the Cooperage in the south to the Marine Lines or barracks for the Marine Battalion in the north. The Plan of the Fortress of Bombay dated 1827 shows the southern part of this belt as "Ground appropriated during the fair Season for Gentlemen's Bungalows with Enclosures," and the northern part as "Encamping Ground during the Fair Season for the Officers of the native Infantry Regiments." Several descriptions of these seasonal houses have been left by visitors. The bungalows were made of bamboo and plaster, and lined with canvas; and detached offices were enclosed in the same compound, filled with plans arranged in tubs. The houses and porches were half concealed by flowering creepers and shrubs which also shaded them from the sun's midday glare. The bungalows were arranged in a row with spaces between them and set at a convenient distance from the road. At the approach of the wet monsoon, the bungalows were dismantled and the construction materials stored away for the next summer, while the occupants shifted to their permanent houses in the Fort or in the European suburbs.[17]

Calcutta

Although Calcutta was the last of the three great British port cities to be established and its trade was of little account until the 18th century, the city's rapid growth shows how access to the rich and well-populated hinterland can overcome the handicap of a late start.[18] The population increased from 10-12,000 in 1710 to an estimated 117,000 in 1752, and 160,000 in 1801.[19] Despite the sacking of Calcutta in 1756 when it was seized by the Nawab of Bengal, the city flourished and in 1773 it came to be the center of administration for the East India Company's affairs in the whole subcontinent.

Calcutta proved from its beginning to be an advantageous place for trade despite the problems of maintaining a navigable river channel about 80 miles from the sea and the devastating health conditions encountered here by Europeans.[20] The Hooghly River served as a meeting place for seagoing ships and smaller inland craft which plied the delta waterways to eastern Bengal and could also proceed up the Hooghly to the Bhagirathi distributary channel, thus connecting to the main stream of the Ganges and so reach Patna and other places in the middle Ganges valley. In the 16th century, the Portuguese had come to the eponymous settlement of Hooghly, a Mughal port and garrison town located on the west bank about 100 miles from the sea. An English factory was set up in Hooghly town in 1658 following expulsion of the Portuguese. But friction with the Mughal administation of Bengal caused the East India Company to shift attention about 25 miles down river to the left (east) bank where in 1686 the rights to trade and collection of land revenue were obtained for three little villages of Sutanati, Kalikata and Gobindpur. Here the tidal currents scooped out a deep pool which could serve as a good anchorage and the river provided a strategic natural barrier against possible incursions of hostile Mahratta land forces from the west. Sutanati, local market center, was chosen to be the location of the East India Company factory, but it had to be abandoned hastily in 1689.

In 1690 the English chose to build their factory in Kalikata (corrupted as Calcutta), the middle village, on a site north of a small stream channel which carried seasonal overflow from the extensive brackish lakes about three miles eastward. Internecine feuding in the Mughal administration of Bengal caused general insecurity. In 1696 the Company began construction of Fort William, named for the ruling monarch of Great Britain in 1700, and completed it in 1712. In 1698 full title and ownership of the three leased villages was acquired by the Company. The Territory of Calcutta, as it came to be known, comprised an area of approximately eight square miles with a frontage of three and a half miles along the Hooghly.

By the turn of the 18th century the stage was set for growth of an English settlement around Fort William and the Great Tank, an artificial pond located on the natural levee a quarter of a mile from the river bank. This European town was enclosed by wooden palisades, while the "native town" grew adjacent on the north, outside the wall. Gobindpur village stood apart on the south near the bifurcation of the Adi Ganga (Original Ganges), a distributary channel which flowed southeast from the main stream of the Hooghly towards the pre-existing Hindu Kalighat Temple. In the mid-18th century Calcutta, both the European and the indigenous towns togther with Sutanati, had become a continuous urban area between the riverfront and Chitpur Road, the old pilgrimage route to Kalighat, while the eastern half of the territory was occupied by fields, groves and outlying farm hamlets, except along the road from the Great Tank through Bow Bazaar to the Baitakkhanna Tree which was a focal point in the trade with eastern Bengal by way of the Beliaghatta waterway. The perimeter of English jurisdiction was marked in part by the defensive Mahratta Ditch, dug by the Company to deter maurauding bands from central India.[21]

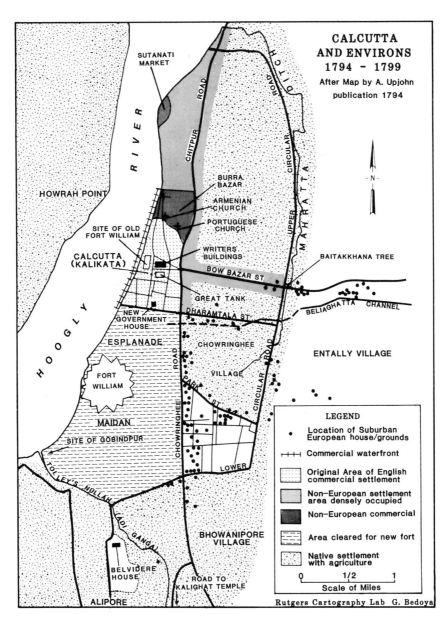

Fig. 2.5 Map of Calcutta and its environs from an accurate survey taken in the years 1792 and 1793 by A. Upjohn, dated April 2, 1794. Inset: Plan of the territory of Calcutta in the year 1742.

A series of changes in the growth pattern was precipitated by the destruction of Calcutta and capture of Fort William by Mughal forces in 1756, followed by restoration of English control in 1757 and expansion of the Company's territory in Bengal. Calcutta Town was rebuilt around the Great Tank, but it was decided that defense required a new larger Fort William to be erected one mile south towards Gobindpur to serve exclusively military purposes. The village was destroyed and the surrounding land cleared to create an Esplanade for free cannon fire over an area measuring some two square miles. The new fort was built between 1773 and 1781 and the old fort demolished, thus providing more space in the center of English business activities and civil government, close to the commercial waterfront and warehouses. New quarters for junior partners of the Company (the Writers' Buildings), the courthouse, town hall, churches and residences of high officers were clustered in this neighborhood, known as Tank Square and subsequently as Dalhousie Square. In 1799 it was deemed appropriate to erect a conspicuous Government House on the northern perimeter of the Esplanade to serve as the official residence and administrative office for the Governor General of the East India Company, beginning in 1803.[22]

English Suburbs

By the last decade of the 18th century suburbanization of the English people had already begun with the building of country houses in several outlying locations at a distance of one or two miles or more from Tank Square. Upjohn's detailed map of 1794 (Fig. 2.5) shows about 100 European houses with gardens or compounds in the quadrant south of the Bowbazar-Baitakkhana axis and east of the old road to Kalighat which bordered the Esplanade (or Maidan). About two-thirds of this number were on or near Chowringhee Road east of the Esplanade. Other lesser groupings appeared in Sealdah village along the road from Baitakkhana to Beliaghata; along Dharamtala Street; and southward towards Entally village along the roadway along the Mahratta Ditch. The southernmost dwelling at this time was Belvidere House, Warren Hastings' country mansion of the 1780's located in Alipur three miles from Tank Square across the Adi Ganga also called Tolley's Nullah.

European residential preference in Calcutta during the 19th century was concentrated in Chowringhee Road, Park Street and vicinity (Fig. 2.6). The English elite built two- or three-storied houses with thick walls of bricks, plastered with cement and coated with whitewash, high flat balustraded roofs and wide pillared verandas and fronted with high porticos, surrounded by gardens and landscaped grounds. Calcutta's Europeans represented a small minority of the population, a mere 3,300 (1.4 percent) in a total of about 230,000 in the police census of Calcutta in 1837[23] and the ruling elite were much outnumbered even in the exclusive European residential sector. Splendor and poverty existed side by side; servants, porters, laborers and shopkeepers necessary for the Europeans lived in low-quality quarters provided in the compounds of the mansions, or concentrated in indigenous-type mud and bamboo dwellings scattered in patches through the European Town. However, color consciousness and prejudice on the part of the English excluded any Indian of high social or economic status from living in the mansions of Chowringhee and vicinity or from enjoying access to clubs and recreational facilities reserved for Europeans only.

In the early 19th century the Indian Calcutta, comprising two-thirds of the area of the city, was focused in the Burra Bazaar (Great Market), a complex and densely inhabited wholesale and retail business area located about half a mile north of Tank Square, immediately east of the northern section of the commercial waterfront. Here the principal entrepreneurs had been at first Bengali cloth merchants and money-lenders, descended in many instances directly from the original Hindu trading castes of Sutanati and Gobindpur. The Bengalis now were in the process of being displaced by North Indian Khatri taders, who dealt in jute exports and a variety of imported goods, paper, and foods of all kinds.[24] Burra Bazaar attacted large numbers of laborers who engaged in goods handling and transport. Since they and their employers came from the northern Hindi-speaking provinces, the language of commerce tended to be Hindi (or Urdu), rather than Bengali which was the prevailing language of the city population.

The Indian Town in the 19th century became a vast complex of contiguous dwelling houses, bazaars with congested main streets and narrow winding lanes. Much of the housing was of poor quality without basic water supply or waste disposal and conditions were hazardous to the health of the inhabitants. Erection of thatched huts was not permitted in Calcutta after 1837 because of the frequency of fires and thatch was gradually replaced by tile roofing.

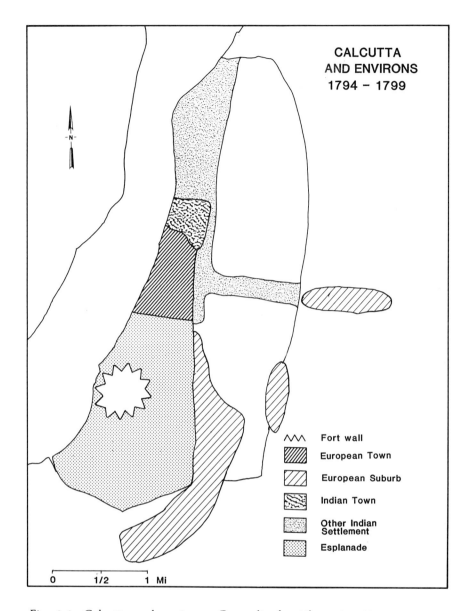

CALCUTTA
AND ENVIRONS
1794 – 1799

∧∧∧ Fort wall

European Town

European Suburb

Indian Town

Other Indian
Settlement

Esplanade

0   1/2   1 Mi

Fig. 2.6 Calcutta and environs. Generalized settlement patterns,
1794-1799.

The European Community

The essence of the European suburbs was their European lifestyle rather than preponderance of European population. In fact, in each of the three cities under review, the European community was numerically small and never exceeded three percent of the total city population. Again, as will be seen later, each European family had a domestic staff several times its own size. The key to the European suburbs was thus an attempt to recreate a European lifestyle as much as the Indian environment would allow and to maintain a separate and superior residential domain clearly segregated from the Indian residential areas.

The European community in India was not only relatively small but its demographic composition was abnormal. The predominance of adult males in the gainfully active age groups was striking. At the same time there were very few children or old people; the absence of the first was due to a high infant mortality rate as well as the practice of sending children to England for schooling; the elderly invariably returned to England after retirement.

In all three cities the British community adhered to a single lifestyle and culture, judging from contemporary accounts, in spite of the striking regional differences as far as the Indian community was concerned. In appearance and dress the Europeans were uncompromisingly European, although it was often informally recognized that their tight fitting clothes were eminently unsuitable to the hot climate. The latest fashions from Europe were avidly copied by the ladies. The diet was as European as the availability of ingredients would permit: No English dinner party at Madras was complete without geese, turkeys and joints of mutton.[25] "Tongues, hams, cheeses and sweetmeats are imported from England; and it is laughable to see how much store is set by raspberry and strawberry jam; but the difficulty of obtaining an article, and the distance whence it comes, wonderfully enhances its worth. English things are considered in Bombay, to be of far more value than Indian."[26] Things Indian (or non-European in general) were despised, to the extent that real Chinese porcelain brought direct from China, so much prized in England, was meticulously avoided as cheap and unfashionable, in favor of English porcelain.

Within the English community, strict notions of precedence and hierarchy, based on official position and status, were observed. Social life consisted of dinners, drives, morning calls, and dances. This found its fullest expression at the eternal dinner party, the most frequent social occasion at all three Indo-British towns. The scale of the party was usually vast, 40 to 50 guests being the norm; and there were about three European men to every European woman present. Since rank and precedence was strictly observed, the same people were usually seated next to each other. This curtailed variety and reduced the conversation to exchanging gossip, general conversation being impossible because of the sheer size of the party. An abundance of dishes was served (stressing meats, poultry, and European delicacies) but not all consumed, because the preceding midday meal was usually eaten rather late in the afternoon. An exotic touch was provided at these dinners by the colorful costumes of the servants who stood behind the masters and attended to their needs, as was the custom.[27]

Another favorite social and recreational activity was the evening drive. The favorite meeting places were the Esplanade and Breach Candy in Bombay, the Course on the Maidan in Calcutta, and Mount Road in Madras. Here the European community turned out in a display of fashionable equipages and clothes, for exercise, gossip, and flirtations. Occasional excursions outside the city were also popular. The theater was rare and good books even rarer. European men favored active sports such as hunts, fox chases, and horse races.

Contact With Indians

European contact with Indians was strictly regulated. European men had occupational contact with several strata of Indians in connection with governmental and business affairs. Social contact was limited to the Indian elite, consisting mainly of the aristocracy and the merchant princes. They could entertain Europeans at dinner parties, usually accompanied by a "nautch" (Indian style dance) and other performances: On these occasions, however, Indian women of high status were almost never present. Indeed, the usual complaint of European women was the almost total lack of contact with aristocratic Indian women who were rarely seen by foreigners. But for both men and women, the most frequent contact was with Indian servants. The domestic staff of an English household was usually a small self-contained community with its own graduation according to status and caste.

The "English menage at Bombay," on the most limited scale, was "far greater than those of persons of equal rank and fortune in Great Britain, and yet the Anglo inhabitants of Bombay are as much behind those of Calcutta and Madras, in expense, and in the superfluit of servants which swell their retinue, as they exceed their countrymen at home in these particulars."[28] The mercantile families generally employed a "dubash" (translator) who acted as a confidential agent responsible both for transacting business in the bazaar for his master, and for supervising the servants in the master's establishment. A high officer employed "purbhoos" or clerks, and "moonshees" or teachers, who doubled as secretaries and accountants: in addition, armed messengers attended him, "chobdars" or mace-bearers, preceded him with silver sticks and announced his titles and names. In private families, the head servant, always termed "boy" irrespective of his age, served as a butler and had several other "boys" or footmen under him. The lady of the house was attended by an "ayah" or maid.

Additional staff included a private tailor or "derjee," "hamauls," bearers to carry palanquins and for household work, sweepers or "halalcors," "massalgees" to attend to lamps and candles and as torch-bearers to run before the carriage at night. The carriage was driven by a coachman, and two "syces" or grooms ran alongside. Finally, there were "sepoys" or peons to guard the house and to carry messages, do marketing, and attend to the removal of goods or furniture.[29]

The domestic staff of an English household at Calcutta was headed by a "sircar" who was an agent and also a money-lender (the equivalent of the Bombay "dubash"). The domestic establishment consisted of a "khansaman" or steward, an "addar" or water cooler, a "sherabdar" or butler, "kitmutgas" or footmen, a "sirdar bearer" or head of all the bearers, and other bearers. A variety of peons known as "chobdars," "sotaburdars," and "hurkarus" carried silver sticks before people of rank, and served as messengers. Carriages were driven by postillions and a groom ran by the side of each horse.[30] In Calcutta it was customary also for European children to have their own servants, which included a nurse, a bearer, a "khitmutgas," a "hurkaru," a cook, a mace-bearer, an umbrella-bearer, a coachman, and groom.

Madras life was no different. The domestic establishment there included the usual "boys," ladies' maids, a tailor, and an array of servants to sweep the rooms and bring water. "There is one man to lay the cloth, another to bring the dinner, another to light the candles, and others to wait at the table. Every horse has a man and a maid to himself — the maid cuts grass for him; and every dog has a boy . . ."[31]

European Housing

Suburban housing consisted of a set of bungalows built in a large park-like enclosure. The main bungalow was the dwelling house, others contained offices, etc., and the servants had their quarters in a rear corner. A pillared gallery or veranda usually ran along one or more sides of the bungalow, protecting it from the afternoon glare and providing additional space to lounge, receive visitors or transact business. In spite of an unimposing, barnlike exterior, the bungalow usually contained a mixture of European style furniture and Indian decor. European architectural styles were by and large reserved for public buildings which appeared in profusion in the 19th century.

In private houses European innovations were limited to glass window panes (superceding the polished oyster shells used in the 17th and early 18th centuries), wooden venetian blinds, and the introduction of European furniture. The air circulating device known as the ceiling "punkah" cannot with certainty be attributed to Europeans, but was liberally used by them. It consisted of a large wooden frame hung from the ceiling and draped with cloth or straw matting, moved to and fro by means of an attached rope running over a pulley, activated by a servant stationed outside the room.

The garden surrounding the bungalow was usually landscaped in the English style although most of the vegetation was local and was laid out with walks and benches from which the view could best be appreciated.

Transportation

Although the transportation was completely pre-industrial, it was relatively fast and efficient and offered a surprising variety.

The most ubiquitous form of transportation confronting the "griffin" or European newcomer was the palanquin, a painted box "very much resembling a coffin in appearance" and carried by special bearers.[32] It had windows and sliding doors, and the passenger could either lie down or sit upright in it.[33] In the 1820's the highest price of an English-built palanquin was Rs. 3,000 apiece.[34] Palanquins were also used for long-distance travel, as for example from Panvel (reached by boat from Bombay) to Poona, a distance of over 60 miles which could be covered in two days and two nights with only short breaks.[35]

In the 19th century the fashionable mode of local transportation became the horse carriages. English buggies, heavy coaches and light landaulets jostled with singular looking ox-drawn shigramps and indigenous bullock carts, or "hackeries."[36] A few English officers and civilians chose to ride spirited Arabian horses.

Dual Patterns of the Later Colonial Period

The dual patterns of separate European and Indian sectors can be traced in the further stages of growth in Madras, Bombay and Calcutta. The European commercial center gradually changed into Western-type business and administrative districts, populous by day and largely deserted by night. The suburbs became elite residential sectors, closely linked by improved modes of transport to the central business district. However, the Indian *bazaar* persisted in its mixed commercial and residential character and the Indians of wealth and social prestige tended to live in or near the main center of the city although in the 20th century there were some exceptions to the residential exclusivity of the European suburbs. Industrial suburbs and satellite towns which appeared in the late 19th and early 20th centuries attracted indigenous mill workers and poor laborers. Time and space does not permit analysis of these phenomena here. The authors undertake in another paper[37] to trace the further evolution of the three Indo-British port cities.

END NOTES

[1]The authors use the term "European" in apposition to "Indian" in the context of this paper although it was the British East India Company officials who exercised authority in the three settlements and people of English national origin were always dominant in the colonial economic and social system. In this paper, therefore, the term "European" may be regarded for most purposes as interchangeable with "British" or "English."

[2]Sten Nilsson, *European Architecture in India, 1750-1850* (New York: Taplinger Publishing Co., 1969), pp. 39-92; and Dilip K.Basu, ed., *The Rise and Growth of the Colonial Port Cities in Asia* (Lanham, MD: University Press of America, 1985),pp. xix-xxx.

[3]Howard Saalman, *Medieval Cities* (New York: George Braziller, 1968), pp. 44-45; and James E.Vance, Jr, *This Scene of Man. The Role and Structure of the City in the Geography of Western Civilization* (New York: Harper & Row, 1977), pp. 159 and 228.

[4]Anthony D. King, *Colonial Urban Development. Culture, Social Power and Environment* (London: Routledge & Kegan Paul, 1976),p. 32; and Pauline Milone, "Allocated or Entitled Housing: Institutional Paternalism and the Growth of the Colonial Port City, p. 213 ff., *et seq.*, in *The Rise and Growth of Colonial Port Cities in Asia*, D. K. Basu, ed., 1985.

[5]B. M. Thirunaranan, "The Site and Situation of Madras," in *Madras 1639-1939*, C. S. Srinivasachari, ed., Madras Tercentenary Committee, 1939, p.325.

[6]S. Muthiah, *Madras Discovered. A Historical Guide to Looking Around* (Madras: East-West Press, 1981), pp. 7-10.

[7]S. Chandrasekhar, "Growth of Population in Madras City, 1639-1961," *Population Review*, Vol. 8, 1964, p. 19

[8]John E. Brush, "The Growth of the Presidency Towns," in *Urban India: Society, Space and Image*, Richard G. Fox, ed. (Duke University: Program in Comparative Studies on Southern Asia, 1970), pp. 93-94, 106.

[9]Susan J. Lewandowski, *Migration and Ethnicity in Urban India. Kerala Migrants in the City of Madras, 1870-1970* (New Delhi: Manohar, 1980), pp. 43-51.

[10]George Kuriyan, "The Distribution of Population in the City of Madras," *Indian Geographical Journal*, Vol. 16, 1941, p. 60.

[11]George Kuriyan, "Growth of the City of Madras," in *Madras 1639-1939. Madras Tercentary Commemorative Volume*, C. S. Srinivasachari, ed., Madras Tercentenary Committee, 1939, pp. 295-315.

[12]Susan J. Lewandowski, "Urban Growth and Municipal Development in the Colonial City of Madras, 1860-1900," *J. of Asian Studies*, Vol. 34, 1975, pp. 341-60.

[13]Meera Kosambi, *Bombay and Poona. A Socio-Ecological Study of Two Indian Cities, 1650-1900* (Stockholm, Sweden: Dept. of Sociology, University of Stockholm, 1980), pp. 25-98; also see Kosambi, *Bombay in Transition: The Growth and Social Ecology of a Colonial City: 1880-1980* (Stockholm, Sweden: Almqvist & Wiksell International, 1986), pp. 30-49, for further details.

[14]S. M. Edwardes, *Rise of Bombay: A Retrospect* (Bombay: Times of India Press, 1902), p. 229.

[15] Mrs. Postans, *Western India in 1838* (London: 1839), vol. 1, p. 30.

[16]Mrs. Colonel Elwood, *Narrative of a Journey Overland from England. . . to India* (London: Colburn and Bentley, 1830), vol. 1, pp. 362-8.

[17]Postans, Footnote 15, vol. 1, pp. 11-15.

[18]Brush, Footnote 8, p. 96.

[19]*Encyclopedia Britannica*, 1910, vol. 4, p. 982.

[20]Rhoads Murphey, "The City in the Swamp: Aspects of the Site and Early Growth of Calcutta," *The Geographical Journal*, Vol. 130, 1964, pp. 241.

[21]A. K. Ray, "A Short History of Calcutta," *Census of India 1901*, Vol. VII, Part 1, pp. 14-16.

[22]Eardley Latimer, *Handbook to Calcutta and Environs* (Calcutta: Oxford Book and Stationery Co., 1963), pp. 24-25.

[23]Cited by Pradip Sinha, in *Calcutta in Urban History* (Calcutta: Firma K L M Private, 1978), p. 43.

[24]Prajananda Banerjee, *Calcutta and Its Hinterland—A Study in Economic History of India 1833-1900* (Calcutta: Progressive Publishers, 1975), pp. 196-97.

[25]Mrs. F. C. Maitland, *Letters from Madras. . .* (London: John Murray, 1843), pp. 48-9.

[26]Elwood, Footnote 16, vol. 1, p. 411.

[27]Maria Graham, *Journal of a Residence in India* (Edinburgh: Constable & Co., 1812), pp. 29-30; Elwood, Footnote 16, vol. 2, p. 97; Maitland, Footnote 25, pp. 47-50.

[28]Elwood, Footnote 16, vol. 2, pp. 1-2.

[29]Graham, Footnote 27, pp. 30-36.

[30]Bishop Reginald Heber, *Narrative of a Journey through the Upper Provinces of India from Calcutta to Bombay, 1824-1825* (Philadelphia: Carey, Lea & Carey, 1828), vol. 1, pp. 52-4.

[31]Heber, Footnote 30, vol. 1, pp. 55-56.

[32]Elwood, Footnote 16, vol. 1, p. 362.

[33]Graham, Footnote 27, pp. 1-2.

[34]Heber, Footnote 30, vol. 1, p. 56.

[35]Heber, Footnote 30, vol. 2, pp. 151-6.

[36]Elwood, Footnote 16, pp. 375-6.

[37]John E. Brush and Meera Kosambi, "Three Colonial Port Cities in India," (forthcoming) in *Geographical Review*, vol. 77, 1987.

3

Planned Cities of India:
A Study of Jaipur, New Delhi and Chandigarh

Neil E. Sealey

Although the majority of the population of the underdeveloped countries is non-urban, these countries have severe urban problems. Indeed, some of the worst, or at least the most quoted, examples are from India where over 75 percent of the population is rural.

Indian civilization has always been active and innovative in the urban sphere, and over the centuries it has consciously created and planned urban settlements. Examples extend as far back as the Indus Valley civilization[1] which created the large capital cities of Mohenjodaro (on the River Indus in Sind), and Harappa (on the River Ravi). Whittick[2] considers these to be the oldest examples of systematic town planning.

However, all these towns and cities have either been overwhelmed by later developments or lie in ruins. The most relevant to contemporary study are Jaipur, built by a maharajah in the eighteenth century, New Delhi, mainly a product of the colonial era, and the incomplete Chandigarh, capital of the Indian Punjab and Haryana. There are at least twenty other new towns or cities in varying degrees of development from this same period of the twentieth century.

The point of this review is that if we look at cities such as these today we are at least starting from a known base — the original plan. The architects' and planners' concepts provide a "control" in respect of what could have been expected to develop, and the reality is there to compare with this view. In this way, perhaps it will be possible to isolate and identify the forces at work in Indian cities and then use them to understand further the complexities of the vast majority of the other, unplanned cities. If the designers of these earlier planned cities identified correctly the forces at work, then their creations should have functioned efficiently, at least during the period for which they were designed. Alternatively, their failures will be apparent. In either case, we have the advantage, in theory at least, of knowing how it was planned to accommodate the various functions of the Indian city and, indeed, just what these were thought to be. Success or failure, alike, can point up the specific elements of urbanism which while unidentified bedevil urban development at present.

Jaipur was started long before the British became a major urban force and their presence in Rajasthan in this respect was always minimal anyway. The study of Jaipur allows us to see the development of a planned city, admittedly in a somewhat unique region of India, over a period of 250 years.

Delhi became the capital of India in 1912 and *New Delhi* was created in the 1920s and 1930s to satisfy the particular needs of the British administration. It represents the majestic might of the colonial forces during the twentieth century.

Chandigarh is entirely post-independence and therefore non-colonial. Built for Indian purposes to Indian specifications (although admittedly by mainly foreign architects), it can allow us to identify both the aspirations and the reality of urban India in the last quarter of a century.

Jaipur

This city was founded in 1727 to replace Amber as the capital of the Rajput state of Jaipur. Its creator was the Maharajah Jai Singh II (1687-1743), noted for his scientific, engineering, architectural and astronomical studies and achievements but especially for his *Yantras*, or astronomical observatories, built at Delhi, Jaipur, Mathura, Benares (Varanasi), and Ujjain.

Given the suitability of the terrain — generally flat, the excellent defensive positions and communications, and the availability of water from rivers such as the Jotwara and Nandi draining into the Raja MullLake in the west, Jai Singh determined that his new city should be centered on his existing buildings. There was otherwise little settlement apart from a few villages towards the east and ample scope for the realization of his own vision of a city at once scientific and harmonious with man and the physical environment (Fig. 3.1).

Jaipur represents a conscious advancement in the evolution of town planning in India. Its two most outstanding characteristics — the sectional layout and the neighborhood units (known as *havelis*) — both succeed naturally from traditional ideas and herald the modern era exemplified by such cities as Chandigarh, with which it clearly has much more in common than the rather anachronistic New Delhi.

Although often described as a square divided into nine blocks, it is clear that this is hardly a realistic description and belies the sensitivity of its creator in placing utility before geometry. The opposite has been said about New Delhi. Thus, the design of Jaipur, despite the absolute authority of its ruler, marks a shift from the epic cities of the Mughal emperors (e.g., Fatehpur Sikri) designed to display pomp, power and glory, to the needs of the people, and the almost continuous growth to a population of 1,004,669 in 1981, making it the twelfth largest city in India, attests to this.

Today the planned city of about three square miles is only part of an urban area of some 25 square miles, but fortunately little of the original identity has been lost. Clearly, in being planned as a walled city its expansion was physically limited, although as will be seen its enlargement within the concepts of the original plan would have been quite possible. In this respect it anticipated Chandigarh and surpassed New Delhi. The city was eventually surrounded by a wall 25 feet high and nine feet thick. This was cut by seven gateways (*pols*), but an eighth was later added between the Ajmer and Sanganer Gates to connect with the important commercial street of Chavra Rasta with the new road known as Sawai Man Singh Highway (Fig. 3.2) leading to Sanganer. Bastions and towers at regular intervals completed the fortifications.

The blocks, or *chowkris*, can be considered as the sectors of modern town planning as in Chandigarh and like them the scale is closely related to movement times. Here it was the human capacity for walking that was considered and the distance along an east-west side is about 900 yards — almost identical to a Chandigarh sector's short axis — and represents about a ten minute walk. This is in fact a much bigger unit than seems to develop traditionally but it is one found in other planned towns such as Fatehpur Sikri and Shahjahanabad. In Chandigarh it is apparent that this distance served both mechanically propelled vehicles — about one minute travel time between sectors — and the pedestrian, for the main shopping street runs the full width of each sector. In anticipation of Le Corbusier's formal road planning (see section on Chandigarh), Jai Singh II divided his sectors with roads 108 feet wide. Within the *chowkris* are successively smaller roads, the access roads being 54 feet wide and dividing the sectors into blocks (*mohallas*) which themselves have lanes half as wide again (27 feet), and this continues down to the narrowest lanes, called *rastas*, only 13 feet wide. The main roads were designed to be, and still are, the main commercial zones, and they are all called *bazaars*. In this respect they are the antithesis of Le Corbusier's throughways, which are designed only for traffic and in many areas deliberately prohibited to the pedestrian. Chandigarh's sectors are inward looking and self-contained. Clearly, traffic has changed and the function of the main thoroughfares with it in Jaipur.

The *bazaars* were obviously not built for fast-moving traffic but rather as the commercial areas of the city. Pavements extended as much as 25 percent of the street width on either side of the road, and land use was restricted to shopping and other commercial uses. No houses were permitted to open onto the main streets and the shops were strictly controlled in respect to size and design, which allowed for about 160 on each side of a sector. Building heights were about half the road widths, 3 or 4 stories, but the ground level shops were surmounted by a terrace reached by steps from the pavement so that the increase in height was achieved in stages and the pedestrian area increased, the whole effect being to enhance the width of the street and maintain proportions. Le Corbusier himself was inspired to incorporate some of these ideas in work he undertook in Ahmadabad. Every detail of the construction was laid out in Vidhyadhar's drawings and strictly enforced. To this end all the shops were initially built by the state.

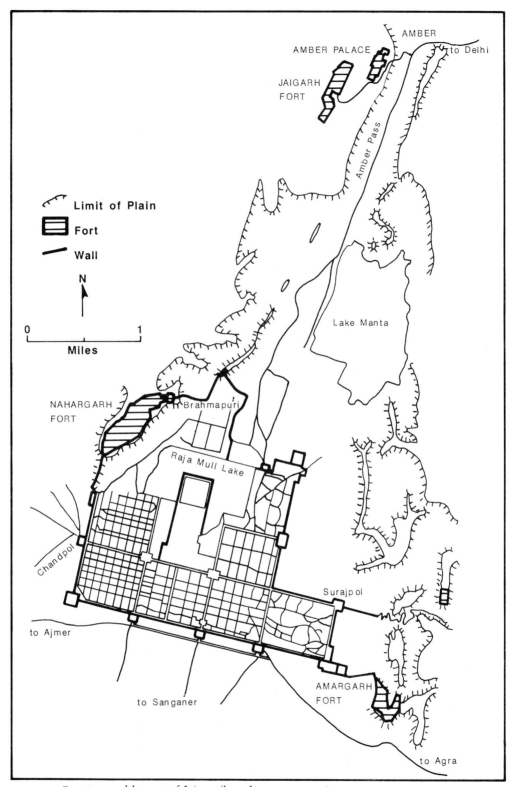

Fig. 3.1 Position and layout of Jaipur (based on 1865 map).

Another contrast with Chandigarh lies in the use of the two main intersections. Instead of having traffic roundabout, the squares or *chaupars* were designed as pedestrian areas for leisure or business. As such they were large, 110 yards square, and contained fountains fed by aqueducts laid beneath the street. These have since been filled in and the squares reduced in size and grassed over. A third *chaupar*, Ramgani Chaupar, was added some time later at the next intersection to the east.

The layout of the residential area has been the key to the future of all these cities, and here there are genuine similarities to Chandigarh. Traditionally Indian society, whether urban or rural, lived in communities distinguished by caste and subcastes which generally reflected occupations. Plots in the *chowkris* were allocated on this basis, with the higher castes being located closest to the palace and the lower castes against the city walls. Despite the disruptions of the last hundred years, this distribution still holds within the walled city, with the northeast sector of Gangapol distinctly low caste and containing many animals, and the whole inner area along the southern wall, known as the Harijan Basti, also of poor quality except where it has been cleared on either side of the New Gate to provide room for two markets, the Bapu and Nehru Bazaars, established for the use of the Sindhi and Punjabi refugees who flocked to the city in 1947 (Fig. 3.2).

Initially, Jaipur was an outstanding success. Its population grew to 130,000 by 1870 and to 160,000 by 1901. In 1879 it was described as a major banking center and money market for all Rajputana[4] based on its trade in precious stones and metals. Gold was imported for a small mint which exported over 100,000

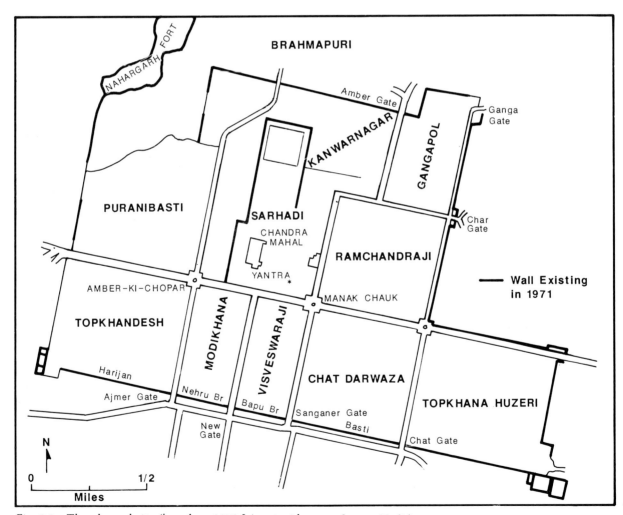

Fig. 3.2   The planned city (based on 1971 Jaipur guide map, *Survey of India*).

gold *mohurs* a year to the rest of India. Jehri Bazaar (Jewelers Market), which culminated in Manak Chauk (Ruby Square), was the center of this activity; and wealth drained from Agra and Delhi as a result of its success. The strength of its markets in other products was also sufficiently notable to attract traders from all parts of India, and overseas links were established through the seaport of Surat, a precursor to Bombay.

Despite this commercial activity, Jaipur never developed any industries of size and there were few other activities of note until the modern period.

A walled city is obviously at a disadvantage when it comes to expansion. Europe abounds with examples of medieval walled cities suffocated by their walls. The simplest remedy is to move outside and, given the topographical setting, it was not surprising that this occurred extensively to the south. The second half of the nineteenth century marked the first serious move outside (as opposed to settlement in existing villages and forts independent of the city) and followed the changeover to rule by the British government in place of the East Indian Company after 1857. The British were no longer prepared to leave the princely states alone and various agents and garrisons were stationed throughout the Agency of Rajputana (the British name for Rajasthan), including Jaipur. In fact, there had been a political agent in Jaipur since 1821, following a rebellion in the city the year before; and this post was maintained until 1947. The residency this agent occupied was a palace just over a mile from the southwest corner of the city which had been built as an occasional residence for the wife of Jai Singh II.

Simple as the expedient of expanding outside the walls appeared, it was in fact very destructive to the original socio-economic structure, which was, as explained, a centripetal one. The new demand for space expressed itself centrifugally and the leap-frogging of the wealthy and ruling classes to the suburbs led to a dualism of old and new separated by a band of low-status housing and functions. Areas such as Brahampuri were entirely abandoned and this settlement is today, in the words of Kohli, "a deserted village presenting a ghastly and shoddy appearance,"[3] and what Indra Pal calls "a slum-like village."[5]

In conclusion it would be fair to say that as a town planning venture Jaipur was initially a considerable success. It managed to provide a spatial framework within which the social customs and economic activity of a large population could function efficiently, and to this added considerable aesthetic character. The inability of the city to cope with subsequent developments should be seen in relation to the pace of change, the scale of change, and the change of function. The rapidity of growth led to a lack of control and haphazard building. The scale of growth could not be accommodated within the existing structure, whether it was housing, retailing or administration. Finally, several new functions, including industry, higher education and state administration, were added.

That the original city has survived this onslaught is perhaps remarkable and justifies the conclusion of a sound original plan that could have been stretched physically (though not socially) using an extension of the *chowkri* layout into the southern area. The width of the main roads was undoubtedly the key factor, for they traverse all areas of the walled city and could easily accommodate modern transport. This is no doubt fortuitous as Jai Singh II could have had no idea of the changes to come. He was, however, a maharajah and elephants were his mode of transport, especially on ceremonial occasions. He built on a grand scale and made certain that the streets were wide enough for his processions and his elephants. (Gangauri Bazaar and Gate were actually named after the procession which passed through them annually.)

In addition to these physical stresses there was a cultural problem, the presence of an alien society which refused to integrate with the existing one and set up its own community outside it. Jaipur's later history certainly illustrates the importance of this and the impact of British settlement must not be underestimated, but nowhere was it to be expressed so forcefully as in and around India's greatest city, Delhi.

New Delhi

Reflecting on the situation in Jaipur, a planned walled city overwhelmed by expansion in all sectors and growing unchecked and largely unplanned into a sprawling suburb to the south, it is hard not to draw some parallels with Delhi. Here too is an old walled city — Old Delhi or Shahjahanabad — equally unable to cope with the forces thrust on it, but in this case the expanded city was laid out and constructed without hindrances by the most reputed power in the field of town planning and yet the result for the Indian people was on almost every count an unmitigated failure.

In Delhi there had been the most profound example of continuous urban development by Hindu and Moslem rulers which culminated in the walled city built between 1638 and 1648, over two and one-half square miles to house 60,000 people at a density of 48 per acre and with an abundance of open spaces, parks and gardens, and roads amply wide for the pedestrian and animal traffic of the time. Had the experience and energy of this creation been combined with the resources and authority of the colonizing power an entirely different picture would have emerged. As is known, however, the two cultures did not combine but chose rather to compete, and in such a situation it was hardly surprising that the result was to the detriment of Indian urban life.

As the concern is with New Delhi, the details of the existing city, usually known as (Old) Delhi today, must be limited. The site had long been used because of its strategic position commanding the route into India from the northwest, and lying on the watershed between the Indus and Ganges Basins. To the northeast lay the Himalayas and to the southwest the desert. Evidence for the sites of at least seven previous cities has been recorded,[6][7] all located in the region between the 60 feet high quartzite Delhi Ridge to the west and the River Jamuna to the east, an area measuring about 5 miles by 11 miles but triangular in shape and tapering to the north.

Because of its strategic significance Delhi had had mixed fortunes by the nineteenth century. Its population has been estimated at 130,000 in 1800, with another 150,000 outside the walled area, although a population of half a million is quoted by Thakore for the fourteenth century.[8] Certainly it was a major commercial center by 1800 and, more so than Jaipur, an industrial center. As the name of its principal street, Chandni Chowk, indicates, silverware and jewelry were important as were other craft products including ivory work, embroidery and wood carving.

The responsibility for the design of New Delhi is credited to Edwin Lutyens and Herbert Baker, two architects largely noted for their designs of large houses for wealthy people, although Baker had been involved in colonial urban development in Africa.

It is apparent that the concepts of modern "garden city" planning as propounded and practiced in Britain at this time were quite absent, and in addition that the function of a town planner per se was confused with that of an architect. In retrospect it would appear that Lutyens and Baker were somewhat inexperienced for the job at hand, although to be charitable much of the design was outside their control and they probably met the required objectives. Unfortunately, the objectives were unsympathetic and inappropriate for the urban needs of the situation and they were neither able to recognize nor to remedy this.

In addition to the questionable choice of architects/planners, the seemingly cavalier attitude of the choice of site was a further indication of the prevailing mood. It was finally decided to locate the new city in the southern and unsettled area (apart from a few villages) rather than to cross the river or extend the already built-up northern area, despite the fact that King George V had already laid the foundation stone there. This in itself seemed a logical choice as much of the area north of the junction of the ridge and river Jamuna, and in the east adjacent to the river and south of Old Delhi, was liable to flood in four monsoons out of ten to a depth of about five feet of water (Fig. 3.3).[7]

Immediately west of the ridge the situation was better. In the north this was occupied by the cantonment and to the south by the same cantonment when it was re-sited. It would seem that the degree of separation from Old Delhi was too great here and presumably the distance would lessen the impact. In the end, the site chosen had good access to the old city, good drainage, and historical antecedents. Room to the south would allow later extension of the built-up area, although this was not a stated factor and the plan did not, in fact, make any such provisions for the future (Fig. 3.3).

The stage had thus been reached where it was just a matter of locating the vice regal palace ("Government House"), the fulcrum of Lutyens' plan; however, this was not in the end a choice to be left to planners or architects although this had been the intention (see footnote 10).

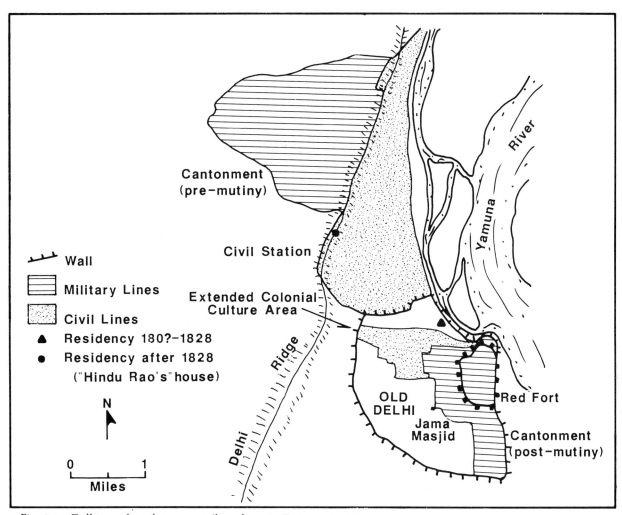

Fig. 3.3 Delhi — after the mutiny (based on A. D. King, 1976).

Viceroy Harding himself rode to the area, rejected out of hand the proposed site as being hot, cramped and without a view, and, in his own words:

> I then mounted and galloped over the plain to a hill some distance away. From the top of the hill there was a magnificent view embracing Old Delhi . . . . I said at once . . . . "this is the site for Government House."[8]

Basically, this was agreed and the location was admittedly appropriate, being a minor spur of the Delhi Ridge known as Raisina Hill and standing 50 feet above the plain (the top 20 feet was in fact blasted away to provide a level and larger surface); but it did illustrate what and who the planning was for.

The prime function of New Delhi was political and administrative and, of necessity but secondarily, residential. Industry was never entertained and is virtually absent even today in New Delhi proper. Indians in practice were a very limited part of the political scene and only the native princes were accommodated. In the administrative field it was reluctantly recognized that there were not enough Europeans to do the clerical jobs and so provision had to be made for housing indigenous clerks. No thought was given at all to housing for the lowest paid workers, the sweepers and such — *peons* — who though universally employed by everyone in power were presumably expected to vacate the city when their day's work was done.

On this basis an explanation of the residential layout can be attempted. It was formal, not functional, and the social axiom that "everyone knows their place" has never been more systematically translated into spatial reality. In Jaipur it was noted how proximity to the center was related to status, giving a

32

gradient of caste downwards from the palace area. This did not override the function of the city or its districts, but in New Delhi the process was carried to its ultimate extreme, based on the "Warrant of Precedence," a sort of social bible which ranked 175 civil and military posts from the Viceroy down. All other nonofficial positions also had some understood hierarchy. Superimposed on this was race. Thus, housing was assigned according to rank in the scale of precedence, and apart from the obvious differences in house style, size, plot and various facilities, of great geographical significance was the weighting given to distance from Government House and the width of road serving it. On the map the naming system, which was also ranked, is indicative of the status of the residences in that road (Figure 3.4).

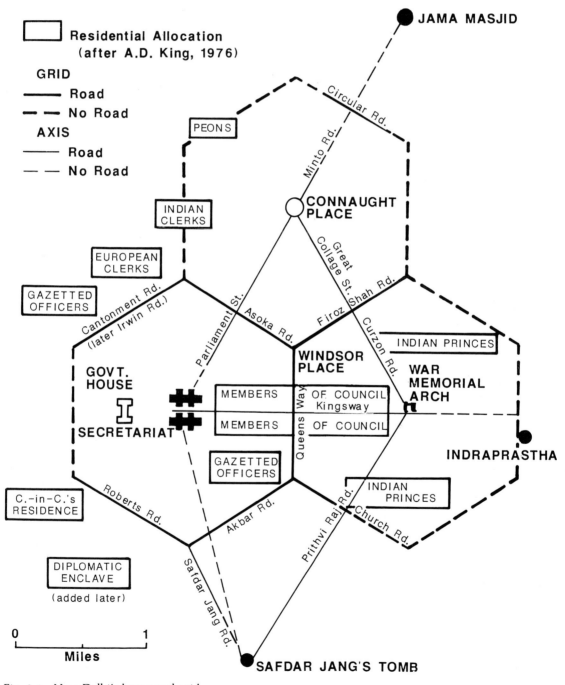

Fig. 3.4 New Delhi's hexagonal grid.

Most of the residential area was completed by 1925 and 3,000 civil servants could be housed. In the interim period the civil lines north of the old city had been adapted as a temporary capital and some important additions were made to it, notably a large secretariat in 1912. The facilities laid out for the Durbar were also put to use, and a Government House was created in the building used to house the King Emperor, while clerks were housed in the various barracks and tent cities of the main Durbar area. These were again brought into use at the time of Partition to house the enormous influx of refugees from Pakistan and, more recently, they have been squatted in by the poorest classes.

Of all the problems faced, housing is by far the most serious. Even the areas provided for in the plan were of poor standard and congested. The typical clerk accommodation wasted space by placing small dwellings in terraces around large squares. These had for the main one story, one room and communal facilities. No provision was made for expansion, an unforgivable omission, and by the mid-1950s half a million people lived in slums and another quarter of a million were squatters spread out over some 500 unauthorized colonies on the outskirts of the city. Sixty-nine percent of the dwellings had only one room (including all parts of Delhi) compared with an average of 44 percent for all India, and over 65 percent had neither kitchen nor toilet.[11] While densities today rarely exceed 100 per acre in New Delhi, they often exceed 1,000 per acre in Old Delhi.[9] In 1978, medium-rise apartments were under construction everywhere — "houses for the civil servants" was the universal explanation. And yet, only 20 percent of the population earned enough to buy the cheapest accommodation unaided. Only 12 percent of the plots handled by the Delhi Development Authority have been sold to the lowest income group despite a policy of setting aside 50 percent of their plots for this group. This largely reflects the insatiable demand from the higher income groups and a waiting list of 27,000 for flats ranging in price from 7,500 rupees to 80,000 rupees. There are in fact few flats available at the lowest price, and a current self-financing scheme is only concerned with those in the 60,000 to 125,000 rupees (about $8,500 to $17,500) range.[12]

Houses are virtually banned and Housing Societies may only form for the purpose of multi-story construction in areas that are miles away from the places of work. As a result a unique reversal of the normal pattern of densities and building heights has taken place and is continuing, for whereas high-rise developments and high densities are normally associated with central areas, the opposite has been the case in New Delhi, and possibly nothing else better expresses the differences in the aims of those who founded the city and those who use it.

It would be unfair to suggest that New Delhi has had anything like a normal pattern of growth, however, and it has particularly suffered from the flood of refugees from Pakistan; from its greatly enhanced importance as the national capital, and from the considerable resultant expansion of government-related commercial and industrial activities. The current Master Plan for Delhi, completed in 1961, foresees a population of 5 million by 1987. It is thus true that much has been forced on this city over which few had control, but with a little justifiable foresight many of the present difficulties could have been limited in their effect.

The Town Planning Organization in 1962[11] reported a deficit of 110,000 houses, 382 primary and 44 secondary schools, and 10 large hospitals. The majority of Delhi's water supply is polluted and intermittent, yet because the British laid out a quite separate irrigation system for the open spaces of New Delhi the parks are always green and the fountains always flowing. The original housing of New Delhi is the exclusive preserve of embassy staff, foreign experts, private company personnel, and senior government staff, in all except the peripheral areas. Guest houses, private companies, banks, airlines, government and quasi-government offices, and hotels (notably the Akbar, Ashoka and Oberoi Intercontinental) have supplanted the rest.

To many, New Delhi is an obstacle separating them from Old Delhi. Even for those who work in it there is no railway station, the railway lines being well clear of the planned area. However much one mourns the loss of such an opportunity to provide India with a fitting monument to Western urban technology, it is nevertheless a fact that New Delhi is little more than a spatial anachronism in the average citizen's life. Indeed, for the most part it is treated as an historic spectacle, displayed to the tourist along with the tombs and ruins of the past and, like them, devoid of a normal life. Only the roads really serve the population and then it is only to take them through the city as quickly as possible.

Chandigarh

There is much that is different and unique about Chandigarh, but its origins, rather than its character, are probably the most fundamental when considering its value to Indian society.

Primarily it was born out of necessity. After Partition the capital of the Punjab, Lahore, lay on the Pakistani side of the border and there was a need to reestablish an Indian Punjabi capital at once. As Simla, the summer capital of the Raj, fell within the new Indian state of the Punjab, this was initially chosen. It was, however, most inappropriate for this task, being difficult to reach, particularly so in winter, isolated from the Punjabi plains, and in its site incapable of modernization or expansion. It has subsequently become the capital of the new mountain state of Himachal Pradesh.

Rather than create a "New Lahore" next to an existing city (which however was very much Pakistan's solution in building Islamabad), it was decided to build an entirely new city; and this was incorporated in India's first Five Year Plan, 1951-56. As early as 1950 an approach was made to Albert Mayer of the United States, a friend of Nehru, and he was asked to prepare a plan. This was done, but unfortunately a shortage of U.S. dollars and the death of Mayer's chief assistant, when returning from India after a detailed study of the site, led to a curtailment of this first scheme.

The architects finally commissioned were Maxwell Fry and his partner/wife Jane Drew. They in turn suggested that Le Corbusier be appointed architectural advisor and after some early difficulty persuaded him to accept the post, together with his partner/cousin Pierre Jeanneret. From within this team it was Le Corbusier who produced the final version of the Master Plan, that of a Sector City. Essentially, this was based on the principal that the city was comprised of semi-independent sectors which could be added to the basic infrastructure as it expanded.

Le Corbusier's and the other architects' objectives were at the simplest level to provide the best possible man-made environment in which to work, reside and relax. The overall structure depended on Le Corbusier's long-held philosophy of the separation of living space from traffic, and the neighborhood provision of all basic services within walking distance. In his role as architect, Le Corbusier designed most of the important public buildings, while his colleagues dealt mainly with the sectors and their housing and public service buildings, such as schools, clinics and shops.

Chandigarh's Master Plan was the product of the evolution of garden city planning in both Europe and the U.S.A. In concept it would have been surprising if anything other than a Sector Design had resulted for a population of about 500,000 or even for the later reduction to 300,000 as this was the only tried and tested model which adequately embodied the four functions accepted as essential in modern urbanism, namely living, working, playing and circulating. (Chandigarh in 1981 had 421,256 people.)

The philosophy behind Mayer's original plan and Le Corbusier's revisions were most important as they explain so much about Chandigarh. In the main, Mayer designed a gaden city following the teaching of Ebenezer Howard whom he had done much to publicize in America. Chandigarh was to be "an essentially peaceful city, not one where complications must be counteracted by other complications."[13] His prime concern was for the quality of domestic life as exemplified by the Indian village and realized in the neighborhood units of his superblocks. He considered many Indian urban dwellers to be still villagers at heart. In the context of his life's work, he at least had an opportunity to build a city which in the U.S.A. was impossible due to vested interests, but in India would be, in Nehru's own words, "free from the existing encumbrances of old towns and old traditions."[14]

In addition, and not surprisingly, he disliked New Delhi's "overscaled sterility and stiltedness" and all that it stood for — "the class stratification and paternalistic symbolism of Lutyens' grandiose early nineteenth century 'White Raj' urban designing."[14]

At first sight it is the formal aspect of the final plan that is so striking, and the regularization of the street lines was a response to two all-pervading elements in Le Corbusier's vision of architecture and planning. The first was his desire to plan for the machine age and thus define a city by its traffic pattern. One of the reasons for the non-fruition of many of his plans was his stated intention "to create architectural machines serving the purpose of government and administration with the greatest efficiency"[15] and into which man then had to fit. Le Corbusier clearly believed that a thorough understanding of physiology and its accommodation through modern technology was sufficient, and after that man would fit the module he had made for him. His own "skyscraper," the Unite D'Habitation in Marseilles, and the sociological failure of high-rise developments in general bear witness to the fallacy of this view. In Chandigarh the principles of the theoretical Radiant City, a vision of skyscrapers served by multi-level, multi-lane, high-speed highways, have been realized, but in two dimensions and not three. As a result it has tended to be a highly compartmentalized and divided entity evoking the criticism that it may well become "a monument to one man's preconceived vision of a tidied-up society" (Fig. 3.5).[15]

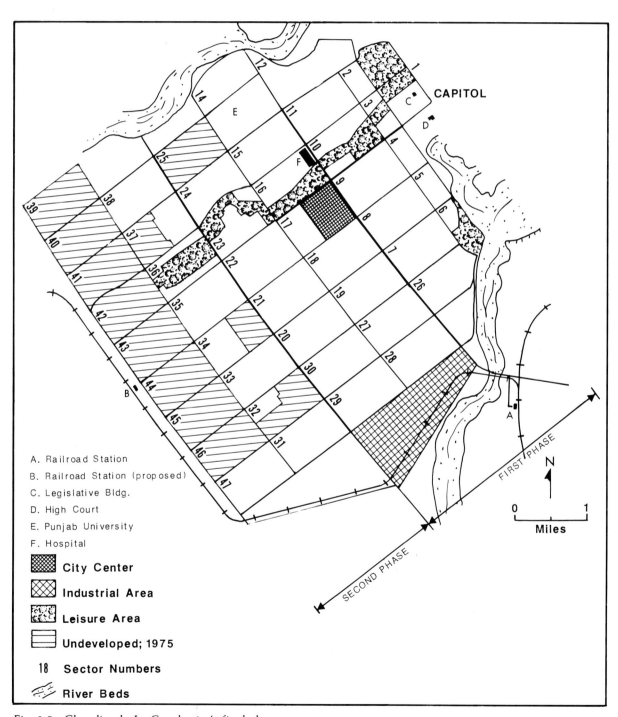

Fig. 3.5 Chandigarh: Le Courbusier's final plan.

Crude as the grid plan of main roads might appear at first sight, it was not only the widths and functions that had been carefully thought out, but also the orientation which provided all the "up and down" roads with a clear view of the Himalayas to the northeast, and so prevents the loss of orientation common to New Delhi's radial system. In addition, the crossing roads, which are in fact slightly curved, run northwest to southeast and therefore shield drivers from the low rays of the setting sun. The distance between intersections has also been carefully considered and is in striking contrast to the traditional Indian grid because it is so big. In most Indian cities the grid system is usually related to pedestrian and animal speeds, and intersections at roughly 100 yard intervals would be common. As motorized traffic moves at about ten times this pace, the sides are that much bigger — about 900 x 1,300 yards.

The residential area is embodied in 30 of the first 36 sectors. Sector 22 was an experimental one, but each sector layout is different in detail, as are housing types and styles. On the debit side must be considered several of the forces already noted, both Indian and British Colonial in origin. Already mentioned (see New Delhi section) was the overlooking of housing provision for the very poorest. Jane Drew, the architect most concerned with this, was originally working with a budget of $585 for a peon's house, the lowest of thirteen grades. She subsequently provided a class of housing for only $370, for the lowest grades of all — the ubiquitous sweepers. This was an astonishing achievement, especially when it is realized that these houses contained two rooms, verandah, kitchen and w.c. plus a courtyard. This was largely made possible by the extremely low labor wages and price of bricks at $3.60 per thousand! Nevertheless, providing housing for the poorest is an intractable problem faced by all cities, and shanty towns both exist and are spreading in Chandigarh despite low construction costs. There is in fact an undersupply of housing of all grades in spite of the rapid early progress.

Regrettably the classic problem, exemplified in New Delhi, is rampant in Chandigarh as well. Although initially the state built the bulk of the housing and 80 percent of this was for the lowest recognized grade of workers, financial problems have led to the auctioning of lots to private builders and today over 70 percent of all construction is in private hands. Given the shortages for all income groups it is inevitable that all this building is for the upper income groups. Even so, prices are so high that every new building, whatever the planning controls in force, is inhabited by multiple tenants or owners and many standards have deteriorated. That the authorities should have so readily relinquished control of the planning process is perhaps the single greatest criticism and the source of greatest conflict among those involved in the project.

Incorporated in the sector concept was the objective that every household should be within 15 minutes walking distance of school facilities. Usually, several schools serving different levels and sexes are found, clear of the bazaar road, and located within the central green band which in general provides leisure space in each sector. Running through the sectors in a longitudinal direction are eight green swathes (Mayer originally had two) which, although at present needing landscaping and organization outside the areas of sports clubs and school playing fields, was Le Corbusier's answer to green belts and park provision. There is a more developed leisure zone, known sometimes as "Leisure Valley," similarly located but broader and based on the presence of a small river bed running from Sector 1 through 5 to 42. This includes some notable developments, including a 30 acre rose garden in Sector 16 (Fig. 3.5).

The capitol (Sector 1) is a natural focus of attention, lying as it does against the panoramic backdrop of the Himalayas; and it is interesting to contrast its impact with that of the capitol buildings in New Delhi. In the latter there seemed to be something of the Washington, D.C. vision of dominance and power, of a commanding presence approached along a sacred and uncluttered mall, while in Chandigarh, for all Le Corbusier's admiration of the scale of New Delhi, the architecture and setting are far more pragmatic and do not command the city. To some the utility of construction may detract entirely from the general regard in which the buildings are held, being for the most part constructed of concrete deliberately left bare to show the shuttering pattern. The recent buildings of the South Bank entertainment complex in London illustrate the style, first introduced by Le Corbusier himself in the 1930s. There is little if any of the detailed decoration of traditional Indian architecture, which is superbly expressed in Jaipur and which Herbert Baker overlaid on his essentially Italianate style secretariat buildings in New Delhi. Chandigarh's secretariat is really nothing more than a rather large office block at first glance, and, sensitive as ever, Le Corbusier oriented it end on so that far from dominating the city it would only minimally interrupt the view to the Himalayas.

To say that development is fully controlled and that Chandigarh will be allowed to evolve in a planned framework would be far from the truth, however. Close control of building is only within the city's power as far as its boundaries, and there is no policy governing settlement in general, either at the state or national level. As a result two potentially disruptive, but perhaps initially complementary, townships have arisen nearby (Fig. 3.6).

Chandigarh provides so much that is absent in India that its main criticism is very much for doing just that[16] and providing a typically middle-class environment. If the suggestion implicit in this is that a city should have been built for India's poorest classes, the endeavor would surely have been hopeless, especially given the context of Chandigarh as a capital city. Houses down to a cost of $150 have been

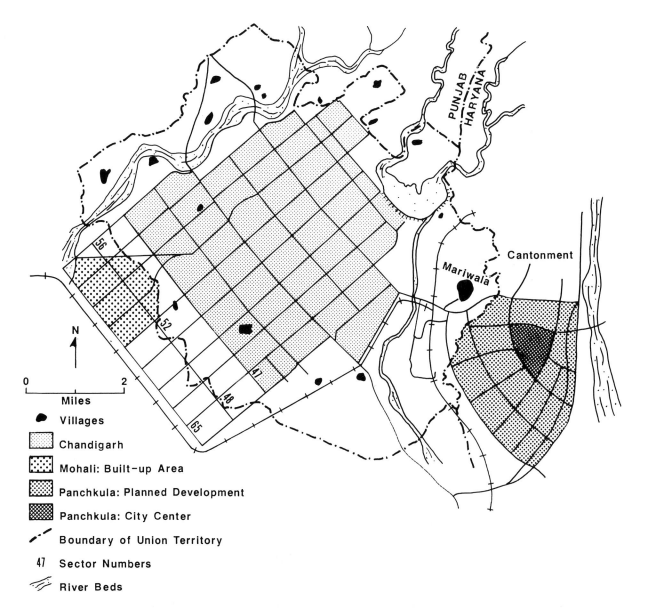

Fig. 3.6 Planned settlement outside Chandigarh: Mohali and Panchkula (based on government of India maps and H. Schmetzer and P. Wakely, 1974).

provided and those who cannot afford them — and many cannot — will need a degree of institutional assistance beyond the scope of the planner to initiate and, so far, outside the ability of poor nations to pay.

The appearance of the city as a sort of Milton Keynes transferred to the Punjabi Plains, simply because certain planning principles are common to both, does not bear inspection in detail; and those who would wish Indian style architecture seem to mean the colonial style bungalow with verandahs all around, cool but expensive in both building costs and space consumption. Difficulties with water supply and the extremely rapid pace of growth so that the demand far exceeds supply have created many problems, but these are circumstantial, not inherent. The grass can be made greener, the dust will be less as building activity declines, and given time the wayside trees will grow. Compared with most Indian cities Chandigarh is clean, attractive and well-equipped. Le Corbusier and his colleagues, in the words of one commentator, have at last "wrung out the heritage of indifference and bad taste left by the Victorian British minds who ruled (India) for two centuries."[17]

END NOTES

[1]T. J. Manicham, et al. "New Towns in India, " in *Selected Papers; Public Administration Problems of New and Rapidly Growing Towns in Asia.* (New York: United Nations, 1962).

[2]A. Whittick. *Encyclopaedia of Urban Planning.* (New York: McGraw-Hill, 1976).

[3]Indra Pal. *Jaipur, A Study in Urban Land Use.* Abstract of Papers, 21st International Geographical Congress, Delhi, 1968.

[4]Major C. A. Baylay. "Jaipur," in *Imperial Gazeteer of India: Rajputana,* Vol. 1, 1879; Vol. 2, 1879; Provincial Series, 1908.

[5]Kohli. *A Guide to Jaipur and Amber.* Undated.

[6]Gordon Hearn. *Seven Cities of Delhi.* Calcutta, 1928.

[7]Ujagir Singh. "New Delhi, Its Site and Situation," *National Geographical Journal of India,* Vol. 5 (3) 1959, p. 113.

[8]Anthony D. King. *Colonial Urban Development.* Routledge, 1976.

[9]King, *op. cit.* The planned population for New Delhi was very low, a mere 30,000 plus dependents, later increased to 65,000, spread over 32 square miles. As dependents were limited it is reasonable to assume 125,000 to be the maximum envisaged, a density of only 6 per acre.!

[10]Delhi Town Planning Committee. *First Report on the Choice of a Site for the New Imperial Capital.* London, 1913.

[11]Town Planning Organization (India). "Delhi, Some Economic Issues in Urban Planning," in *Selected Papers; Public Administration Problems of New and Rapidly Growing Towns in Asia.* (New York: United Nations, 1962).

[12]V. K. Dethe. "Delhi Development Authority Performance Belies Promise," *The Times of India,* August 5 and 6, 1978.

[13]Norma Evanson. *Chandigarh.* University of California Press, 1966.

[14]A. E. J. Morris. "Chandigarh: The Plan Corb Tore Up?," *Built Environment Quarterly,* Vol. 1, No. 3 (Dec. 1975), pp. 229-234.

[15]Russell Walden. *The Open Hand — Essays on Le Corbusier.* M.I.T. Press, 1977. Includes (1) Maxwell Fry, "Le Corbusier at Chandigarh;" (2) Madhu Sarin, "Chandigarh as a Place to Live In;" (3) Stanislaus von Moos, "The Politics of the Open Hand."

[16]Michael Madgwick. "India's New Town: Le Corbusier's Chandigarh," *Building Design,* No. 420 (Nov. 1978), p. 16.

[17]Marg. Editorial Comment, 1974.

[18]H. Schmetzer and P. I. Wakely. "Chandigarh: 20 Years Later," *Architectural Design,* Vol. 44 (June 1974), pp. 350-361.

[19]Survey of India. *Chandigarh Guide Map.* 1:20,000. 1972.

4

Reflections on Primacy: Cases from Asia

Norton Ginsburg

The reasons for reconsidering primacy as an issue in understanding the developing polities in Asia are: (1) the considerable differences of opinion as to what its implications are, (2) a recent spate of literature relating directly or indirectly to the concept, and (3) a range of definitions as to what the term means. With regard to the last of these, for the most part it refers to a particularly dominant city in a national urban hierarchy, usually as measured in terms of a population size commonly several times larger than that of the next largest city.

With regard to the first reason, the causes and significance of primacy are shrouded in uncertainty. To be sure, there have been reviews of the subject, in a measured way by Richardson among others,[1] but primacy continues to have a bad name, at least with regard to development and what might be termed "spatial justice." Most of the recent literature, as well as some of the older, regards the Primate City as a villain, interfering with national development and exacerbating the inequalities in incomes that characterize all countries but particularly those in the "developing" category. As exemplars of this literature, I refer to works by Bruce London,[2] Dennis Rondinelli,[3] and Lee de Cola,[4] whose article in *Economic Development and Cultural Change* nonetheless is a technical *tour de force*. To be sure, these works and others like them do not focus necessarily on primacy alone; they also are concerned with the nature of urban hierarchies overall, with rank-size relationships among cities, and with the relations between urbanization and development, for the most part in developing countries.

With regard to current usage, I was taken aback when reading Chauncy Harris' excellent piece on urbanization in Japan in which he refers to Tokyo as "clearly the Primate City" of Japan,[5] since the Tokyo metropolitan area (Kei-hin) is less than twice the size of its nearest rival (Kei-han-shin); and this led me to go back and read Mark Jefferson's seminal statement again.[6] Harris, of course was right, in that Jefferson clearly refers to a condition of "double primacy" and cites New York, *inter alia*, as an example. However, conventional usage would require a much higher proportion of population for a first-ranking city in a national urban system if the term "Primate City" were to be applied to it. Moreover, there have been frequent references in recent years to "regional primacy," as in China or India, and this usage also has been thought-provoking.[7]

Given these stimuli, I sought out what I had to say on the subject before. As it turns out, 25 years ago I wrote for the *Atlas of Economic Development*:

> The conclusion is inescapable that primacy is not a simple correlate of national income and political status. The Primate City is found in more prosperous and long-established, as well as in poorer, newer countries, but it does appear to be more common in the latter than in the former, especially where the state is small enough in population and territory so that some one city combines the functions of national capital, commercial metropole, chief port, and center of the Great Tradition (or nationalism) of the country concerned. On these grounds one could reasonably postulate a high probability for the development of Primate Cities in countries newly independent and with changing economies, as a result of the high localization of increasing political and economic functions in them. This prediction would better fit those states which are comparatively small and compact, with few barriers to areal integration, and with small to medium populations of relative ethnic homogeneity, but without a deep-rooted urban tradition. Only time will tell.[8]

What time appears to tell is that were one to write such a statement today, certain changes would be in order if not essential, especially if one were to speak solely of Asian cities, since the quotation refers to a global pattern. At the same time, most of the generalizations, explicit or implied, would, in my view, still stand. What I propose to do in the rest of this paper is to explore what some of the changes and additions might be. To this end, Table 4.1, which contains some useful information (as well as some that might not be as useful), has been prepared. Among other things it lists indices of primacy based on data for the mid-1950s compiled for the *Atlas of Economic Development*[9] and another set of indices based upon more recent data, in addition to some general population data and information about urban and economic growth. One should be well aware, as I will point out further below, that these data are highly suspect and might not be entirely comparable. Since most of the countries with which we are dealing fall into the category of "underdeveloped," and a prime hallmark of underdevelopment is scant or unreliable information, that is understandable. Still, caution is the word.

However, before looking at this information and using it as a basis for some general comments, it might be well to quickly review what has gone before and what are some of the problems of definition and interpretation of primacy.

Mark Jefferson first introduced the concept of primacy in his *Law of the Primate City* published in 1939. Jefferson clearly had in mind a conception of the great city as the bearer of high civilizations, as a symbol, as an expression of high culture, as the generator and purveyor of ideas within a given culture. His models were such cities as London and Paris, which were world cities and which dominated the urban systems in their respective countries. He noted, however, that, although these were many times larger than their nearest rivals, cities of lesser size relative to second cities, such as New York, also could qualify; and he observed that outside of Europe and North America there were a number of cities which would satisfy the criteria for primacy. His implied thesis was that inevitably such cities would come into being, unless prevented from doing so by presumably unusual if not abnormal circumstances.

Although Jefferson's proposal struck a respondent chord among geographers, it is not clear what its impact was among other social scientists. Fei, Hsiao-tung, the distinguished British-educated Chinese sociologist, knew of Jefferson's work and referred to it in his *China's Gentry*, written in the late '40s; but in the version edited by Margaret Park Redfield and Robert Redfield, an editorial footnote by the Redfields to Fei's reference to Jefferson reads simply, "The Mark Jefferson reference has not been found."[10]

Two years after Jefferson's article appeared, George Zipf proposed a so-called "rank-size rule" for cities, which was a special case of a more general proposition that many phenomena were rank-ordered in the same way.[11] In 1947 John Q. Stewart applied the principle to the cities of the United States,[12] and despite reservations the formula quickly found its way into the urban geographical literature as an idealized expression of a Pareto or log-normal statistical distribution for cities in given countries. This formulation coincided with a burgeoning interest among geographers in quantitative methods, and it carried remarkable appeal at a time when the ideas of Christaller and Losch also were having their effect. Although the notion of hierarchy was in fact at variance with the concept of continuous rank-size relations, the two sets of propositions reinforced each other operatively on the American scene. Many attempts were made to reconcile the two, with mixed results, but the idea became commonly held that departures from one or the other of these formulations were unnatural, dysfunctional, or, better, disorderly, that is, lacking in order. This was not, of course, what Jefferson had in mind at all. To him order did not simply mean regularity; it meant comprehensibility. Still, the appeal of a principle of regularity was strong. If rank-size regularity were indeed the consequence of innumerable forces moving more or less in the same direction toward some state of long-term equilibrium as suggested by Stewart,[13] then one would have a standard against which to compare divergencies or, if you like, residuals. One might even be able to relate urbanization and city systems to economic development.

The difficulty with this view, and it would be well to state it early, is the strongly implied assumption behind it, that social processes lead to an "ideal-typical" state of equilibrium, a comforting notion if true. However, most thoughtful social scientists would reject such a proposition, would regard it as suspect and simple-minded, and would seek some alternative formulation. Within the little knowledge we have about societal change and its geographical concomitants is the fact that all social systems are in a state of continuing disequilibrium. There is no equivalent of a "climax vegetation," for example, in human affairs. This is what distinguishes human behavior and its consequences from those of other elements in nature. To be sure, a standard such as a rank-size distribution might be useful in making certain kinds of comparisons, but its utility in *explaining* such differences inevitably would be small, unless some equilibrium state could be demonstrated.

TABLE 4.1

Asiatic Triangle: Population and Urbanization

Country	1982 Population (millions)	Area (000km²)	Density (per km²)	Annual Increase Rate (1975-82)	Per Cent Population Urban	Annual Urban Growth Rates (1975-80)	Primacy Index (1950s)	Primacy Index (ca. 1980)	Alt. Primacy Index (ca. 1980)	Annual Growth of GNP/ca. (ca. 1970-79)
EAST ASIA										
1. China (inc. HK/Macau)	1,031.88	9,597	106	1.4	20.5	3.2	44.8	47	.89	2.8
(Taiwan)	18.14	36	411	2.0	69.3	--	49.7	48	.94	7.3
2. Japan	118.45	372	314	0.9	78.3	1.7	454.7	49	.97	3.9
3. Korea, North	18.75	121	156	2.4	59.7	4.0	42.1	n.a.	n.a.	n.a.
4. Korea, South	39.33	98	399	1.8	54.8	4.3	47.9	59	1.43	8.1
5. Mongolia	1.76	1,565	1	2.9	50.4	4.1	62.5	n.a.	n.a.	n.a.
SUB-TOTAL	1,210.17	11,753	100	1.4	32.8	2.9				
SOUTHEAST ASIA										
1. Brunei	.25	6	43	5.5	76.3	8.6	n.a.	n.a.	n.a.	4.6
2. Burma	37.06	677	55	2.2	27.2	4.3	68.1	72	2.5	2.0
3. Cambodia	6.98	181	39	-0.2	13.9	0.9	81.6	n.a.	n.a.	n.a.
4. Indonesia	153.05	2,027	80	1.7	20.2	3.6	45.6	57	1.3	4.6
5. Laos	3.90	237	16	2.4	13.4	5.7	n.a.	58	.65	n.a.
6. Malaysia	14.76	330	45	3.1	29.4	3.6	60.8	54	1.2	5.4
7. Philippines	50.70	300	169	2.7	36.2	3.8	82.0	80	4.1	3.9
8. Singapore	2.47	(.581)	4,254	1.3	74.1	1.2	n.a.	n.a.	n.a.	6.7
9. Thailand	48.45	514	94	2.1	14.4	3.5	94.2	95	12.6	4.4
10. Vietnam	56.21	330	171	2.3	19.8	3.3	n.a.	55	1.2	n.a.
SUB-TOTAL	373.81	4,069	80	2.1	22.8	3.6				
SOUTH ASIA										
1. Afghanistan	16.79	647	26	2.6	15.4	5.8	46.5	71	2.4	n.a.
2. Bangladesh	1.36	47	29	2.2	3.9	4.8	n.a.	n.a.	n.a.	n.a.
3. Bhutan	92.62	144	643	2.3	11.2	6.7	n.a.	58	.95	0.8
4. Ceylon (Sri Lanka)	15.19	66	232	1.7	26.6	3.8	78.0	58	1.4	2.5
5. India	711.66	3,288	216	2.2	22.2	3.4	44.4	50	.50	1.6
6. Nepal	15.02	141	100	2.9	5.0	4.9	73.9	n.a.	n.a.	0.3
7. Pakistan	87.13	804	109	3.0	28.2	4.2	n.a.	59	1.4	1.5
SUB-TOTAL	939.77	5,137	183	2.2	22.5	3.6				
TOTAL	2,523.69	20,959	120	1.8 (est.)						

Nevertheless, as noted earlier, the recent geographical, sociological and planning literatures, especially about developing countries, are highly pejorative with regard to primacy.[14] London describes Bangkok as having "historically been parasitic throughout Thai history," although, to be fair, he recognizes different types and degrees of parasitism.[15] Salah El-Shakhs views primacy as a part of a stage of development through which developing countries pass and then, presumably happily, move on to an Elysian state of "balanced hierarchy" as they develop economically and politically.[16]

I should like to propose that primacy, on the contrary, may well better fit the general case, at least in Asia, but only under certain conditions, than a rank-size or "balanced hierarchy" formulation. Let me couch the argument in this way.

Every central place is primate in and for its hinterland. This is easily seen in instances of local market towns, for example. As one moves up the size-ratchet of settlements, this proposition continues to make good sense. Settlements that perform a multiplicity of functions above and beyond those of smaller, lesser neighbors within their hinterlands are likely to be much larger in size and in range of services rendered and territory commanded.

The towns that studded the margins of archipelagic Southeast Asia, for example, in the pre-modern period all were primate to their immediate hinterlands. However, as they established relations with their peers, they took on additional functions which stimulated their growth and led increasingly to their becoming more substantial centers of processing and exchange in their own right. Melaka is a case in point.[17] Thus their early thrust toward primacy was reinforced with these changes. Angkor Thom, also a Primate City, was neither a port nor a mercantile center; however it was in a political-cultural sense a "navel of the Universe" and that universe was defined in terms of the extent of its control over territory and population as well as by its significance as a symbol of the divinity of its rulers. Similar examples might be drawn from South Asia as well.

There were, then, in effect two kinds of urban centers in this over-generalized picture: those that were primarily administrative centers and entrepots, with small immediate landward hinterlands, and those that were administrative centers with extensive hinterlands. Both of these, however were "parasitic" in the sense that Hoselitz used the term, in that they were not producers of wealth but organizers of it and mediators in its distribution.[18]

The colonial city that followed from these was in smaller countries modeled more after the first type than the second, but in both instances they were less actively engaged in the production of wealth than in siphoning it off to the metropoles. It is important, however, to note that very quickly, and following the decline of Portuguese power in Asia, the colonial powers and the cities which were the "head-links" to and for them, became actively engaged in the production process. British imperialism in South and Southeast Asia, as well as Dutch and French, introduced new patterns of production upon the old and in many ways left the old largely alone. British policy toward the Malays in Malaysia is a conspicuous case in point. Who the wealth benefited is another matter, but the great cities evolving during the colonial period everywhere in Asia became the focal points *both* for administration of dependent territories *and* for coordinating the production of new wealth, oriented toward export to be sure, in the form of estate products, forest and mineral products, and new lands brought under cultivation, as in southern Burma, for the production of traditional crops like paddy, but under new management so to speak. Such cities, primate in the smaller territories but not in the larger, reached out into the national hinterlands under colonial rule through improved inland waterway facilities, railways, and to some extent roads, and they became, in the larger entities at least, linked with one another more effectively than they were to their immediate settled hinterlands, which remained in many ways little touched by these new developments. They also were generative, as were the pre-colonial entrepots, and therefore were modernizing agents in that they brought together diverse populations with a broader world view than that of the rural peasantry. This was the pattern even in non-colonial Thailand, although there the drive of the monarchy toward national integration as a device for partially countering prospective partitioning and dependency played an important role.

One of the consequences of these developments was an increasing coincidence of the overall distribution of population in most Asian countries with that of the great cities. In the few instances where hierarchies of cities, including some great ones, antedated the expansion of Europe into Asia, as in China and Japan and, to a degree, India (although the late Nisith Kar argued that such a hierarchy came into being in India only within the last two centuries, that is, during the British period), cities were located for the most part in or immediately adjacent to areas of major population concentration, a condition associated in turn with heavy reliance on local wet-paddy cultivation. In those without such indigenous urban systems, population came to be concentrated in areas near the evolving colonial capitals and other centers. Such was the case in Burma, Malaya, the Philippines, to a lesser degree Vietnam, and Thailand.

The former centers of colonial administration and coordination for the most part also became the centers of power, authority and, in a sense, the management of the newly independent states. As governmental bureaucracies flourished, both people and investment have been concentrated in these centers which continue to exert influence, if not strict control, over not only their more immediate hinterlands but over the peripheral territory of the national polity as well.

Improved technology has intensified the dominance of these large urban centers. In transportation no portion of national territories is inaccessible to central authority by rail, air or road. Moreover, governments control communications media such as radio, and these have fed back upon metropolitan dominance and further stimulated it and the primacy with which it is often associated.

That technology also affected relations between the city and the areas contiguous to it. Formerly these were poorly connected. As time has passed, they have become increasingly well articulated, particularly through the proliferation of bus services. What this means is that the immediate hinterlands of these cities — their umlands — have been extended some 100 kilometers from the outer limits of their built-up areas, and commuting between city and hinterland has increased at astronomical rates, even where, as in the case of Calcutta, it had already been important. In short, Asian cities now are not only relatively well connected with remote hinterlands of specialized production and with each other but also increasingly are associated, even as they themselves grow rapidly, with a large part of their national populations, if not a majority of them.

The fact that metropolitan populations themselves are growing rapidly and that the per capita income and therefore purchasing power are so much greater than those of populations in small towns and rural areas has been related to a concentration of manufactural industry in the larger cities, which then act as major markets for goods domestically consumed as well as for products to be exported. Most manufacturing other than that which has a clear and direct raw material base is located in the larger cities, whether or not national policies are oriented toward export or import substitution. Although manufacturing employment remains a minor element in most Asian countries, as it grows its impact is bound to be greatest on cities and particularly on the larger ones. Although there is nothing surprising about such a generalization, it should not be overlooked. The continued growth of the larger cities, including those that are primate, is associated with a process of "cumulative causation," to use Gunnar Myrdal's phrase, which is unlikely to be reversed or substantially modified through decentralization to smaller places though there are somewhat ambiguous evidences of such a trend in China, the Koreas, and, of course, Japan. But even in those cases, decentralization tends to appear more in cities of a satellite character with regard to the metropolitan areas than those in more distant locations.

With these propositions in mind, one can look at the accompanying table of Asian populations and urban characteristics. Almost all countries in the region display varying rates of population growth, higher in the South and Southeast Asian realms than in the East Asian realm; and urban population growth rates are considerably higher than those of overall national rates.

With regard to primacy itself, it is possible in most cases to compare primacy indices for both the mid-1950s and for approximately 25 years later, depending on the data available. These indices show the percentage of population in the four largest cities in each country that is accounted for by the largest city, an index developed originally for the *Atlas of Economic Development*, which permitted the calculation of a weighted world mean, 55 percent in the 1950s. This figure appears to be a reasonable one for the later period as well. It is striking how few changes there have been over time. A small shift upward in the case of Burma and Malaysia (*sans* Singapore), a larger one in the case of Indonesia, a slight shift downward (unexpectedly) in the case of South Korea and substantially downward in the case of Sri Lanka are among those worth noting. In some other countries, e.g., Afghanistan and Cambodia, changes appear to be associated with domestic unrest if not disaster. In any event, the ranges in both periods appear comparable.

Moreover, there appears to be little relationship between rates of economic growth and primacy, but some countries that have been doing well economically show more of it, like South Korea, or continue moving toward primacy, like Indonesia and Malaysia. Also, there continues to be a strong inverse relationship between primacy and size of country. Smaller countries continue to show a strong positive relationship or are moving in that direction, as in the case of Malaysia; larger countries continue to show low levels of primacy.

The table does not show measures of regional primacy within large countries, but even though there are indications of positive change in India and China, these are modest enough to make generalization uncertain. Still, primacy on a regional basis would seem to be in the natural order of things even in countries with well-developed urban systems like China. Although transportation improvements are bound to take place in China, for example, it is difficult to forecast what the effects will be on regional primacy. Better transportation would permit great dispersion of industry to be sure, but it also might stimulate a more rapid growth of the regional centers, the centrality of which could be reinforced. In short, technological innovation could go either way, and government policy can be expected to be the factor deciding the direction of change rather than classical Weberian location theory.

Envoi

Now that we have gone through this exercise, a look back at the quotation from 25 years ago seems appropriate. Though time tells us that some changes are in order, the basic propositions appear to hold up quite well. Indeed, there seems to be no relationship between primacy and development. Size, however, clearly matters; the larger countries do not generally display primacy. Territorial compactness alone, however, may not matter much. What does matter is the *distribution* of population. In most Asian countries with a high incidence of primacy, e.g., Thailand, a large proportion of the national population is localized almost within commuting range of the metropolis, where with higher incomes, commercial services, and government offices the market is and where its parameters are determined. The same point holds with regard to the phrase, "barriers to areal integration," which appear to matter little. Ethnic homogeneity also seems to have little relevance. Like all very large cities, Primate Cities tend to rank high on the multi-ethnicity scale, though probably more so in Asia than elsewhere.

Those cities that are primate or near-primate have, despite their colonial past, shifted universally toward becoming symbols of national identity as well as of government. It is readily comprehensible, therefore, that they should continue to grow, especially as government continues to play a dominant role in most Asian countries in the development of manufacturing industry which tends to locate in them as well. Under these circumstances what is surprising is the modest extent of national primacy in Asia, contrary to much received wisdom, where only half a dozen countries are characterized by it.

One of the reasons that primacy is thought to be more widespread than it is, is the fact that the term has come to be applied to any largest city in a given country whether or not it satisfies the conventional definition which assumes its being considerably more than twice the population of the second largest city. In Japan, one finds a rank-ordered statistical distribution of cities, and in that urban system Tokyo is scarcely primate, only very large, as the more than 17 million residents of the rival Osaka/Kobe/Kyoto, or Keihanshin, conurbation would assure us. In China, Shanghai is not primate, nor in India, Calcutta, although the importance of these great cities to their respective countries is immense, Shanghai alone accounting for more than 12.5 percent of China's industrial product and for 25 percent of its foreign exchange earnings.[19]

Above all, the model of a rank-size statistical distribution of cities or a so-called "balanced hierarchy" being the end product of development appears to be ill-founded, though still attractive to many. Primate cities, wherever they appear, and indeed any of the great cities of Asia, constitute vast resources, despite their problems, for the polities and space-societies of which they are a part. This proposition underscores the need for rethinking strategies for urban development in Asia even as the outmoded "received wisdom" is rejected.

END NOTES

[1]H. S. Richardson, *City Size and National Spatial Strategies in Developing Countries*, World Bank Staff Working Paper No. 252 (Washington: IBRD, April 1977); also, *The Economics of Urban Size* (Lexington: Lexington Books, 1973), as well as several articles on the same theme.

[2]Bruce London, *Metropolis and Nation in Thailand: The Political Economy of Uneven Development* (Boulder: Westview, 1980).

[3]Dennis Rondinelli, *Secondary Cities in Developing Countries* (Los Angeles: Sage, 1983), especially p. 24ff.

[4]Lee De Cola, "Statistical Determinants of the Population of a Nation's Largest City," *Economic Development and Cultural Change* (October 1984), v. 33, 1, pp. 71-98.

[5]C. D. Harris, "The Urban and Industrial Transformation of Japan," *Geographical Review* (January 1982), v. 72, 1, p. 80.

[6]Mark Jefferson, "The Law of the Primate City," *Geographical Review* (April 1939), v. 29, 2, pp. 226-32, a remarkably succinct statement, considering its impact on thinking about cities and their relationships to the societies which have produced them.

[7]For example, refer to S. D. Chang's fine paper for these meetings: "The Changing Patterns of Chinese Urbanization, 1953-82," in which he develops a two-city primacy index for provincial capitals and other major cities. Less soundly based is a paper by T. Banerjee and S. Schenk, "Lower Order Cities and National Urbanization Policies: China and India," *Environment and Planning A*, April, 1984, pp. 485-509.

[8]N. S. Ginsburg, "Urban Population II: A Measure of Primacy," in *Atlas of Economic Development* (Chicago: U. of Chicago Press, 1961), p. 36.

[9]S. K. Mehta also makes use of these data in his "Some Demographic and Economic Correlates of Primate Cities: A Case for Revaluation," *Demography*, 1964, v. I, pp. 136-47, in which Mehta arrives at many of the same conclusions noted in the Ginsburg quotation above.

[10]Fei, Hsiao-tung, *China's Gentry* (Chicago: University of Chicago Press, 1953), p. 92.

[11]G. K. Zipf, *National Unity and Disunity* (Bloomington: Principia Press, 1941). In the same year, John K. Wright published a paper covering much the same ground, but in a more rigorous way, for the United States. J. K. Wright, "Certain Changes in Population Distribution in the U.S.," *Geographical Review* (July 1941), v. 31, 3, pp. 488-90.

[12]J. O. Stewart, "Empirical Mathematical Rules Concerning the Distribution and Equilibrium of Population," *Geographical Review* (July 1947), v. 37, pp. 461-85.

[13]*Ibid.*, pp. 484-5. It is worth noting, however, that Charles T. Stewart, Jr. expressed extreme scepticism of this proposition and argued that "the rank-size rule, although in many cases a reasonable approximation to the actual distribution of towns by size, has no logical basis." See "The Size and Spacing of Cities," *Geographical Review* (April 1958), v. 48, 2, p. 244. Charles Stewart took into account both the Christaller and the Losch schema.

[14]N. V. Sovani reviews some of this early literature in his provocative "The Analysis of 'Over-Urbanization'," *Economic Development and Cultural Change* (January 1964), v. 12, 2, pp. 113-22.

[15]Bruce London, *Metropolis and Nation in Thailand: The Political Economy of Uneven Development* (Boulder: Westview Press, 1980).

[16]S. El-Shakhs, "Development, Primacy and Systems of Cities, *Journal of Developing Areas*, 1972, v. 7, pp. 11-36.

[17]N. Ginsburg, "The Changing Meaning of Modernization in Southeast Asia," Chapter 37 in K. S. Sandhu and P. Wheatley, eds., *Melaka: The Transformation of a Malay Capital c. 1400-1980* (Kuala Lumpur: Oxford University Press, 1983), pp. 285-99.

[18]B. F. Hoselitz, "Generative and Parasitic Cities," *Economic Development and Cultural Change* (April 1955), v. 3, pp. 278-94.

[19]*The Economist*, 30 March, 1985, p. 51. In that reference the figure "12.5 per cent" is given incorrectly as a percentage of GNP, not industrial output.

5

Trends in Urbanization and Urban Development in Sri Lanka

Bernard L. Panditharatne and Allen G. Noble

In Sri Lanka an urban area is defined, not by size of population or other physical characteristics, but as a legal entity defined by the Minister of Local Government. It is a political-administrative definition. In 1971 there were 12 municipal councils, 37 urban councils and 86 town councils making a total of 135 urban settlements. In 1979 the town councils were grouped with the rural and village councils, but, in the census of 1981, the population of such areas was counted as urban. Most settlements of more than 5,000 were classified as urban, although three settlements with more than 10,000 population were not raised to urban status.

Historically, Sri Lanka evolved two urban systems: one of traditional, pre-industrial cities functioning as regional administrative centers and market towns, developed in the irrigated rice economy of the 'Dry Zone' centered on the first capital city of Anuradhapura (300-1017 A.D.). The other, the colonial urban system, which began with the Portuguese (1505-1658) and was further developed by the Dutch (1659-1795) and the British (1796-1948), focused on Colombo, in the Wet Zone (the southwest quadrant). Colombo continued to be the capital and chief port during the entire colonial period (e.g., up to 1948) and thereafter in independent Sri Lanka.

Urbanization was the outcome of administrative centralization and commercialization and was characterized by a proliferation of towns, the growth of urbanized villages in the southwest lowlands and, above all, by movement of people to the city of Colombo, the center of employment and opportunity. Consequently, Colombo experienced rapid growth up to 1950, despite its limited economic base, inadequate infrastructure, lack of housing supply and increasing environmental pollution.

Urbanization and urban development followed three phases. First, urbanization was polarized on Colombo as the administrative, commercial, business and industrial center for Ceylon (Sri Lanka). The international and transhipment trade of the Indian Ocean resulted in extensive port, city and metropolitan development (Greater Colombo) and urban spread to produce the Colombo district.[1] Second was a phase in which decentralization and depolarization trends operated stimulating the growth of several satellite/dormitory towns and urbanized villages, particularly in the Colombo district[2] and along the southwest coastal lowlands. Third, counter urbanization trends were tied in with policies, programs and projects directed at agricultural development, which resulted in the growth of several medium- and small-sized towns as service centers for the developing agricultural hinterlands and in the reactivated urbanization of the Dry Zone. These counter urbanization trends have contributed to maintain a rural-urban population balance in the proportion of 80-20 percent (approximately) within the past 25-30 years.

Growth of Urban Population

Sri Lanka had a total population of 14.8 million in 1981, of which 11.6 million or 79.6 percent was rural, distributed in 18,681 villages, and 3.2 million or 21.4 percent urban in 135 urban places (Fig. 5.1).[3]

Before independence, Sri Lanka's level and rate of urbanization were relatively low and more or less conformed to the macro-regional trend of South Asia.[4] Sri Lanka's urban population in 1946 was 1.02 million, which represented 15.4 percent of the total population. By 1971, although the urban population had more than doubled to 2.84 million, it represented only 22.4 percent of the total population. In 1981 the urban population increased to 3.2 million, but the urban ratio had further decreased to 21.4 percent (Table 5.1). The urban rate of increase was higher than the national population rate of increase up to

48

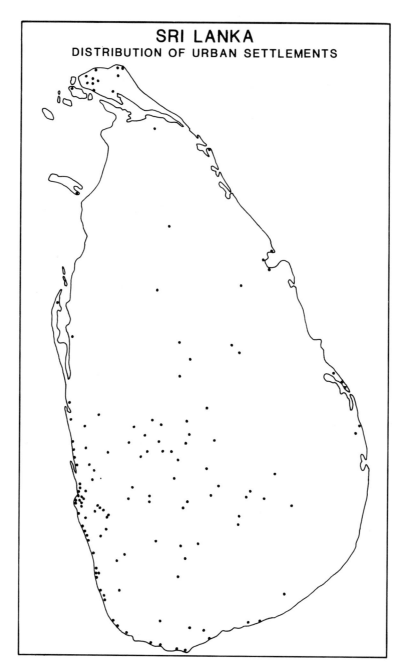

SRI LANKA
DISTRIBUTION OF URBAN SETTLEMENTS

Fig. 5.1 Distribution of urban
settlements in Sri Lanka.

1971, but thereafter the national rate exceeded the urban. The increase of urban population reflected the interplay of three sets of factors: natural increase, migration increase and increase resulting from changes in the boundaries of urban areas or in the upgrading of villages to urban status.

Natural increase was the chief reason. Death rates declined from 21.5 per 1,000 in 1946 to 8 per 1,000 in 1981. Birth rates also decreased from 38 to 28 per 1,000 during the same period, producing a population increase of 2 percent per year. Migration patterns in 1981 showed significant movements to the Colombo district and other densely populated districts of the Wet Zone, especially Kalutara, Galle, Matara and Kandy. Migration contributed to nearly 20-35 percent in the population increase of the towns of the

TABLE 5.1

Growth of Population - 1953-1981

Sri Lanka	1953	1963	1971	1981
Total Population	8,098,637	10,582,063	12,711,143	14,850,007
Percentage Increase		(31.4)	(20.5)	(14.28)
Total Urban Population	1,473,985	2,016,258	2,842,077	3,194,999
Percentage Increase		(36.7)	(40.0)	(11.02)
Percentage of Urban Population to Total Population	[18.2]	[19.1]	[22.4]	[21.5]
Colombo City Population	426,127	511,644	562,420	585,776
Percentage Increase		(20.06)	(9.92)	(3.98)
Percentage of Colombo's Population to Total Urban Population	[28.9]	[25.38]	[19.79]	[18.3]

Colombo district and 50 percent in the new towns of the Dry Zone, particularly in the Anuradhapura, Polonnaruwa and Moneragala districts. Up to 1963, migration accounted for 5-10 percent of the increase of population for Colombo, but during the 1963-1981 period it was extremely small due to: (a) the very limited "pull" as a result of the restricted employment base and (b) the high land values and consequent rents which prevented even middle income earners from becoming residents in the city.

Recently, migration streams have flowed to the development project locations in Sri Lanka and have been noticeably concentrated in the Dry Zone towns as centers of administration, technical and educational innovations, and service. Particularly important centers of growth have been Anuradhapura, the ancient capital city and the regional center of the northern plain which has been redeveloped and zoned as both a "sacred city" and a new town; at Trincomalee, the fast developing port of the east coast; at the state-managed industrial locations; and at the new towns associated with the multi-purpose developments in the Galoya, Uda Walawe and Mahaweli river basins.

Extension of town limits due to reorganization into wards, particularly in the 12 municipalities, and the increase in the number of towns from 81 in 1953 to 98 in 1963 and 135 in 1971 contributed to the increase of urban population. For example, Kandy increased its area by 1.5 square miles and Dehiwala Mt. Lavinia by 212 square miles. The relatively high numerical urban increase of 826,000 during the 1963-71 period was attributed partly to the increase of 37 towns during that period, and partly to the natural increase of urban-residential population and the migration increases in the Dry Zone towns. In contrast, during the 1971/81 period the urban increase was reduced to 353,000.

TABLE 5.2

Sri Lanka Urban Population

Categories	1953			1963			1971			1981		
	Nos. of Towns	Pop.	% of Total U. Pop.	Nos. of Towns	Pop.	% of Total U. Pop.	Nos. of Towns	Pop.	% of Total U. Pop.	Nos. of Towns	Pop.	% of Total U. Pop.
500,00	--			1	510,947	25.4	1	563,705	19.79	1	585,776	18.3
100,000	1	426,127	34.4	1	111,631	5.5	2	260,093	9.1	5	631,054	19.8
50,000	6	383,038	30.9	5	379,265	18.8	5	411,311	14.4	3	195,094	6.1
20,000	6	154,727	12.5	18	487,986	24.2	25	781,874	27.5	31	976,957	30.6
10,000	15	213,150	17.2	21	278,153	13.8	34	499,561	17.5	35	511,138	16.0
5,000	4	29,691	2.4	23	158,280	7.9	30	215,848	7.6	28	199,189	6.2
2,000 (and below)	11	32,400	2.6	30	90,023	4.5	38	114,914	4.1	31	95,671	3.0
All Towns	43	1,239,133	100.00	99	2,016,285	100.00	135	2,848,116	100.00		3,194,879	100.00

From Census of Sri Lanka, 1981

U = Urban

Urban Population According to Size of Towns

In Sri Lanka's urban system, Colombo always has held a position of primacy (Table 5.2). Colombo's population reached 426,127 in 1953, which represented 28.9 percent of the urban population and nearly 5 percent of the total national population. By 1981 the population had increased to 585,776 but represented only 18.4 percent of the country's urban population and 3.8 percent of the total national population. However, Colombo had nearly four times the population of the second largest city, Dehiwala Mt. Lavinia (174,000), and the third ranking city Moratuwa (136,000) and more than five times that of Jaffna, Kotte or Kandy (each exceeding 100,000).

TABLE 5.3

Population Growth in the Six Largest Cities of Sri Lanka

Name of City	Census Year	Population	Percent Increase	Average Annual Growth Rate %
Colombo	1946	362,074		
	1953	426,127	17.69	2.5
	1963	511,644	20.0	2.0
	1971	562,420	9.9	1.2
	1981	585,776	4.1	0.4
Dehiwela-Mt. Lavinia	1946	56,881		
	1953	78,213	37.5	5.3
	1963	110,934	41.8	4.2
	1971	154,194	38.9	4.8
	1981	174,385	13.0	1.3
Moratuwa	1946	50,698		
	1953	60,215	18.7	2.7
	1963	77,833	29.0	2.9
	1971	96,267	23.7	3.0
	1981	135,610	40.8	4.1
Jaffna	1946	62,543		
	1953	77,811	24.4	3.5
	1963	94,670	21.6	2.2
	1971	107,184	13.0	1.6
	1981	118,215	10.0	1.0
Kotte	1946	40,218		
	1953	54,318	35.0	5.0
	1963	73,324	34.8	3.5
	1971	93,680	27.7	3.5
	1981	101,563	8.4	0.8
Kandy	1946	51,266		
	1953	57,200	11.6	1.7
	1963	68,202	19.0	1.9
	1971	93,303	36.8	4.6
	1981	101,281	8.5	0.9

Thirty-one towns had populations between 20,000-50,000 and 35 towns between 10,000-20,000. These were widely dispersed and in terms of size were the typical Sri Lankian towns. In addition, there were 59 towns with populations below 10,000 and of these, 31 towns were below 5,000.

Growth Rates

Colombo registered moderate rates of increase in population up to 1961 (Table 5.3). The inter-census increase initially exceeded 2 percent per year, but decreased to 1 percent per year during the 1961-1971 period and to a very low rate of 0.4 percent per year between 1971 and 1981. In comparison, the annual rates of increase of the national urban population were 3.6 percent for 1953-63 and 4 percent for 1961-71, but they decreased to 1.1 percent in the 1971-81 period.

Four big cities, those with populations exceeding 100,000 (i.e., Dehiwala Mt. Lavinia, Jaffna, Kotte and Kandy), recorded increases of urban population at decreasing rates. For example, Dehiwala Mt. Lavinia showed a decrease from 4.2 percent during 1953-1963 to 1.3 percent in 1971-1981. Similarly, Jaffna from 2.2 percent to 1 percent; Kotte from 3.5 percent to 0.8 percent; and Kandy from 1.9 percent to 0.9 percent. Moratuwa at the southern fringe of the Colombo urban region, however, was the exception. Towns in the Greater Colombo region registered the fastest growth rates (i.e., 8.8 percent per year). Towns with populations between 50,000-20,000 recorded 6.7 percent and those with populations 20,000-10,000, 6.9 percent. The small towns in the Dry Zone with populations below 10,000 recorded very high increases, more than 8 percent per year.[5]

The Distribution of Urban Population
and Density Characteristics

Colombo district accounted for more than 50 percent of the total urban population, Jaffna district about 8 percent, and Kandy, Galle and Kalutara more than 5 percent each. Most of the districts in the Dry Zone had very small urban populations, although the rates of growth of these towns were high (Fig. 5.2).

The average population density for Sri Lanka was 230 per square kilometer in 1981. Colombo district had the highest density (2297 per sq. km.) which was nearly ten times the national average density. Colombo city's average density was 64.7 per acre (approximately 30,720 per sq. km.), which was more than ten times that of Colombo district and more than one hundred and twenty times that of the national average density.

Urban Zones

Sri Lanka may be divided into four urban zones which have different levels in intensity of urban development. The zones are: (1) the *urbanized wet zone* accounting for more than 65 percent of the entire urban population including (a) Colombo city and Greater Colombo, (b) the towns of Colombo and Gampaha districts, and (c) towns and urbanized villages of the southwest coastal region; (2) Jaffna and towns of the Jaffna peninsula; (3) the Matale-Kandy-Gampola Zone of the Central Highlands; and (4) the *least urbanized Dry Zone* with 60 percent of Sri Lanka's total area but accounting for only 14 percent of the total urban population.

In the urbanized wet zone each town or service center served about 150 villages spread over 0.6 square miles, whereas in the Dry Zone, each town served 231 villages in an area of 1-6 square miles.[6] The spacing between the towns was fairly regular, about 10-20 miles in the Wet Zone and 8-12 miles in the compact Jaffna peninsula and 20-30 miles in the Dry Zone.[7]

Phases of Urbanization and Urban Development

Phase 1: Polarization in Colombo

Colombo was a port before it became the capital of Sri Lanka. However, its national administrative functions made the townscape. The political, economic and financial power accruing to the capital city was the chief stimulus to the port. Its early history, colonial rule, export-import trade, island-wide hinterland, and the elaborate route system connecting it with all parts of the island, all have contributed to make Colombo not only the chief port and capital of Sri Lanka, but its greatest urban concentration as well.

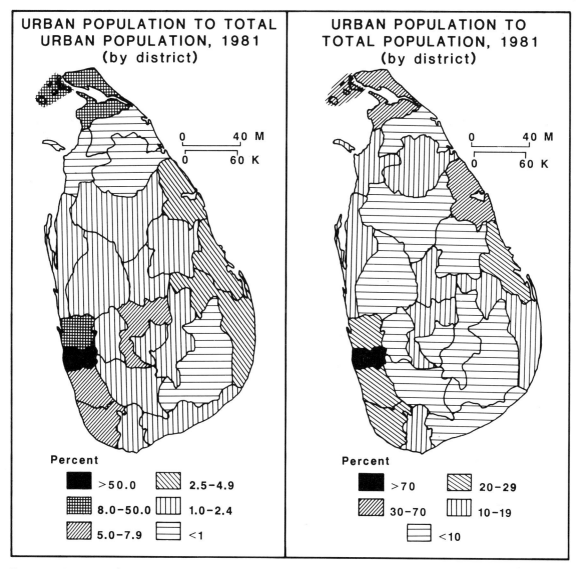

Fig. 5.2   Percent urban population by district, 1981.

Colombo city passed through several stages of change, reorganization and expansion as a Portuguese "fort and royal city" (1518-1658); as a Dutch port-capital of the maritime provinces (1659-1795); as the capital and chief port under the British (1796-1948); and as a national capital in independent Sri Lanka since 1948. Colombo was raised to municipal status in 1866. The growth of the tea, rubber and coconut plantations in Colombo's hinterland and the export-import trade channelled through the port of Colombo broadened its urban-economic base and created a variety of employment opportunities. The urban population increased from 95,843 in 1871 to over half a million in 1981. A multi-ethnic urban community grew up, with Sinhalese as the majority community (51%) and Jaffna Tamils (22.2%); Moors (21%); Malays (2.2%); and Indian Tamils (1.9%) making up the minority groups.[8]

Colombo occupied the apex of the political, socio-economic and administrative structure. At the national level, central and high level functions, i.e., those of the Prime Minister (later the President), the legislature, the judiciary, the administrative bureaucracy and the military forces, were centralized in the city. About the beginning of this century, Colombo functioned as the most important coaling port in the Indian Ocean, by virtue of its central location. It was also the main port for water bunkering and stevedoring, and for ship repair and fitting. It ranked as the third port of the British Empire and seventh in the world.[9] It was, however, subject to changes. The closure of the Suez Canal in the 1956 affected it adversely and the canal's reopening in 1975 reactivated Colombo's shipping. However, the city declined as a port of call for passenger liners, although it compensated for this by the increasing tanker traffic between the Middle East and Japan and as a port of transhipment for containerized cargoes to India, Pakistan, Bangladesh and the Gulf states. Colombo's functional dominance as the chief port for the Sri Lankan exports of tea, rubber and coconut produce, and imported goods, such as food, textiles, machinery and luxury items, and as the chief distributing center for the wholesaling and retailing trades, remained unchallenged during this phase.

Colombo experienced a rapid growth of medium- to small-scale industries associated with the processing of agricultural raw materials, such as tea, rubber and coconut produce; marine engineering, repairs and boat building; assembling and fitting of machinery, and equipment repairs and maintenance; market-oriented consumer industries and the economic infrastructure activities of electricity, water, sewerage, gas, telecommunications, bus, tram and railway transport. Colombo's superior internal accessibility, its external focality, the availability of power and utilities, and labor supply, capital and market have made it the hub of commercial, business, financial and industrial activities.

Phase 2 Depolarization Trends: The Growth of Greater Colombo and the Urbanization of Colombo District

In Colombo city, depolarization trends have operated along with and at the same time as the polarization trends which resulted in the metropolitanization of Colombo and the growth of Greater Colombo. These trends have produced the growth of towns as 'counter magnets' to Colombo and the suburbanization and rural development of the Colombo district. Certain administrative decisions and policies have contributed to this trend. Among these the most important have been the policy with regard to the location of industries outside the city limits; the policy of reinforcing and upgrading the health and educational institutions at regional centers in the Colombo district; decentralization measures resulting in the moving out of offices from the Fort to peripheral locations; the shift of the political functions, e.g., the Parliament, from Colombo the new political capital city of Sri Jayawardhanapura (Kotte); the policy of administrative devolution to the District Development Councils; the shifting of stores and warehouses to locations outside the city, and the improvements to public transportation services in Colombo's commuting areas. Some of these are discussed in greater detail below.

Policy of decentralization of industries from Colombo city. Industrialization in Sri Lanka has been closely related, both to the country's balance of payments position because of the importation of machinery, equipment and raw materials, and to the local market, especially to local incomes invariably from agricultural and state employment sources. Agricultural sector performance was vital to the performance of the industrial sector, as well as for urbanization. In the first phase, Colombo city, because of its advantageous factors, attracted to the city many industries which contributed to its growth. To avoid the over-concentration of industries in the city, the state around 1960 adopted a decentralization policy based on the principle of "import substitution." This action resulted in several towns around Colombo, e.g., Ratmalana, Katubedde, Moratuwa, developing as new loci for industries. Further, the growth of two state-sponsored industrial estates at Ratmalana (south of Colombo) and at Ekala (to the north) intensified the decentralizing trend. Since 1978 the state has encouraged "export promotion," international investment and private sector participation by establishing two investment promotion zones (I.P.Z.), also referred to as "Free Trade Zones," at Katunayaka and Biyagama. Both are within the area of the jurisdiction of the Colombo Economic Commission. The favorable investment climate, the comparative advantage of abundant labor, and the favorable terms to foreign investors, all have contributed to substantial foreign investments in labor-intensive textile and apparel industries, electronic assembly, and several consumer industries and services-oriented businesses, all providing employment to about 25,000 females[10] within the Free Trade Zones.

In other districts, the state-managed industrial ventures based on raw materials have led to the concentration of other related ativities and the growth of industrial townships. Examples are the cement and chemical industries at Kankesanthurai and Paranthan, respectively, in the Jaffna district, the paper industry at Valaichena in Batticoloa district, salt in Hambanbota and Puttalam districts, and ceramics at Negombo, Gampaha district.

Growth of Satellite and Dormitory Towns

About 30 towns in the Colombo district have been developed as satellite and dormitory towns to Colombo City. As the population of these towns has increased, their services and functions have proliferated and certain institutions have been upgraded. As growth continues, these towns begin to act as counter magnets to Colombo.

Upgrading of the Health and Educational Institutions in Towns of the Colombo Region

The over-concentration of hospitals and special clinics for outpatient services and specialized treatment in Colombo made necessary a government program to establish or upgrade regional hospitals at selected centers. The success of this program has checked to a great extent the over-concentration of patients at the Colombo hospitals and has brought about an even and fair distribution of patients at these institutions. A similar effort has been made in education. Colombo held a dominant position as the center of excellence in higher education when English was the medium of instruction. The free education policy implemented in the mid-1940's and the switch over of the medium from English to Sinhala and Tamil altered Colombo's dominance. Rural schools with facilities in arts subjects and selected schools for science subjects have been established for the education of the rural peoples. As regards the admissions of students to the universities, the advantages once enjoyed by the schools of Colombo have been reduced considerably by a policy which has a spatial bias distinctly in favor of undeveloped districts. Fifteen percent of the total admissions is reserved for the twelve undeveloped districts and a further fifty-five percent is distributed among the twenty-four districts on the basis of population.

Shift of Parliament from Colombo to Sri Jayawardhanapura

The shift of the Parliament to Sri Jayawardhanapura and its development as the political capital marked a significant point in devolution. It is expected that, in the future, foreign embassies also will move to this new location, along with several State ministries and departments. The reclamation of nearly 1,000 acres, will be required before other urban land uses, such as residential, services, recreational and institutional, can be located here. As these uses grow, the town will assume a look of maturity.

Colombo and Commuting Areas: Improvement in Transportation

Colombo has always been the largest center of employment in Sri Lanka. Out of a total of 351,000 employed, nearly 180,000 were resident in the city. The balance commuted daily to their jobs in the city. Altogether it was estimated that nearly 600,000 commuted daily to the city for various purposes including employment. The public transportation services have been able, up to now, to cope with the transportation of this commuting population, despite the heavy overloading, frequent breakdowns and constraints faced in replenishing the rolling stock/vehicles. Recently, private enterprises have entered the transportation business. This has not only relieved the State of a great burden, but also has greatly improved transportation services

Phase 3 Counter Urbanization Trends: Rural-Regional Development

Sri Lanka, as early as the 1930's, followed a progressive welfare policy in health and education and had established a fairly adequate infrastructure in respect of these two services. Control of malaria, vaccination and immunization programs, a network of rural hospitals and dispensaries for the administration of Western medicine, in addition to the indigenous medical facilities for basic rural medical care, all have resulted in the lowering of the mortality rates to 8 per 1,000, one of the lowest in Asia. A policy of free education implemented in the mid-1940s, coupled with compulsory primary education and *swabasha* (regional vernacular languages) as the media of instruction in the 1950s, have improved the literacy rate in Sri Lanka to 85 percent. Universal adult franchise was in operation as early as 1931, making rural folk politically conscious and sensitive to the politics of 'State welfare'. Free rice and subsidized foodstuffs to everyone up to 1977 compounded the cost of the welfare package, which to a great extent erased the spatial disparities between the urban and rural areas and ensured spatial equivalence in the distribution of welfare. Although the annual per capita income was low ($300),[11] the physical quality of life index was high, an average of 82 on the scale of 100, one of the highest in Asia, which indicated the impact of welfare and development efforts on the rural scene. The lowest local index was 64 for the mountainous district of Nuwara Elia, whereas some of the rural districts of the Dry Zone, such as Anuradhapura, Moneragala, Hambantota, Polonnaruwa, Puttalam, Mannar, Trincomalee and Vavuniva, recorded indices above 80.[12]

Another realistic picture of the quality of the rural environment of some districts may be demonstrated by the major socio-economic indicators (Table 5.4). Jaffna district has scores above the average in respect to all criteria except water supply. The highland districts of Nuwara Eliya and Kandy had below average scores for housing, nutrition, and infant and child mortality. Galle district in the Wet Zone and Kurunegala in the Dry Zone fared adequately and Batticoloa district showed below average scores.

Agricultural development in the plantation areas was mostly for export crops in the Wet Zone, and mostly for food production in both the Dry Zone and Wet Zone coastal lowlands. As regards plantation agriculture, measures such as rehabilitation of marginal and low yielding acreages, modernization of machinery, higher wages for laborers, better housing, improved amenities, and transport facilities have improved agricultural production and increased per capita income, standards of living and mobility. Agricultural modernization in the plantation areas has contributed to urban functional vitality, the upgrading of towns, and greater interaction between the estate and urban sectors.

Agricultural development of the Dry Zone has involved irrigation, land development, colonization and multipurpose projects, all directed towards transforming a low productivity, subsistence agriculture into a high productivity system. All these projects were administered through Dry Zone towns which played an active and generative role in the developmental process. Further, these towns functioned as centers of innovation and diffusion of knowledge to the developing regions, as centers for repairs to agricultural machinery and for spare parts, as storage and distribution centers for fertilizer, weedicides and pesticides. These towns were also the centers for education, health, cultural and recreational diversions (especially the cinema) and the sites of ancient temples and shrines.

Integrated multipurpose projects, such as the accelerated Mahaweli River development, Uda Walawe and Galoya, have improved the physical, socio-economic, cultural and institutional infrastructure of the rural areas. The modern agricultural systems are integrated into an evolving agro-industrial structure with planned central places and townships. The success of rural development has led to relative stability of labor in rural areas.

Whatever have been the factors, forces or circumstances in Sri Lanka's urbanization, they have operated to maintain an equilibrium between urbanization and counter-urbanization resulting in a rural-urban population in the approximate ratio of 80 to 20. Corey calls it "more a case of policy serendipity than a result of intentionally planned and coordinated counter-urbanization policy."[13]

Present Institutional Framework and Urban Development

The state's liberalized trade policy in 1977, particularly the relaxing of controls on imports, has stimulated urban activities. Colombo projected a busy scenario of activities and progress visible in the new high rise buildings, the new shopping plaza, and the fullness and variety of goods displayed in the shops, duty free shops and busy hawker stalls at the "World Market Area" in the Fort and along the pavements in the Pettah and the other centers of the city. New housing policies have led to increasing private sector participation in house construction. Transport also has improved as a result of private sector enterprises. Finally, improvements in the theater, cinema, television, and sports stadiums and in religious ecumenism shared by the four major religions in the city were profound.

Tourism has made Colombo an unavoidable focus for tourists, accounting for an annual turnover of more than half a million persons. Colombo's hotel accommodation capacity has increased to 2,000 rooms, accompanied by the expansion of employment in tourist-allied services and trades in both the formal and informal sectors. Tourism has spread to other geographical locations, resulting in the centralization of

TABLE 5.4

Status of selected districts in relation to some major socio-economic indicators

(C = Average, C+ = Better than average, C- = Worse than average)

	Jaffna	Betticalcoa	Kandy	N'Eliya	Galle	Kurunegala
Infant Mortality	C+	C-*	C-	C-	C	C+
Child death rate	C+	C-	C-	C-	C+	C
Nutritional levels	C+	C-	C	C-	C+	C
Life Expectancy	C+	C-	C-	C-	C+	C+
Literacy	C+	C-	C	C	C+	C+
Nature of Housing	C+	C-	C-	C-	C+	C
Owned Housing	C+	C-	C-	C-	C+	C
Water Supply (Tap and Well)	C-	C-	C+	C+	C	C
Electricity	C+	C+	C+	C+	C+	C-
Toilets	C+	n.a.	C+	C+	C	C
Primary School enrollment	C+	C-	C+	C+	C+	C+
Primary School drop out	C+	C-	C+	C+	C+	C+

*Batticaloa infant mortality rate is recorded at 35.5 in 1979, a significant improvement over 1977 (50.8) and 1978 (45.6).

Source: "Socio-economic Indicators of Sri Lanka", Dept. of Census and Statistics/FAO, Feb. 1983.

activities along the beaches of the southwest coast such as Negombo, Bentota-Kogalla; along the eastcoast at Nilaweli-Kalkudah; at the historical and archaelogical sites and towns of Anuradhapura, Polonnaruwa, Sigiriya and Kandy; at the salubrious and scenic highland towns of Nuwara Eliya, Bandarawella and Hatton; and at places of religious significance as Kataragama and Kelaniya.

Considering the rather rapid urban growth and accompanying changes, and the need to monitor such changes systematically, the *Urban Development Authority (U.D.A.)* was established by law in 1978 and entrusted with the planning, regulation and control, and implementation of integrated economic, social and physical development of designated urban areas. The scope of activities of the U.D.A. cover the following : (1) planning and developing of Colombo, district capitals and the urban centers of Sri Lanka,

(2) redevelopment of central areas of Colombo City, (3) formulation and execution of programs of slum and shanty upgrading, (4) reclamation of marshes and the establishment of new administrative centers, (5) execution of industrial and integrated development projects, and (6) development of public amenities in urban areas.

The U.D.A. has been influenced considerably by the general directions as specified in the Colombo Master Plan, namely:

(1) to give priority to physical development planning in order that the projected population and economic growth can be accommodated in the most functionally effective manner, while at the same time minimizing the demand for capital investments for the public sector to meet the infrastructural needs;

(2) to encourage the location of economic activities in the metropolitan region which will enjoy the advantages of forward and backward linkages, skilled labor, access to financing, entrepreneurial resources and a full range of services, thus maximizing the potential output to the economy from private capital investment so generated;

(3) to accrue social benefits from planning to the population; and

(4) to incorporate tourist promotion measures.

The U.D.A. plays a major role in reorganizing the urban space of Colombo city, and thus in changing its morphology. Several projects have been undertaken including:

(a) construction of a 30 story building in Echelon Square in the Fort to provide an additional 1.9 million square feet for business-oriented enterprises, institutions and residential uses;

(b) conversion of Chalmes Granaries in the Pettah, which once stored rice imports, into a national cultural center and commercial complex;

(c) two new markets, one at St. John's fish market and a vegetable market at Kachcheri Road, to be constructed with modern facilities; and

(d) warehouses and stores which occupied prime land in the central part of the city to be shifted to peripheral locations.

One of the major problems of Colombo has been housing. Several state agencies, including U.D.A. and N.H.D.A. (National Housing Development Authority), in collaboration with the Municipality of Colombo, have improved the housing stock and the city's environmental sanitation. However, the demands for housing, especially of the urban proletariat, have remained unsolved. Out of a total 2,925,625 houses in Sri Lanka,[14] Colombo city accounted for 84,530 housing units, only 3 percent of the country's housing stock. There were nearly 25,000-30,000 unauthorized living units referred to as "slums and shanties" which accommodate approximately 40-42 percent of the city's population. More than 50 percent of the houses were not supplied with electricity and 49.26 percent of the slums and shanties used kerosene for lighting. Forty percent had no cooking facilities. The average per capita floor area varied from 4 square feet in the congested wards, with the average density exceeding 200 per acre, to 17.5 square feet in the moderately populated wards, with densities of 60 per acre.

The slum upgrading program was designed to improve the living conditions of slum dwellers. The projects provided amenities, such as water, toilets and electricity, and community services such as education, health and family planning to reach a target group of about 6,500 low income families. Despite these measures, the housing problem remains unsolved because of (a) the magnitude of the problem, especially in Colombo city; (b) a shortage of urban land which results in high land prices; (c) the high cost of construction; and (d) the politically and socially impolitic step of evicting on a mass scale the poor families who have lived in improvised homes for so long. The Peliyagoda project, based on the reclamation of 500 acres, has reduced considerably the pressure on Colombo's land by shifting warehousing, stores, industries and related uses to this location. Similar projects are being executed in Onigodawatta, Ratmalana, and Athurugirya in the Colombo district.

The U.D.A., in collaboration with the councils of Kandy, Nuwara Eliya and Batticoloa, have completed development plans to improve the commercial, residential, civic and recreational facilities of these towns. It also assists urban areas in raising funds required to implement commercial development projects and in the preparation of designs for several regional towns. The U.D.A. thus acts as a catalyst for development by generating and promoting contacts between land owners, and private developers at the metropolitan, district, regional and country-town level.

Prospect

The current projections of population growth in the Colombo district, *vis-a-vis* the other districts, indicate an increasing growth tendency for the Colombo district and for those of the southwest lowlands. Based on these trends, the Master Plan for Colombo proposed four strategies to reduce inequalities in spatial development:

1. to allow high concentrations of people in nonagricultural activities in the Western Province (Colombo, Gampaha and Kalutura districts) and to create infrastructure facilities for the growth of industry and generation of employment;

2. to establish a major growth pole with population of 250,000-500,000 as a counter magnet to Colombo and to determine where it should be — Kandy, the traditional regional center of the Central Highlands, or Anuradhapura, the ancient capital in the heart of the developing Dry Zone, or at Trincomalee, one of the best natural harbors in the world located on the east coast — at what cost, and what the economic base should be;

3. to establish a series of regional growth centers, each with a population of 75,000-150,000, with productive and viable nonagricultural enterprises;

4. to establish a growth corridor with Colombo as its base and to determine the axes of growth. Also to determine the feasibility of implanting 'growth axes' to promote the zonal developments extending from Colombo to Negombo; Kandy through Dambulla to Anuradhapura, and Anuradhapura through Pollonnaruwa to Trincomalee.

Two problems, one of resource management, the other of urban management, also have to be considered. First, the deterioration of revenue generation at the city level has been one of the major reasons for the inadequacy of finances, though the per capita expenditure on urban services including administration, urban planning and welfare services was only Rs 8 in 1983, a relatively small amount for the maintenance of the existing services. Second, the proportion of expenditure covered by local taxes has been declining over time from 29 percent in 1979 to 26 percent in 1982 and to an estimated 18 percent in 1987. Third, central government agencies gradually have been taking over some of the functions of the local authorities leaving the latter in some cases limited only to refuse collection and disposal. Thus it will be necessary to restore the financial viability of the local authorities by restructuring property taxes, tax ratios and other fiscal measures. New investments in urban areas are necessary to arrest the deterioration now taking place due to overuse of the existing infrastructure and to enable future expansion of facilities to match population increases.

Certain investments, especially the items included under economic overheads, social overheads, and urban development, have an urban emphasis. Some important examples are the direct dialing telephone facilities between major towns, Colombo area development project and outer-Colombo area development project, Colombo airport expansion, Colombo port development, fishery harbors development, urban house construction and upgrading of state buildings, water supplies, and sewerage works (Table 5.5).

Conclusion

Developmental planning in Sri Lanka has been based on the exploitation of physical resources, and this seems to be logical as long as Sri Lanka as a producer of agricultural raw materials is so dependent on world market forces. However, as planning progresses and is able to achieve high growth rates, and as the areas reach high stages in the development of physical resources, it is to be expected that the planning is

TABLE 5.5

Allocation of Government Capital Expenditure 1984/88

SRI LANKA	(in Million Rupees)	
	Treasury	Foreign
General Allocation Heads (selected items only)		
Agriculture	36,330	24,245
Mahaweli Project	21,187	15,370
Irrigation	2,750	1,841
Plantations	5,057	3,624
Fisheries	280	51
Field and Minor Crops	4,200	1,599
Industries	280	51
Housing, Water Supply and Water Development	7,796	7,730
Economic Overheads	29,700	13,366
Social Overheads	5,894	979
Specific Projects (directly and indirectly) having a bearing on urban development		
Housing	2,925	14
Urban Sites and Services	966	
Urban Construction	245	
Rural Housing	1,550	
Slum and Shanty Upgrading	164	14
Other Construction	1,565	91
Industrial Training Project	234	
Other Constructions	999	
Upgrading State Buildings	320	
Water Supply	3,306	1625
South West Coastal W.S.S.	48	
Greater Colombo	1,150	473
Haris Pattuwa W.S.S.	165	81
Jaffna W.S.S.	241	158
Matale-Polonnaniwa W.S.S.	255	216
Matora-Dickwella W.S.S.	62	
Trincomallee W.S.S.	78	

	Treasury	Foreign
Negombo W.S.S.	318	217
Mannor W.S.S.	37	15
Other W.S.S.	292	35
Rehabilitation of Existing W.S.S.	660	430
Railways		
Railway Technical Training Center	55	
3rd Line from Maradana to Regame	47	
Power		
F.T.Z. Bujagama	6	
Training School	53	88
Posts and Telecommunications	2,471	1,065
CADS I, II, III	672	336
Rural Exchange (Kandy)	30	
Training Center	12	4
Air Port Development	3,750	250
Colombo Port Devlopment		
Stage I	422	422
Stage II	748	748
G.C.E.C.	300	
Social Overheads (Technical Education)	739	396
Integrated Rural Development (12 districts)	2,171	1,754

Source: Public Investment, 1984/88. Selected from Table 7.1 pp 146-159.

likely to acquire an increasingly urban industrial structure characterized by the emergence of the town region as the unit of economic development.[15] However, the physical resources have to be developed sufficiently to reach a stage so that the urban region will be the most appropriate form for planning.

END NOTES

[1] B. L. Panditharatne, "Growth Morphology and Ethnic Characteristics of Colombo Agglomeration," in *Urbanization in Developing Countries*, Manzoor Alam and V. Pofishisshevsky (eds.) (Hyderabad, India: Osmania University, 1976), pp. 427-453.

[2] V. Samaravingha, V., "Spatial Polarization of Colombo—A Study of Regional Inequality," *Journal of Social Sciences, Sri Lanka*, Vol. 1 (1982), pp. 75-94.

[3] Sri Lanka, Department of Census and Statistics, *Census of Population and Housing of Sri Lanka*, Colombo, 1981.

[4] B. Renaud, *National Urbanization Policies in Developing Countries* (Washington: World Bank, 1979).

62

[5]D. Abeysekare, "Urbanization and Growth of Small Towns in Sri Lanka, 1901-71," *Papers of the East-West Population Institute*, No. 67, 1980.

[6]W. P. T. Silva, "Land Settlement and Urban Development in the Dry Zone," *Journal of Social Sciences, Sri Lanka*, Vol. 2, No. 1 (1979), pp. 55-76.

[7]B. L. Panditharatne, "Trends of Urbanization in Ceylon," *Ceylon Journal of Historical and Social Studies*, Vol. 7, No. 2 (1964), pp. 203-217.

[8]Sri Lanka Census, footnote 3.

[9]B. L. Panditharatne, "The Harbor and Port of Colombo: A Geographical Appraisal of Its Historical and Functional Aspects," *The Ceylon Journal of Historical and Social Studies*, Vol. 3, No. 2 (1960), pp. 120-143.

[10]Sri Lanka, National Planning Division, *Public Investment, 1983-87*, Ministry of Finance and Planning, Colombo, 1983.

[11]World Bank, *World Development Report 1984* (New York: Oxford University Press, 1984), p. 218.

[12]H. D. Sumanasekara, "Measuring the Regional Variation of the Quality of Life in Sri Lanka," *Journal of Agrarian Studies, Agrarian Research Institute*, Vol. 2, No. 1 (1974), pp. 27, 40.

[13]Kenneth E. Corey, "Deconcentrated Urbanization in Sri Lanka: A Case of Policy Serendipity," *Urban Studies Working Paper*, No. 2, 1984.

[14]Sri Lanka Census, footnote 3.

[15]Brian J. L. Berry, "The urban growth and economic development of Ashanti," *Urban Systems and Economic Development*, University of Oregon Press, 1962, pp. 53-64.

6

Urban Development Issues in Asia with Special Reference to Sri Lanka

Ved Prakash and Jack Huddleston

Rapid urbanization, a low level of income and net savings, and high costs associated with urban development and urban services are critical factors contributing to the deteriorating urban environment in most developing countries. Although the seriousness of the urban situation is recognized, public policy, planning, programming, resource allocation, and financing aspects of urban development are generally unintegrated and disjointed. In this paper we will identify and discuss the strategic urban development issues in the developing countries of Asia in general, and in Sri Lanka in particular. This is done in the context of four interrelated perspectives or frameworks:

1. Demographic and urbanization processes and prospects;
2. Planning approaches for national development and urban development, with an emphasis on their institutional setting;
3. Urbanization policy responses; and
4. Economic and fiscal/financial aspects.

We conclude by summarizing and synthesizing each of these in terms of their major policy implications for financing urban development.

Demographic and Urbanization Processes and Prospects

Urbanization is basically a twentieth century phenomenon. In 1920, of the total world population of 1.9 billion, only 360 million or 19 percent lived in urban areas. By 1950 urban population increased to 712 million or 28 percent of the total world population of 2.5 billion. In 1980 total urban population stood at 1.8 billion or 41 percent of the total world population of 4.4 billion. By the end of the century it is anticipated that the majority of people will be living and working in urban areas (3.2 billion out of the total world population of 6.3 billion). Among the more developed countries the level of urbanization (percent of total population living and working in urban areas) was 39, 52, and 71 percent in 1920, 1950 and 1980, respectively. By the year 2000, the comparable percentage is likely to be 80. For the less developed countries taken together, the level of urbanization increased from 8 percent in 1920 to 16 and 30 percent respectively by 1950 and 1980. At the end of the century this percentage is likely to be 42.[1]

Developing countries, have and will continue to register very rapid increases in urban population during the second half of this century — a ten-fold increase, more than twice the total population growth rate and more than four times the rate of increase in rural population. Among the developing regions of the world, Asia will continue to have the lowest level of urbanization such that in the year 2000, 39 percent of its population will be urban, followed by Africa (43 percent) and 75 percent in Latin America (Figure 6.1). Although the level of urbanization in less developed countries will continue to be significantly lower than the level in developed countries, the total number of urban dwellers in less developed countries exceeded the total number of urban dwellers in developed countries for the first time in 1980. By the year 2000, it is anticipated that two out of every three urban dwellers will be in the less developed countries (reverse of the situation that existed in 1950). Urban population in the less developed countries of Asia was 90 million in 1920, 342 million in 1950, 689 million in 1980, and is likely to increase to 1.4 billion by the end of the century. During the second half of this century, the rate of growth of urban population is likely to average around 4 percent per annum, more than doubling itself every two decades. It may be noted that during 1950-2000, more than 60 percent (or 1.2 billion) of the 1.8 billion increase in

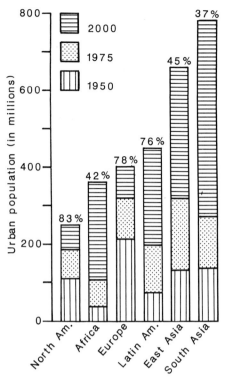

Fig. 6.1 World urban population growth and percent urban in year 2000, by region.

SOURCE: United Nations, 1982

urban population in developing countries is expected to be in Asia, and of the 1.2 billion increase in Asia, two countries—India and the People's Republic of China—will account for a significant majority of the incremental urban population in Asia.

A salient feature of the urbanization process in the developing countries has been the invariable trend towards concentration of population in the capital cities and large urban centers.[2] The developing countries in Asia, however, vary widely in terms of the level and tempo of urbanization, and the primacy of the cities. Despite these variations, however, a few generalizations can be made:

> First, generally countries in the middle income group (Republic of Korea, Malaysia) have a higher percentage of urbanization. Second, population concentration in the metropolitan and large cities is common in most DMC's (Developing Countries Members of the Asian Development Bank)—a feature on which the concern for the problems of urbanization is largely focused. Third, large cities have generally been growing as rapidly as the total urban population of the country, and there is no evidence that today's very large cities (population above five million) are encountering any natural or technological limits to this growth.[3]

However, the respective patterns of urbanization (in terms of concentration of population in different city-sizes) in the developing and developed countries were quite different until recently. But the patterns have become very similar such that by the year 2000 the largest cities (1 million-plus and 5 million-plus) are likely to account for a larger percent of the total population in the developing countries (including Asia) than the developed. To underscore this point, it may be pointed out that of the world's 15 largest cities in 1950, 11 were in the developed countries. In the year 2000, 12 of the 15 largest cities will be in developing countries—eight in the Asian developing countries.

In many respects the demographic and urbanization processes in Sri Lanka followed less developed countries' trends through 1970. For example, the annual rate of growth of population during the 1950s was 2.7 percent and during the 1960s it declined slightly to 2.3 percent per annum. The comparable rates for urban population were 5.2 and 4.4 percent respectively. However during the period 1971-1980, the growth of population declined to 1.6 percent per annum, with rural and urban populations growing at 1.7

and 1.2 percent respectively, lower than the rural and average rates of growth.[4] The World Bank suggests that the urbanization process may accelerate somewhat during the rest of this century. In 1980, in Sri Lanka, the urbanization pattern was also different, showing below average concentration of population in cities of 20,000 plus and 100,000 plus respectively. According to the 1981 census, the population of Colombo, the largest city, was just under 600,000 (Tables 6.1, 6.2 and 6.3). The slowing down of the population growth, as well as the urbanization process in Sri Lanka, has been attributed largely to successful efforts of the government which have resulted in geographically dispersed social services and nearly equal social welfare indicators in urban and rural areas.[5] Demographic and certain other indicators in the context of income are quite impressive in Sri Lanka relative to several comparable countries.

Review and analysis of demographic and urbanization processes suggests the following four major concerns for public policy and planning with respect to urban development:

1. Urbanization process (rate) cannot be influenced to any appreciable extent.
2. Although there is literature concerning the pattern of urbanization and the need to develop an appropriate hierarchy of urban centers, no theoretically generalizable models exist. In the majority of developing countries, urban development strategies are random efforts at altering the pattern of urbanization and no empirical evidence suggests that policies have been effective.[6]
3. Management problems of very large cities in terms of providing accessibility of urban services and facilities for large segments of poor households, and improving environmental conditions.[7]
4. Size and level of urbanization may result in different policy concerns in different countries.

When the above concerns are analyzed within the perspective of the urbanization process in Sri Lanka, only the third item above is of crucial importance. Although concern is at times expressed that Colombo is too large and/or has some attributes of being a primate city, we believe that concern about the pattern of urbanization in Sri Lanka (item 2 above) should not be very serious.[8]

TABLE 6.1

Total Population and Urban Population Growth 1953-1981

| | 1953 | 1963 | 1971 | 1981 | Annual Growth Rates | | | |
					1953-1963	1963-1971	1971-1981	1963-1981
Population (000)	8,098	10,582	12,690	14,848	3.1	2.3	1.6	1.9
Urban Population (000)	1,239	2,016	2,848	3,194	6.3	4.4	1.2	2.6
% Urban	15.3	19.1	22.4	21.5				

Source: World Bank, Sri Lanka Urban Sector Draft Report (July 1983)

TABLE 6.2

<u>SRI LANKA</u>
<u>POPULATION OF THE MUNICIPAL COUNCILS AND URBAN COUNCILS IN 1981</u> *

(above 14,000 persons)

Name of Town	Population 1981 Census	Average Annual Growth Rate (%) in the Inter-Censal Periods	
		1963-1971	1971-1981
Colombo Municipal Council (MC)	585,776	1.24	0.42
Dehiwela - Mt. Lavinia (MC)	174,385	4.88	1.27
Moratuwa (UC)	135,610	n.a.	n.a.
Jaffna (MC)	118,215	1.65	0.98
Kotte (UC)	101,563	n.a.	n.a.
Kandy (MC)	101,281	4.60	0.82
Galle (MC)	77,183	1.15	0.61
Negombo (MC)	61,376	2.64	0.75
Trincomalee (UC)	44,913	n.a.	n.a.
Batticaloa (MC)	42,934	7.45	1.68
Matara (UC)	39,162	n.a.	n.a.
Ratnapura (MC)	37,354	5.23	2.83
Anuradhapura (UC)	36,248	n.a.	n.a.
Badulla (MC)	32,954	3.85	-0.49
Kalutara (UC)	31,495	n.a.	n.a.
Matale (MC)	29,745	2.19	-0.31
Kurunegala (MC)	26,519	1.88	0.53
Puttalam (UC)	21,463	n.a.	n.a.
Nuwara Eliya (MC)	21,319	1.46	3.04
Chilaw (UC)	20,830	n.a.	n.a.
Nuwara Eliya (MC)	21,319	1.46	3.04
Kegalle (UC)	14,920	n.a.	n.a.

* There are 12 Municipal Councils, 38 Urban Councils, and 24 Development Councils.
Source: Census of Population and Housing, Sri Lanka - 1981 and M.W.J.G. Mendis, <u>op.cit.</u>

TABLE 6.3

Sri Lanka: Comparison of Demographic Indicators in Income Context

	Per Capita Income (US$) 1980	Crude Death Rate Per 1000 Population (1980)	Life Expectancy at Birth (1980)	Average Annual Population Growth (1970-1980)
Zaire	220	18	47	2.7%
Malawi	230	22	44	2.9%
Mozambique	230	18	47	4.0%
India	240	14	52	2.1%
Haiti	270	14	53	1.7%
Sri Lanka[1]	270	7	66	1.6%
Sierra Leone	280	18	47	2.6%
Tanzania	280	15	52	3.4%
China	290	8	64	1.8%
Guinea	290	20	45	2.9%
Industrial Market Economies	----	9	74	0.8%

Source: World Development Report, 1982

[1]The data for Sri Lanka differ slightly from most country sources but are included here as contained in the World Development Report, for purposes of comparison.

Planning Approaches for National and Urban Development and Their Institutional Setting

National planning is grounded in economic development planning with a sectoral orientation, while urban planning conventionally focuses upon physical/spatial development with an inter-sectoral, comprehensive emphasis.[9]

National plans are of two types—general policy and sectoral plans and administrative agency functional plans prepared by ministries and departments. The latter are typically inputs to the national plan but are prepared more frequently, are more specific, and are keyed into a national fiscal allocation cycle. National planning is characterized by stronger vertical relationships, with horizontal coordination at the general policy level. It is commonly deficient in project specifics. It is generally dominated by a top-down planning system in which the flow of decisions emanates from a central authority.

Local urban planning has had a physical emphasis, with an orientation toward individual projects. Because of the specificity of project planning and execution, there are often better horizontal ties and informal coordination among line agencies at the field or project implementation level.

The shortcomings of national planning have been widely described in the literature and generally include at least the following:

1. limited utility, i.e., lack of specificity and project content, essentially no linkage to national budgetary decision making, and a seeming emphasis in macro-economic planning on the production of the published plan versus a plan as an implementable action program;
2. the failure to deal with interregional (urban) disparities; and
3. a dismal record in addressing the needs of the poorer segments of society.

Urban planning has experienced its own problems. The consequences have been poor project design and execution, a myopia regarding the nature and scale of the underlying developmental problems, limited staff capacity, insufficient fiscal resources, and an inability to deal with the fragmented and complex line agency budgets and programs to achieve areal integration.

At the risk of overstating the situation, the personnel legacy of national and local planning to date are economists at the national level who have become enthralled with elegant econometric modelling and physical/town planners at the local level who are concerned with their notion of "comprehensive planning." Both of these groups of planners have been largely divorced from decision making and programmatic considerations, although there is increasing evidence of an evolution towards action-oriented planning at all levels.[10]

The prevalent national and local planning approaches point to the near intractable issues of integrating/coordinating economic and spatial planning. This is equally true of horizontal and vertical intergovernmental relations for urban development policies and programs.

Institutional Setting

The majority of developing countries have unitary systems of government. Constitutionally, all powers rest with the central government. Only a handful of countries have a federated system where subnational governments are constitutionally assigned certain functions and revenue powers. Even in the latter group, subnational levels of government are largely dependent upon the national government for financial resources. From the fiscal dependence perspective, almost all developing countries either are or resemble unitary systems of government. Consequently, division of responsibilities and allocation of resources among different levels of government becomes a serious problem for intergovernmental coordination. In most countries, policies and programs do not exhibit the needed dynamism and flexibility and thus are unable to cope with the diversity among different urban areas.

The institutional problem is further compounded by the fragmentation of responsibilities dealing with urban planning and development programs at national and subnational levels. In a majority of cases, individual projects and programs are planned, approved, and financed by different agencies and statutory bodies, severely limiting the coordinated approach to urban development.

We believe, however, that this situation is less serious in Sri Lanka. Existing institutional arrangements encompassing urban development functions are far less fragmented and provide unmatched opportunities toward formulating coordinated urban development strategies, public policies and investment programs. Currently the overall national urban development policy is decided by the Subcommittee of the Cabinet of Ministers, which is directly concerned with activities related to urban development, under the chairmanship of the President. The Prime Minister is in charge of the Ministry of Local Government Housing and Construction (MLGHC) and is the key member of the Cabinet Subcommittee. The Secretary of the MLGHC serves as secretary to the subcommittee. All the important departments, authorities, boards, corporations and funds at the national level that are involved in urban development programs are either under the MLGHC, or report directly to it.[11]

Project planning and management for urban development is generally inadequate in most of the concerned agencies. We believe that the serious shortcomings are the lack of attention to financial, investment and, when appropriate, economic aspects as well as monitoring and evaluation phases. This is especially the case for projects for which the Urban Development Authority has the lead responsibility. Consequently, the potential opportunity for a coordinated set of urban development strategies, policies, investment programs and financing measures, mobilization of resources for financing capital outlays and maintenance and operating expenditures is currently not being utilized. The input of the MLGHC appears to be minimal in the public investment programming process.

A brief history of the role of the Urban Development Authority (UDA) is essential in understanding the institutional setting for urban development projects. The UDA was established in 1978. The UDA is entrusted with planning regulation and control, and implementation of integrated economic, social and physical development of designated urban areas. Its powers and functions include:

1. to formulate and submit development plans, including capital investment, for government approval;
2. to implement development and capital investment plans approved by the government;
3. to formulate capital improvement programs;
4. to acquire, develop and dispose of land in the urban development areas; and
5. to approve, coordinate, regulate, control or prohibit development schemes or projects, or development activity of government agencies (including local government authorities), or other persons in designated urban development areas.

Since its inception, the UDA has played the crucial role in the formulation, design and implementation of major urban development projects (e.g., the Parliamentary complex, the administrative complex, fish market, and other commercial and residential development—including upgrading of slums and sites and services programs). The main emphasis to date has been on the physical design and engineering aspects of urban development projects. The economic and financial aspects have been given little if any attention. This has led to the adoption of standards on the basis of "desirable quality targets," rather than relative to costs, economic capacity, and adequate measures for resource mobilization. Consequently, the opportunity costs associated with the above-mentioned major urban development projects may be quite high. This, in fact, has been borne out by the cost over-runs for all the above and other urban development and housing projects, and their dismal performance in terms of cost-recovery.

Public Policy Responses

The developing countries in Asia, like most other developing countries, are undergoing rapid socioeconomic changes, and most are engaged in varying forms of planning for national development. A review of some of the recent national development plans indicates that most do not contain clearly defined objectives and targets for urbanization. The concern is primarily expressed in terms of altering the pattern of urbanization. These plans concentrate on the problems of economic growth and increasing financial resources, while giving inadequate attention to relating economic development to spatial consequences. Some aspects of urbanization are discussed in the plans in conjunction with industrial location policy, as problems associated with housing or slums or the need to prepare "master plans" for all cities above a certain size. From a public policy point of view, Dotson defines this lack of attention to urbanization and urban development in national planning as either unconscious, partial, uncoordinated or negative.[12]

Balanced regional development and elimination of disparities among regions have been major objectives expressed in most national plans. But only in a few instances are concrete suggestions presented with regard to the methods for achieving these objectives. The Indian and some other national development plans, for example, include explicit location policies as a means for distributing investment in new industry more equitably among regions. Similarly, small-scale industry is identified and considered in the context of either rural or small town development. Despite these locational attempts, many Indian national planners admit that decentralization efforts have failed, that the aggregation of industry of different scales has continued in the large cities, and that regional disparities have increased rather than decreased.

Another aspect of this quest for decentralization is evident in the continued interest in the development of new towns, particularly in conjunction with large-scale industrial investment and administrative reforms requiring new capital cities. The model for planning most of these new towns has generally been the British "garden city" in its manifold company town varieties. The resultant opportunity cost of this kind of urbanization is enormous, both in economic and in social terms.[13]

At the metropolitan level, urban planning has largely been modelled along the lines of European and North American examples. As a result, most of these "master planning" efforts have produced, at best, some interesting compilations of information about the nature of urban problems, and at worst a colorful map and picture books, some of which have become much sought after as collector's items. The conceptual poverty which has long dominated Western urban planning has been exported to the Asian metropolis despite, or perhaps because of, the considerable interest which organizations like the United Nations, the Ford Foundation, and some of the bilateral technical assistance programs have shown in problems associated with the fast growth or the primate centers of the developing countries.[14]

Until recently, the developing countries, as well as multilateral and bilateral aid/donor agencies, dealt with urban shelter and infrastructure on a sectoral basis. A recent report of the World Bank points out that:

> The sector-by-sector approach by itself, however, has been found to have certain weaknesses, and it has been necessary to develop comprehensive integrated ways of providing shelter to make programs more effective in meeting the needs of low-income groups. Most of the previously mentioned services taken by themselves are important to the provision of shelter, but they are considerably more effective when they can complement one another. The provision of water supplies alone, for example, has only a minimal effect on health unless complementary measures are taken to improve the disposal of human waste . . . To bring these services together requires a high degree of planning and integration of investments in urban services that by and large is lacking in most urban areas . . . The purely sectoral approach, moreover, does not lend itself to addressing the problem of land tenure . . .

> To improve the provision of shelter and complementary services, the Bank has put its greatest effort into financing of the upgrading of dwellings in existing settlements and sites and services projects for the development of new settlements. The salient feature of these projects has been the coordination of land tenure, public services, and private investment, along with the improvement of employment opportunities. The outstanding element of policy behind these projects is an emphasis on cost recovery and the development of shelter programs that can be replicated on a large scale.[15]

Past approaches, in a majority of the developing countries have by and large been inappropriate and ineffective. Another recent World Bank report summarizes the situation by stating that:

> . . . Unfortunately, the need for sound policy and strategic investment was not fully appreciated in the 1960's in most countries. Governments frequently mounted expensive public housing schemes, extended water supply networks, and built roads on an *ad hoc* basis, without a long-term view of how they fit together in relation to anticipated needs. Policymakers and technicians lacked adequate technical and financial solutions to the problems they anticipated.

> By 1970, the urban dilemma appeared particularly intractable because awareness of urban needs had developed at the same time as an international consensus was emerging that the rural sector should be the priority for assistance. Urban investment which used scarce public funds would divert needed resources from the rural sector. This view was supported by the fact that urban investment was

frequently subsidized at the time and benefitted only a minority of the population. Moreover, urban services with high unit costs, provided on a subsidized basis, could not be extended to the urban masses. It was, therefore, essential that a new approach be found which acknowledged that the urban sector could and should pay for itself and which provided services which were affordable to the urban poor and thus permitted replicability for the sector as a whole.[16]

As pointed out in the preceding section, in the case of Sri Lanka the public policy response to urban development problems has been similar to other developing countries in general. In recent years it has become evident that lack of coordination among government departments, agencies and authorities with regard to urban development projects and programs, especially inadequate attention to financial aspects, has led to unprecedented and accelerated shortfalls with respect to mobilization of resources for financing urban facilities and long-run maintenance and operating expenditures. Thus there is an urgent need for a systematic review of current urban development strategies and programs.

Economic and Fiscal Aspects

Policies and strategies for resource mobilization for financing urban development must be viewed within the broader framework of national income and social accounts; national (central), state (provincial), and local government revenues and intergovernmental fiscal transfers; and capital and· annual maintenance and operating costs associated with urban service requirements.

The scale and rapid growth of urban population translates into massive capital investment requirements and resulting long-term, reoccurring costs in most developing countries. When these costs are juxtaposed with extremely low levels of income and net savings, the severity of constraints and the importance of resource mobilization come into focus.[17]

It may also be pertinent to point out that, during the 1970-1980 period, population and Gross National Product both grew at average annual rates of 2.7 percent in the less developed countries, whereas the GNP grew at 3.2 percent per annum and population at 0.8 percent per annum in the more developed countries (Table 6.4). The less developed countries taken together are thus faced with an extremely difficult situation, i.e., limited resources in the face of rapidly rising urban populations and related facilities and service requirements.

Per capita GNP (1981) and average annual rates of growth during the last two decades for 16 Asian countries are presented in Table 6.5. The World Bank's 1983 Report on World Development divides the 117 countries or market economies into five groups: (1) low-income countries (per capita GNP of US$400 or less); (2) lower middle-income countries (per capita GNP between US$420 and 1,630); (3) upper middle-income countries (per capita GNP between US$1,700 and 5,670); (4) high-income oil exporters (per capita GNP between US$8,500 and 24,660); and (5) industrial market economies (per capita GNP between US$5,230 and 17,430). Of the 16 countries included in Table 6.5, eight, including Sri Lanka, belong to group 1 (low-income) countries, four to group 2, and the remaining four to group 3.

In a majority of the countries (including Sri Lanka), the average annual growth rate has been under three percent. Only three countries (Hong Kong, Republic of Korea, and Singapore) had annual growth rates around seven percent. In real terms, per capita GNP may have declined in several countries.

Given the low level of income and pattern of income distribution, the incidence of poverty (both urban and rural) is relatively much higher in the developing countries of Asia than other regions (Table 6.6). Thus the level of net savings in most of the developing countries is extremely low. Even if urban development infrastructure is accorded a high priority in the developmental context, available resources may be quite deficient in most of the countries.

Analysis of public sector data indicates that the size of the public sector relative to the national income is rather small in many developing countries in Asia. In about half, total public expenditures constitute less than 25 percent of the Gross Domestic Product. In 1981 there were three countries where this percentage was just over 30 (Malaysia, Singapore and Sri Lanka). The total public expenditure relative to Gross National Product has changed only slightly during the last two decades in most of the developing countries in Asia. Government revenue receipts (all levels) constitute less than 20 percent of the Gross Domestic Product in a majority of them. In Sri Lanka, per capita total current revenue in 1975

TABLE 6.4

Per Capita Gross National Product in Selected Developing Countries in Asia

Country	GNP Per Capita		Rank[1]
	Dollars in 1981 prices	Average Annual Growth (Per Cent) - 1960-81	
Afghanistan	170 [2]	0.5	9
Bangladesh	140	0.3	5
Burma	190	1.4	8
China[3]	300	5.0	21
Hong Kong	5,100	6.9	91
India	260	1.4	17
Indonesia	530	4.1	41
Korea, Republic of	1,700	6.9	74
Malaysia	1,840	4.3	77
Nepal	150	0.0	7
Pakistan	350	2.8	30
Papua New Guinea	840	2.5	51
Philippines	790	2.8	49
Singapore	5,240	7.4	93
Sri Lanka	300	2.5	24
Thailand	770	4.6	48

[1]Lowest to highest per capita GNP among the 125 countries included in the World Bank Report.

[2]for 1979 in current prices.

[3]Excluding Taiwan, whose per capita GNP was US$890 in 1975 and average growth rate, 6.9 per cent (1965-74).

Source: International Bank for Reconstruction and Development, World Development Report 1983, (Washington, D.C., 1983).

TABLE 6.5

Income Distribution in Selected Developing Countries in Asia

Country	Year	Percentage Share of Household Income by Percentile Groups of Households						
		Lowest 20 Percent	Second Quintile	Third Quintile	Fourth Quintile	Highest 20 Percent	Highest 10 Percent
Bangladesh	1973-74	6.9	11.3	16.1	23.5	42.2	27.4
Nepal	1976-77	4.6	8.0	11.7	16.5	59.2	46.5
India	1975-76	7.0	9.2	13.9	20.5	49.4	33.6
Sri Lanka	1969-70	7.5	11.7	15.7	21.7	43.4	28.2
Indonesia	1976	6.6	7.8	12.6	23.6	49.4	34.0
Thailand	1975-76	5.6	9.6	13.9	21.1	49.8	34.1
Philippines	1970-71	5.2	9.0	12.8	19.0	54.0	38.5
Republic of Korea	1976	5.7	11.2	15.4	22.4	45.3	27.5
Malaysia	1973	3.5	7.7	12.4	20.3	56.1	39.8
Hong Kong	1980	5.4	10.8	15.2	21.6	47.0	31.3

Source: World Bank, World Development Report, op. cit. pp. 200-201.

was US$31, of which US$26 was through taxation. The tax structure relies heavily on indirect taxes in most of the developing countries in Asia.

Investment in urban development in Sri Lanka has been concentrated in a small number of large projects in Colombo and a few other selected urban centers. For example, a large proportion of the total planned investment in urban development during 1979-1984 has been in three projects in Colombo, i.e., the Parliamentary complex, the new administrative complex, and the new fish market.[18]

Public sector housing during the corresponding period has been about the same as in the above three projects and is concentrated in Colombo and Kandy. Water supply and sanitation accounts for most of the remaining investments in a few selected urban areas. It appears that this investment in a few large areas has constrained investments in many of the smaller urban centers. It seems that planning for urban development projects has been seriously lacking in financial and investment aspects.

The most serious issue that emerges from the discussion above underscores the need for strict adherence to affordability, cost recovery, and replicability as they become paramount in the context of public policies and programs for urban development. It is all the more important that physical, economic and financial aspects of urban development plans and projects *must* be considered as integral elements of the planning and public policy processes.

Summary

The scale and rapidity of the urbanization process in the Asian developing countries is unparalleled in history. The problems of planning, resource mobilization and financing urban development should be differentiated in terms of different city-sizes. Investment requirements and fiscal efforts for financing long-run expenditures are so massive that urban facilities and services in the large cities must be largely self-financing. Per capita income is generally positively associated with city size; thus the economic capacity in these cities may be two, three or more times that of their respective national average.

The prevailing worldwide attitude among politicians and other major participants in public policy arenas is generally anti-urban, and particularly anti-big city. This attitude is commonly shared by planners of all kinds. The suggestions and arguments by various commissions, committees and others in many countries that large cities should get a very high priority in allocation of investment and other financial resources from the national government have not been heeded. Politically, they may not be feasible in the near future.

The size of the public sector is relatively small and many countries in Asia rely heavily on indirect taxes. It is likely that the overall incidence of taxation is not very progressive. Since income levels in large cities are generally several times that of the national average, it may be argued that there is room for much greater fiscal effort in large cities; thus the case for complete reliance on national allocation of resources is not a strong one and cannot be justified. Rapidly growing cities must, therefore, bear a large proportion of the fiscal burden of financing urban facilities and services. The task of planning and resource mobilization for financing urban development may thus be best accomplished by giving the large cities more revenue-raising authority and more responsibility for their own expenditures.

Assignment of additional revenue and expenditure authority to local governments in large cities must be concomitant upon a marked improvement in assessment and collection administration of tax and other resources that are already available to them. In respect to additional assignment of tax and other revenue authority to local bodies, intergovernmental fiscal cooperation devices may provide many advantages over local administration in the case of specific tax and non-tax revenues.

Intergovernmental fiscal relations will continue to be of increasing importance, although their objectives may be different for smaller urban areas and big cities. Intergovernmental fiscal cooperation devices such as tax supplements, tax credits, and tax sharing have necessarily to play much larger roles than they do at present. A suitable system of grants-in-aid must be developed to supplement the tax cooperation devices towards achieving broad policy coordination and functional cooperation; stimulating, controlling, and supervising local public agencies; and equalizing costs and opportunities among local governments to minimize the externalities and spillover effects.

The land situation is extremely critical in Asia. Urban land resources and rising land values offer major constraints and tremendous opportunities for urban growth management as well as mobilization of fiscal resources for urban development. Land taxation has a tremendous potential as a source of revenue and may provide important policy instruments towards achieving other public policy objectives, e.g., cross-subsidization for poor households.

The importance of taxation of land and buildings as a financing resource is considerable. Currently, property tax is a minor source and of little importance in terms of revenue in most of the developing countries in Asia. Property taxation should thus occupy an increasingly important place in efforts to finance urban services. The bases of exemptions, rates, assessment and collection of real estate taxes must therefore be carefully examined in each country; and some radical changes may be called for. The recent experiences in Taiwan and the Republic of Korea with integrated land and property tax systems provide a basis for optimism in resource mobilization through similar fiscal devices.

Local tax revenues have generally been found to be less income-elastic than the provincial and particularly national taxes. Imbalances between expenditure requirements and resources available to urban local bodies are thus likely to continue and become cumulatively more accentuated in the future. Non-tax revenues, especially user and beneficiary charges, can potentially provide more elastic sources of revenue in the face of rapid additions of population in the large cities and rising incomes with economic development. Thus, the role of pricing policies and cost recovery methods, along with increased reliance upon other non-tax revenues, may be extremely important in the resource mobilization context.

Rapid growth of large cities would require increasingly heavy amounts of investment in urban infrastructure facilities. In many of the countries there are no capital markets from which the funds can be borrowed directly by the municipal governments. Only a handful of cities are able to secure even partial long-term financing against the issuance of their own bonds. Careful examination of alternative institutional arrangements (e.g., revolving funds and infrastructure development banks) to facilitate loan finance for urban capital improvement programs in a particular country would thus be crucial.

END NOTES

[1]Philip M. Hauser and Robert W. Gardner, "Urban Future: Trends and Prospects" in Hauser et al., *Population and The Urban Future* (Albany, New York: State University of New York Press, 1982), pp. 1-58.

[2]*Ibid.*

[3]Asian Development Bank, *Bank's Strategy for Assistance in Urban Development* (Manila, draft, 1980)

[4]M. W. J. G. Mendis, "An Analysis of the Inter-Censal Growth of Towns in Sri Lanka," *Development Planning Review*, Vol. 1, Nos. 1 and 2 (Dec. 1982), pp. 1-13.

[5]World Bank, *op. cit.*, and G. V. S. deSilva, *Some Heretical Thoughts on Economic Development* (Colombo, Sri Lanka: Lake House Investments Ltd., 1973).

[6]H. Richardson, *City Size and National Development Strategies in Developing Countries* (Washington, D.C.: World Bank Staff Working Paper No. 252, 1977); and Bertrand Renaud, *National Urbanization Policies in Developing Countries* (Washington, D.C.: World Bank Staff Working Paper No. 347, 1979).

[7]See for example Johannes F. Linn, *Cities in Developing World: Policies for Their Equitable and Efficient Growth* (Oxford University Press, 1983).

[8]Primacy index for Sri Lanka on a four city basis in 1981 is only 1.1.

[9]For a more detailed discussion, see Stephen Born and Ved Prakash, "Integration of Local and National Level Development Planning," a paper presented at the Conference of Integrated Rural/Area Development Planning, Arusha, Tanzania, March 10-15, 1980.

[10]See, for example, Bendavid-Val, Avrom and Peter Waller (eds.), *Action Oriented Approaches to Regional Development Planning* (new York: Praeger Publishers, 1975); and Leo Jakobson, *The Sketch Plan: A Method for Programming Action* (Madison, Wisconsin: Regional Planning and Area Development Project, University of Wisconsin, 1981).

[11]Departments of Local Government, Local Government Service, Town and Country Planning, National Housing and Buildings; Urban Development, National Housing Development, Central Environment, and Town Hall Foundation Authorities; National Water Supply and Drainage, Common Amenities, Local Government Service Advisory and Local Government Service Disciplinary Boards; State Engineering Corporation, Building Materials Corporation, and the Government Owned Business Undertakings of the Colombo Commercial (Engineering) Ltd.; and Local Loans and Development, and National Housing Funds.

[12]Arch Dotson, "Urbanization and National Development in South and Southeast Asia," Report of the Southeast Asia Development Advisory Group (Urban Development Panel Seminars, New York: Asia Society, 1972), pp. 1-2. See also Bertrand Renaud, *National Urbanization Policies in Developing Countries* (Washington, D.C.: World Bank Staff Working Paper No. 347, 1979); and H. Richardson, *City Size and National Spatial Strategies in Developing Countries* (Washington, D.C.: World Bank Staff Working Paper No. 252, 1977).

[13]Ved Prakash, *New Towns in India: Monograph on Southern Asia No. 8* (Durham, North Carolina: Duke University, 1969).

[14]Leo Jakobson and Ved Prakash (eds.), *Metropolitan Growth: Public Policy for Southeast Asia* (Beverly Hills, California: Sage Publications, 1974), pp. 259-286.

[15]*Shelter: Poverty and Basic Needs Series* (Washington, D.C.: World Bank, September, 1980).

[16]*Learning by Doing: World Bank Lending for Urban Development* (Washington, D.C.: World Bank, 1983).

[17]A recent study by the World Bank and the WHO estimated incremental per capita capital costs for urban water supply to be around US$121 (1977 prices) for house connections and US$48 for street standpipes. The sanitation costs were estimated to be around US$112 for house connections and US$35 for household systems. A somewhat conservative estimate for minimal standards for the very basic facilities such as water supply, sanitation, roads, street lighting, drainage, and schools may range between US$350 and $500 per capita. Maintenance and operating (reoccurring) costs may be around US$50 per capita per annum.

[18]Total public sector planned outlays (for the country as a whole) during 1983-1987 are around Rs 128 billion, of which housing, water supply and urban development accounts for Rs 12 billion (or 10 percent of total). The cost of the above three projects (1979-1984) is estimated to be around Rs 3.0 billion.

7

The Intermediate City Concept Reviewed and Applied to Major Cities of Sumatra, Indonesia, 1961-1980

William A. Withington

Several usages of intermediacy have been applied within studies of cities and city systems. Among these have been Hildred Geertz' use of "metropole" to denote sizable and functionally diverse Indonesian cities identified in the 1930 Dutch Census;[1] Kingsley Davis and associates at the International Urban Institute in Berkeley, California;[2] Phillip Hauser and others in United Nations urban data discussions;[3] Dennis Rondinelli in recent articles and books;[4] the present author in a number of papers dating from 1969;[5] James Osborn in his Ph.D. dissertation publication;[6] as well as many others.[7] While several of the intermediate city usages agree on a lower or upper population threshold, most show considerable variation in other defining bases.

The purpose of this chapter is first to review and restate the intermediate city concept; and second, to demonstrate the application of the concept to cities in a particular developing world area, in this case the large western island region of Sumatra in Indonesia (Fig. 7.1). Questions posed and at least partially answered are:

1. What guidelines seem most appropriate for defining intermediate or second-level cities in Asia?

2. In Sumatra what cities should be included as major cities fitting the intermediate city concept?

3. For these major cities, what are the distinctive characteristics and changes during the 1960s and 1970s?

4. To what extent are the Sumatran cities in their characteristics and changes representative of intermediate cities in the broader urban systems of Indonesia, Southeast Asia and Monsoon Asia?

The Intermediate City Concept

Thirty years ago, Donald Fryer used the term "millionaire cities" in discussing the primate and other larger cities of Southeast Asia.[8] T. G. McGee's *Cities of Southeast Asia* focused mainly on the region's primate cities.[9] My own interest evolved from residence in Honolulu, Hawaii, primate only as the then territorial and now state capital; in Lexington, Kentucky; and during the years 1957 to 1959 in Medan, capital of North Sumatra province and largest Indonesian city outside the national core area of Java.[10]

How does one define intermediate importance when much larger cities near or far may dominate? The *United Nations Demographic Yearbook* enumerates cities worldwide if their populations exceed 100,000.[11] Kingsley Davis and his associates likewise used a population of 100,000 as the lower threshold for any metropolitan area having a central city of 50,000. This is also the usage of the U.S. Census Bureau for metropolitan population clusters and is reflected in Borchert's "American Metropolitan Evolution."[12] Beginning in the late 1960s I discussed intermediate cities, applying a lower threshold of 100,000 people and an upper one of one million people.[13] In the 1970s James Osborn's focus on the "middle city" of Malaysia included cities ranging from less than 20,000 people to Kuala Lumpur's city figure of more than 500,000.[14] In recent articles and books Dennis Rondinelli's "secondary cities" have a lower threshold of 100,000 and include all cities of a nation except its primate and/or capital largest city in Less Developed Countries.[15]

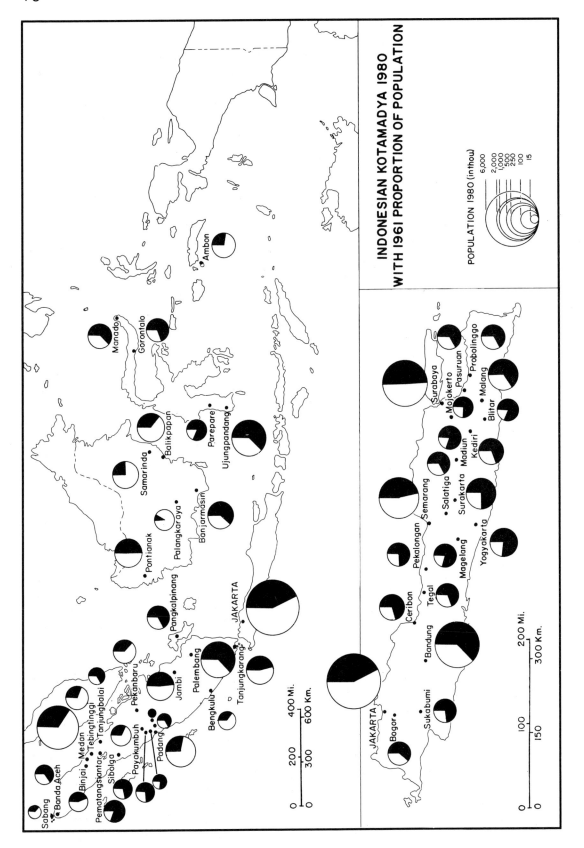

Fig. 7.1 Municipalities/Kotamadya of Indonesia, 1980 (1961 population by segment of proportional circle of 1980 city population).

The frequency of its application suggests the analytic value of the intermediate city concept. What should the limits by population or other criteria be? My own answer is illustrated in detail using cities of Sumatra, Indonesia. In this discussion, all or almost all cities of larger population, except the primate and usually capital city, are included at the upper end of the population range. At the lower end, 100,000 people frequently seems appropriate as a minimum for metropolitan character. However, capitals of provinces or equivalent principal administrative divisions as in Indonesia have sufficient functional diversity and circulation infrastructure, if not population, to warrant inclusion as intermediate, middle range, secondary or "major cities."

Sumatra's Major Cities, 1961-1980

Sumatra in western Indonesia is that nation's largest outlying region in population and also in amount and diversity of products generating foreign exchange from exports.[16] What are Sumatra's major cities, fitting the definition of an intermediate city? Seven of Sumatra's cities had more than 100,000 people in the 1980 Census of Population (Table 7.1). In descending rank order by population these cities are: Medan, Palembang, Padang, Tanjungkarang-Telukbetung, Jambi, Pekanbaru and Pematangsiantar. Among these, only Pematangsiantar in eastern North Sumatra is not a provincial capital city. The largest in population is Medan with nearly 1.4 million, ranking fourth in Indonesia, below only the three Java cities of Jakarta, Surabaya and Bandung (Fig. 7.1).[17]

Among Sumatra's twenty *kotamadya* (municipalities) for which 1980 population data are available, two cities having fewer than 100,000 people must be included on any list of Sumatra's major cities (Table 7.1, Fig. 7.2). These two are the provincial capital cities of Banda Aceh in Daerah Istimewa Aceh (D.I. Aceh) near the northern tip of the island, and Bengkulu, the seaport city on the southwestern coast of Sumatra and capital city of Bengkulu Province. Each is the "primate city" of its political unit and as such is the major city in diversity of functions and in political, economic and cultural nodality.[18]

Eleven other *kotamadya* across the length and breadth of Sumatra have considerable importance in both current and historical terms. Most have localized hinterlands and limited diversity or nodality compared with the nine major cities. All are identified here as "Lesser Cities" often as satellite or tributary centers in relation to the provincial capitals. The one possible exception is Bukittinggi in upland West Sumatra, the Fort de Kock of the Dutch colonial era. Bukittinggi has continued to be a cultural and religious center of the Minangkabau people, the dominant ethnic group of West Sumatra.[19]

Characteristics and Changes in Sumatra's Major Cities

The nine major cities of Sumatra ranged in population in 1980 from Medan with nearly 1.4 million people to Pematangsiantar eighty miles away with about 150,000, and to Banda Aceh's 72,000 and Bengkulu's nearly 65,000 (Table 7.1). Two decades earlier in 1961, populations of these cities were as low as 25,000 in Bengkulu, not yet a provincial capital, to almost 480,000 in Medan, with Palembang only a few thousand people less. At that time six cities exceeded 100,000 in population, while Pekanbaru's population was about 71,000 (Table 7.1).

Urban population growth for Sumatra's major cities has been generally rapid during the 1961-1980 period. Six of the nine major cities more than doubled their populations as compared with only three of the eleven "lesser cities" (Table 7.1, Fig. 7.2). Thus, six of the nine major cities grew in population by more than 100 percent. Only Pematangsiantar (30.4%) and Palembang (65.7%) increased at a rate below Sumatra's population growth rate of 78 percent. The rapid population growth in these major Sumatran cities, as in most Third World cities, resulted from high levels of natural increase combined with large volumes of net in-migration.[20] However, at least four of the six cities (six of nine among all *kotamadya* in Sumatra) having population increases of over 100% also had urban area expansions during the 1961-1980 period. The fivefold increase in Medan's urban area in 1972 was greatest, but Padang, Pekanbaru and Bengkulu also had sizable additions both in urban area and populations.[21] Among the lesser Sumatran cities, Sabang, Payakumbuh and Tebingtinggi had very large percentages of population growth, large enough to result in very small or negative growth in the population of associated *kabupaten*.[22]

TABLE 7.1

Intermediate and Lesser Cities of Sumatra, 1980

INTERMEDIATE CITIES

Municipality (Kotapradja-1961; Kotamadya-1971, 1980)	Province	Population 1980	Population 1961	Percentage Change	1961 Population % of 1980
Banda Aceh	D.I. Aceh	72,090	40,067	80.0	55.6
Medan	North Sum.	1,378,955	479,098	187.9[a]	34.7
Pematangsiantar	North Sum.	150,376	114,870	30.4	76.4
Padang	West Sum.	480,922	143,699	234.0[a]	29.9
Pekanbaru	Riau	186,262	70,821	162.0[a]	38.0
Jambi	Jambi	230,373	113,080	103.5[a]?	49.1
Palembang	South Sum.	787,187	474,971	65.7	60.3
Bangkulu[b]	Bengkulu	64,783	25,330	160.0[a]	39.1
Tanjungkarang-Telukbetung[b]	Lampung	284,275	133,901	111.9[a]?	47.1

LESSER CITIES

Sabang	D.I. Aceh	23,821	8,500 (e)	180.2[a]?	35.7
Binjai	North Sum.	76,464	45,235	69.0	59.2
Tebingtinggi	North Sum.	92,087	26,228	251.1[a]	28.5
Tanjungbalai	North Sum.	41,894	29,152	43.7	69.6
Sibolga	North Sum.	59,897	38,655	55.0	64.5
Payakumbuh	West Sumatra	78,836	21,031	274.9[a]	26.7
Bukittinggi	West Sumatra	70,771	51,456	37.5	72.7
Padangpanjang	West Sumatra	34,517	25,521	35.2	73.9
Solok	West Sumatra	31,724	18,909	67.8	59.6
Sawahlunto	West Sumatra	13,561	12,276	10.5	90.5
Pangkalpinang	South Sumatra	90,096	60,283	49.5	66.9

Banda Aceh - Provincial Capital City in 1980.

[a]City known or believed to have expanded its urban territory since 1961.

[b]Lampung Province was established in 1964 with Tanjungkarang-Telukbetung as its capital; Bengkulu in 1968 with Bengkulu (city).

Sources: Indonesia, Biro Pusat Statistik, Sensus Penduduk 1980 (Jakarta: May, 1981); and Sensus Penduduk 1961 (Djakarta: June, 1962). Author's computations of percentages.

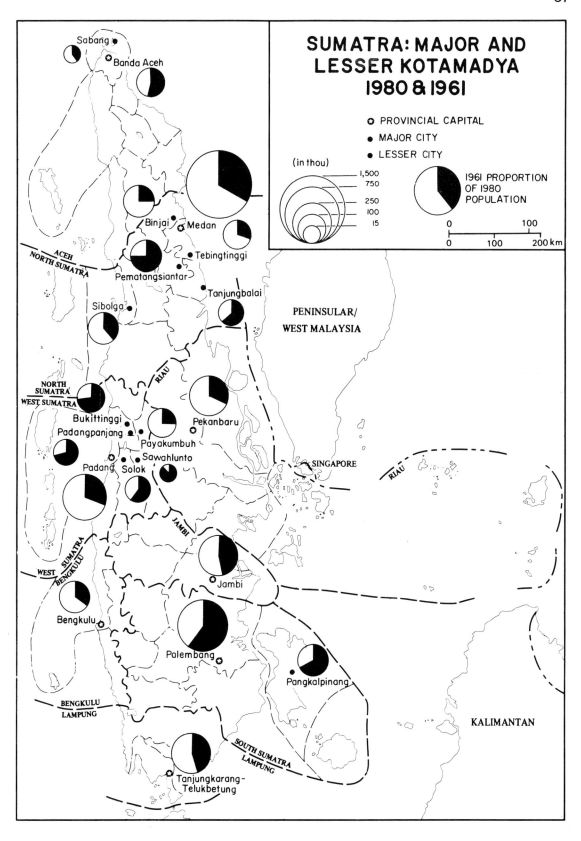

Fig. 7.2   The major cities of Sumatra, 1980 and 1961.

Other urban changes have included:

1. Both forced and voluntary outmigration flows, by non-ethnic Indonesians including Chinese, South Asians and Westerners, plus educated Sumatrans attracted to Jakarta or other extra-Sumatra places and opportunities.[23]

2. Considerable urban development in both the older central city areas and in expanding peripheries where residential areas, factories, sports stadia and university campuses have been added.[24]

3. For some of these cities, sizable immigrations related to Indonesia's "transmigration" program have brought many additional people from Java, Bali and southern Sulawesi.[25]

4. The eight provincial capitals, all on or near coastlines or major river arteries, show generally rapid growth. The one non-capital city of Pematangsiantar in eastern North Sumatra has a low upland site at the center of a commercial estate area and the lowest major city rate of population growth (Table 7.1).[26]

These points and others which might be added give strong evidence of advantages for some cities; handicaps for other cities. The most notable advantage for a city is to serve in the role of administrative capital of a province. Except for Pekanbaru these provincial capital cities are long-established cultural, political and economic centers.[27] Favoring most of the major cities is an accessible site on a coastal plain, well served by both natural and developed transportational facilities and linkages.[28] Though the Sumatran western coast has had historical periods of considerable importance, in recent decades this coast has been more nearly a "back door" in contrast to the eastern coast. Bengkulu, Padang and to some extent Banda Aceh (Kutaradja) are handicapped by locations not served by major routes or large traffic flows. The twin city of Tanjungkarang-Telukbetung with the nearby outport of Panjang/Srengsem faces the busy Sunda Strait and western Java; Palembang, Jambi, Pekanbaru and Medan are on or near the Strait of Malacca on the east, a heavily traveled corridor served also by the nearby major entrepots of Singapore, Penang and Luala Lumpur or its Klang outport.

Major Sumatran Cities as Surrogates for Asian Intermediate Cities

The final question posed in this discussion is to what extent can Sumatra's major cities — in their associations, characteristics and trends of change — serve as surrogates for intermediate cities more broadly across Asia? The reasonable answer is, "in part, yes; in part, no." On the positive side, Sumatra's major cities do represent many aspects characteristic of Asian intermediate cities in general.[29] These Sumatran cities are important regional administrative, cultural and economic nodes. Most are well served by nearby airports and seaports, though three — Pekanbaru on the Siak, Jambi on the Batang Hari, and Palembang on the Musi — are eastern plain cities more than forty kilometers inland on a large navigable river. Only Pematangsiantar in the low uplands of eastern North Sumatra has no airport or seaport. Like most intermediate cities of the Less Developed World, Sumatra's major cities have had rapid population growth from a combination of high natural increase and sizable net immigration flows. Each is involved in public and private attempts to improve its internal urban structural elements and remove any circulation blockages or other deterrents to internal and external services.

On the negative side, that is, that Sumatra's major cities cannot appropriately be considered surrogates, these Sumatran intermediate cities have specific site, situation and national or international linkages different from those of other Asian intermediate cities. In Java, Indonesia's core, for example, its intermediate cities increased in population far more slowly, enough so to suggest problems including economic stagnation.[30] Several cities of Java with high female to male population ratios have had sizable out-migration losses as men left to search for economic opportunities elsewhere. The diversity among Sumatra's nine major cities — in population size, rates of growth in the 1961-1980 period, and in diversity of ethnic and religious patterns — can also be cited as reasons why these cities should not be considered as surrogates or models for Asian cities.

Returning to positive reasons why Sumatra's major or intermediate cities can represent a broader universe of Asian cities, two need to be stressed. These are: (1) the regional setting away from the national core area provides insights into recent peripheral urban development; and (2) these cities represent real world conditions, providing an understanding of particular cities or groups of cities in their own spatial setting, physical, cultural, political and economic.

Summary

What has the application of flexible threshold limits for the intermediate city concept contributed as illustrated in its application to the major cities of Sumatra? First, rapidly increasing cities such as Medan, which have exceeded the one million population level, continue to be considered an intermediate city until or unless the city emerges as the national capital, largest or primate city. Within Indonesia, Medan has long been a regional capital, larger than any other Indonesian Outer Island or periphery city but containing not more than one-fifth of Jakarta's population.

Second, significant regional centers, such as Banda Aceh and Bengkulu, are included as intermediate cities. The focal functional qualities associated with administrative capital of a province, economic center, hub of communications and cultural nodality all reinforce the importance of these cities, despite populations considerably below the 100,000 level.

In effect, no arbitrary population — or functional — range should be stated as controlling the inclusion or exclusion of urban centers as intermediate, middle-range or secondary cities. The national capital, most populous and/or most functionally diverse city or cities, should be excluded at the upper end of the urban system, just as the many smaller regional cities generally are too limited in nodality, functions or population to attain intermediate city status.

END NOTES

[1]Hildred Geertz, Chapter 2, "Indonesian Cultures and Communities," pp. 24-41, in Ruth T. McVey (ed.), *Indonesia* (New Haven, CT: Human Relations Area Files, 1963). A table on page 19 in a chapter by Karl Pelzer lists cities of Indonesia with populations in excess of 100,000 in 1961, as well as their 1930 populations.

[2]Kingsley Davis, *World Urbanization, 1950-1970*, Institute of International Studies, Population Monographs Nos. 4 and 9; (Berkeley, California, University of California, 1969, 1972).

[3]Phillip Hauser, "World and Asian Urbanization in Relation to Economic Development and Social Change," *Urbanization in the ECAFE Region* (New York: United Nations, July 18, 1956); Gerald Breese, *Urbanization in Newly Developing Countries* (Englewood Cliffs, N.J.: Prentice Hall, 1966); and *United Nations Demographic Yearbook* (New York: United Nations, annual), lists by nation all cities of 100,000 or more.

[4]Dennis A. Rondinelli, *Secondary Cities in Developing Countries: Policies for Diffusing Urbanization* (Beverly Hills, California: Sage Publications, 1983), especially Chapter 2 defining secondary cities.

[5]William A. Withington, "The Intermediate-Size Urban Center: Its Significance and Role in the Developing World of Southeast Asia," unpublished paper read at the annual meeting, Association for Asian Studies, Boston, Massachusetts, March 29, 1969; several others on Sumatran and Indonesian intermediate cities; and "The Intermediate City of Southeast Asia," unpublished paper read at the 13th Pacific Science Congress, Vancouver, BC, Canada, August 26, 1975.

[6]James Osborn, *Area Development Policy and the Middle City in Malaysia* (Chicago: University of Chicago, Department of Geography, Paper No. 142, 1973).

[7]J. T. Fawcett, R. J. Fuchs, R. Hackenberg, K. Salih, and P.C. Smith, *Intermediate Cities in Asia Meeting: Summary Report* (Honolulu: East-West Center Population Institute, 1980); and Richard Ulack, "The Impact of Industrialization upon the Population of a Medium-Sized City in the Developing World," *Journal of Developing Areas*, 9 (January, 1975), pp. 203-220.

[8]Donald W. Fryer, "The Million City in Southeast Asia, *The Geographical Review*, Vol. 43 (1953), pp. 474-494.

[9]T. G. McGee, *The Southeast Asian City* (New York: Frederick Praeger, 1967).

[10]My residence was in Hawaii from 1927 to 1941; Lexington, Kentucky, 1955-1957 and 1959-present; and Medan, Sumatra, Indonesia, while a Ford Foundation Visiting Professor, Faculty of Economics, Nommensen University.

[11]*United Nations Demographic Yearbook* (New York: annually).

[12]John R. Borchert, "American Metropolitan Evolution," *The Geographical Review*, Vol. 57, 1967, pp. 301-332.

[13]William A. Withington, footnote 5 above.

[14]Osborn, footnote 6 above.

[15]Rondinelli, footnote 4 above.

[16]Sumatra in 1980 had 28 million people, second only to Java-Madura's 91.3 million in a total national population of 147.5, Biro Pusat Statistik, *Penduduk Indonesia 1980 . . .* (Jakarta: May, 1981). During the 1973-1977 period exports from Sumatra accounted for between 53 and 64 percent of Indonesia's values by value, Biro Pusat Statistik, *Statistical Pocketbook of Indonesia, 1977/1978* (Jakarta: 1978), p. 278.

[17]*Penduduk Indonesia, 1980*, Series L, No. 2, p. 5, see footnote 16.

[18]For a 1960s perspective, prior to the establishment of Bengkulu Province, see W. A. Withington, "The Major Geographic Regions of Sumatra, Indonesia," *Annals of the Association of American Geographers*, Vol. 57, 1967, pp. 534-549, for the regions served by Banda Aceh and Bengkulu cities.

[19]Hildred Geertz, footnote 1, pp. 78-85, provides a useful statement. The author's fieldwork in June, 1964, in Bukittinggi, West Sumatra, provided a strong perception of cultural centrality for the Minangkabau people. An earlier statement is that of Edwin M. Loeb, *Sumatra, Its History and Peoples* (Wien: Verlag des Institutes fur Volkerkunde der Universitat Wien, 1935), pp. 97-99. Fort van den Capellen (now Batusangkar), Fort de Kock (now Bukittinggi) and Payakumbuh (Pajakumbuh) are stated by Loeb to form the kernel of Minangkabau.

[20]Immigration data at the provincial level are available in Biro Pusat Statistik, *Penduduk Indonesia 1980*, Series S/2, *Hasil Sensus Penduduk 1980* (Jakarta: 1983), tables on population by place of previous residence five years earlier and place of birth according to place of present residence. Transmigration, also at the provincial but not at the city level, has been stated in successive *Statistik Indonesia* and *Statistical Pocketbooks of Indonesia* annually (Jakarta: Biro Pusat Statistik, yearly to the early 1980s). A recent study providing some sample population mobility and growth answers for Medan, Pematangsiantar and Tebingtinggi, eastern North Sumatra, is that of Thomas R. Leinbach and Bambang Suwarno, "Rural-Urban Mobility and Employment: Indonesia," Ottawa, Canada, A Final Report to the International Development Research Centre, 1984).

[21]Comparisons by author of earlier and current Sumatra city maps or plans and of 1961, 1971 and 1980 Indonesia Census data, some specific and some indicative of urban area expansions.

[22]Payakumbuh's increase in population during 1961-1971 was largely at the expense of Limapuluh Kota kabupaten, West Sumatra. Tebingtinggi's growth along with that of Medan, resulted in a decreased population in Deli Serdang kabupaten between 1971 and 1980. Data for *kotamadya/kotapradja* and *kabupaten* from 1961, 1971 and 1980 census sources.

[23]From the author's knowledge of employment locations of many students trained under the Ford Foundation project at the Faculty of Economics, Nommensen University, Medan, who were hired by the Central Government in Jakarta, and others who have been employed by Indonesian or international oil companies, and in consulting positions.

[24]Western-standard hotels in central city areas; stadia and university campuses usually in urban peripheries; factories and enlarged airports, also peripheral; along with new residential areas have been added in most major Sumatran cities.

[25]See footnote 20 comments. Nearly 250,000 persons are listed in the seven years for which I have data as coming to Sumatra. Lampung (95,000), South Sumatra (75,000), Bengkulu (33,000), Jambi (over 17,000) and Riau (12,000) were the principal provinces of destination, but no specific data indicate urban destinations.

[26]Pematangsiantar is the cultural center of the Simelungun Batak, but large numbers of Toba Batak and "Javanese" have also come in, as noted in Leinbach and Suwarno, footnote 20.

[27]Pauline D. Milone, *Urban Areas in Indonesia, Administrative and Census Concepts* (Berkeley, California: University of California, Institute of International Studies, Research Series No. 10, 1966), pp. 118-119. Pakanbaru/Pekanbaru was not listed as urban by the Dutch jn 1930.

[28]United Nations, ESCAP, *Asian Highway Route Map: Indonesia, Route A2/A-25* (Tokyo: Bridgestone Tire Co., Ltd., for UN ESCAP, 1978).

[29]A broad overview of the interplay of urban characteristics and cultural settings, though not specifically on Southeast Asia, is provided by John Agnew, John Mercer and David Sopher (eds.), *The City in Cultural Context* (Boston: Allen and Unwin, 1984).

[30]Biro Pusat Statistik, *Penduduk Indonesia 1980* (Jakarta: May, 1981) and also *Penduduk Indonesia 1971* (Djakarta: June, 1972) and *Penduduk Indonesia 1961* (Djakarta: June, 1962) provide comparisons at the municipality or *kotamadya/kotapradja* level for female/male ratios. The municipalities having the highest female/male ratios tend to be those with slowest population increases and limited new economic development.

8

The Program Planning Model: A Tool for Policy Planning and Policy Research in South Korea and Sri Lanka

Kenneth E. Corey

Introduction

The purpose of this chapter is to enable the reader to obtain an introductory understanding of qualitative generic planning methods within the context of planning development programs in a newly industrialized country and a less developed country. In order to accomplish this, the chapter has been organized into four principal parts. These include: (1) background and context to these qualitative methods; (2) a brief description of the Program Planning Model; (3) an application of this method to the development of a regional planning strategy for Seoul, South Korea; and (4) the use of the Program Planning Model to assess the development planning and urbanization patterns of Sri Lanka.

Background and Context

For purposes of providing context, the reader is referred to some definitions used recently by Miles and Huberman. They view *qualitative* analysis as being concerned with data that "appear in words rather than in numbers."[1] Qualitative data can be collected by: review of literature, content analysis, "observation, interviews, extracts from documents, tape recordings," and the like. Miles and Huberman go on to state that they *analyze* qualitative data by means of data reduction, data display and conclusion drawing, and verification.[2] These applications are congruent with the qualitative approaches used in the planning methods and the two development planning cases analyzed below.

A qualitative planning research methodology is adopted here because it was intended that the findings from the case studies might actually be *utilized* by policy planners. Douglass B. Lee, Jr. and others in planning research have observed that effective and operational decisions are more likely to result if the recommendations from planning analysis are couched in terms that are understandable — especially to decision makers and clients.[3] With this lesson in mind, the qualitative planning methodology of the Program Planning Model was used here both *to plan policy* and *to analyze policy* in the Asian case studies that follow. Before developing the cases it is necessary to introduce the qualitative planning method that was central to this research.

A few background comments are in order about planning methods and qualitative research. In the current and recent literature on qualitative methods there is scant reference to qualitative research methods that properly can be labeled action research.[4] Using Peter Clark's definition of *action research*, the researcher addresses practical problems with theoretical relevance *and* is concerned with transferring the knowledge from the research findings to the participant-objects of the research. "Thus, action research must possess an aspect of direct involvement in organizational change, and simultaneously it must provide an increase in knowledge."[5] In contrast, most qualitative research methods seem to fall under the categories of *basic research, applied research,* and *evaluation research.*[6] This observation is made to suggest that the development and application of planning methods and related interventionist research technologies may well be a neglected area of qualitative methodologies. It is intended that this brief exposure to a select set of planning methods might serve to stimulate others to consider experimenting with qualitative planning approaches in their own research — both applied research and action research.

Program Planning Model

Andre L. Delbecq and his colleagues, especially Andrew H. Van de Ven, have been developing these qualitative planning methods for more than a decade. The Program Planning Model (PPM) was introduced in 1971.[7] PPM offers program planners and managers a generic, effective means for introducing *innovation*[8] and coping with, and directing change in dynamic and uncertain organizational and societal environments. PPM can be used to break down organizational and societal problems into manageable parts, and sequence them into stages that produce new programs and projects. It is an incremental, decentralized and socio-technical approach that involves the assignment — by stage — of the most appropriate *roles* and *actors* to the specific planning task that needs to be completed in an interdependent sequence of problem-solving activities. The process requires the timely participation of those who need to be involved (i.e., clients, such as citizen organizations) for the successful execution of a new program or innovation.

The Program Planning Model has changed and been developed over the years. The 1971 edition of PPM has evolved and, through systematic experimentation, has been modified. In 1975 the qualitative techniques of nominal group and Delphi were linked to PPM.[9] The program evaluation component of PPM was developed and explicated in 1976.[10] The program implementation strategy was detailed in 1978.[11] The funding, grantsmanship, and resource-development functions of PPM were developed further and advocated in 1979.[12] In 1979 also, the importance of mediating the perspectives of the various actors in the program-development policy process was clarified.[13] In 1980, (a) PPM was tested empirically and compared to traditional planning and management methods,[14] and (b) new propositions for PPM were derived and suggested to provide guidance for implementing collective action in organizations.[15] In 1986, the out-of-print 1975 *Group Techniques for Program Planning* book was reprinted, thereby giving a new generation of planners easy access to some of PPM's techniques.[16]

It is assumed here that planning takes place from an organizational base — usually large complex organizations. One should consider using PPM in planning organizational activities — if the organization is characterized by most of the following attributes that have been listed by Andre L. Delbecq and his associates:

- The organization has limited time.
- The organization has few staff.
- The program has a limited budget.
- The programs serve multiple groups.
- The staff have different values.
- The program will be affected when needed changes are made.
- The environment and technology affecting the organization and its activities are not fully understood.
- There is low readiness in the organization to adopt an innovation or a new activity.
- Initiatives have to face a large number of reviewers and approvers for proposed activities to be sanctioned and funded.

PPM can be of assistance in addressing these issues, because it is a transferable conceptual framework that simplifies the planning task and makes planned change manageable. One can use PPM to understand and to play one's role as planner *and* researcher in conducting effective planning and in researching planning processes.

Stage 1: The Initial Mandate

The result of this PPM stage is to secure elite (i.e., top design makers and resource controllers) understanding and the official sanction of the organization to begin planning the new program or project, and to form a planning coordinating committee to link the program planning to policy makers, the administrators, the controllers of resources, the key clients/citizens, and the ultimate program implementors.[17] The method used during this stage is to share information about the prospective innovation, to obtain endorsements, to build alliances, to harness diversity to the planning task, and to identify potential threats to, or opportunities for, the planning organization. The role of the planning coordinating committee is to monitor and advise the planning staff, and to review the evolving programmatic innovation throughout its development. The planning coordinating committee reports to the organization's governing body or to the delegated developmental program manager.

Stage 2: Problem Exploration

The task during this phase of PPM is to assess, document and to provide evidence of the citizens' and clients' need. This can be done by observation, and by interviews and structured meetings (i.e., nominal groups) especially with clients and consumers, as well as providers, decision makers and resource controllers.[18] (9). Problem exploration can be aided by searching existing information and prior surveys on needs. It may be necessary also to conduct new surveys via hearings or use of media.

The key actors in this stage are the citizens and/or clients with the needs; their role is to tell about their problems and to specify their needs. The key listeners here are the program planners whose function it is to ensure that this needs assessment drives the plans and new programs that are generated later in this process. The planning coordinating committee reviews the resulting problem-exploration report, suggests modifications to it, and recommends continuation or termination of the program planning process.

Stage 3: Knowledge Exploration

The contribution of this phase to the PPM process is to obtain the most effective state-of-the-art solutions to the needs and problems identified. An initial approach that can be employed during this stage is the use of telephone surveys to obtain nominations of key knowledge-resource people, such as funders, service providers and content experts; Delphi would be an example of another knowledge exploration technique that might be used.[19] The experts are asked to recommend potential solutions and the innovations necessary to meet the needs identified by citizens/clients during the earlier problem-exploration stage. The key actors here are the external experts telling the program planners what actions can be taken to solve the problems explored in Stage 2. The planning coordinating committee again reviews the report from this PPM stage and suggests modifications and continuation (or not) of the program planning effort.

Stage 4: Proposal Development

The outcome of this PPM stage is a written strategic proposal that speaks to the initial mandate and incorporates the Stage 2 needs and their Stage 3 best solutions.[20] To accomplish this, the task is to prepare a proposal that covers the history to date of the proposed innovation. The document should not be a polished detailed report, rather it should look like an early sketch draft; it must be perceived and should be able to be modified easily. It should be in outline form; it might contain simple illustations; it should include a clear summary statement; and it should be accompanied by endorsements from respected individuals both from within and from outside of the planning organization.

This phase also should include the planing coordinating committee review of the proposal — one that produces an adoption/approval for the innovation. This review *also* must incorporate the needs and commitments of external funders and/or commitments from the organization's resource controllers and agreement from all who will be needed during later implementation to cooperate in the realization of the objectives of the new program. Importantly, this PPM phase should produce ownership, i.e., a shared sense of excitement in the potential, and the ultimate achievement of the needed innovation. The nominal group technique[21] can be used to conduct a systematic proposal review. It is essential that the proposal be able to be modified and strengthened by others who are not part of the planning team. Negotiation of proposal elements and the resources needed to implement the proposal should characterize this stage.[22] The key actors of this stage are the program planners, the internal and external resource controllers, and the organization's elites.

Stage 5: Program Design

The result of this phase of PPM is a plan — in operational and tactical detail — to be used in the implementation of the new program. The task here is to select from the programmatic alternatives to the needs identified earlier, and then to develop a single action program or intervention that is most likely to meet these needs.[23] This stage begins to specify the management requirements of the proposed program during implementation. At this time the design for the program evaluation is completed.[24] The principal actors in this phase are the program planners; they are responsible for the technical microdesign of the new program; their main concern is to continue to insure that their operational plans directly address the earlier-identified needs of the citizens or market. The planning coordinating committee reviews the plan and sanctions (or not) the design of the program for further development in the next stage of PPM.

Stage 6: Program Implementation and Program Transfer

The outcome here is to execute the new program, but in a way that systematically and experimentally tests the innovation before going to full implementation. The concern in this phase is to avoid making the big mistake and to derive systematic lessons from the experimental design. A small-scale *pilot project*, followed by a slightly enlarged and more broadly applied *demonstration test*, combine to provide the background necessary before going to *full program implementation*.[25] The key actors are the program planners and representative program implementators and service providers. The planning coordinating committee assesses the pilot and demonstration subphases and their findings before recommending full program implementation.

Program Evaluation: Spans Stages 4 through 6

The issue here is the monitoring and evaluation of the planned and tested new program activities relative to the stated program objectives.[26] The findings obtained during these evaluations are used to improve the program design and implementation. The key actors in this activity are the citizens/consumers/clients or their representatives, the program planners and/or outside evaluators. This activity serves the audit function of determining the extent to which the originally-stated needs have been reduced by the action resulting from the implemented new programs. With the review and sanction of the planning coordinating committee, the new program can be transferred from the developmental part of the organization to the routine, functional side of the organization.[27]

PPM Summary

The chapter to this point has sought to introduce the reader to a select set of developmental planning tools. These developmental methods are designed to introduce innovation, that is *new* programs to societies, communities and organizations. These qualitative planning methods are recommended here because they have been tested, assessed and documented extensively.[28] These methods have proven effective in sensing external and internal forces of change and harnessing them so as to reduce the needs of citizens and an organization's clients. In a few words, "these methods work."

By pursuing this introduction with additional reading from the references cited herein, and by extensive practice and experience in one's own organizational/environmental context,[29] the researcher and planner alike can become more effective in their respective roles.

The Asian Case Studies

The purpose of this part of the chapter is to demonstrate briefly how the Program Planning Model, used as an organizing conceptual framework, aided in the execution first, of a piece of policy planning research, and in the second case, a piece of policy analysis research.

Seoul, South Korea

In this case, PPM was used to plan policy. This is considered an example of action research, or at least it suggests a strategy for the execution of an action research effort.

The Seoul initial mandate. With the clients and sponsors being the Metropolitan Government of Seoul and the Korea Planners Association, a project was initiated to develop and present an overall strategy that could be used in planning for Seoul in the year 2000.[30] The author was the planner in this context. The PPM framework was used to make the planning task manageable. PPM was applied both to research the issues and its approach was recommended to the clients in Korea to be used in the implementation of the strategy for Seoul.

The Seoul problem exploration. The clients took the lead in specifying the problems and in providing the initial data and information on Seoul's needs and problems. The researcher used independent documentary sources to corroborate and elaborate on the provided material; this resulted in a comprehensive problem exploration. The explicated problems included: large population growth and rapid population growth, water and air pollution, the need for land use and transportation patterns that minimize energy consumption, and the requirement to be able to finance Seoul's new programs that are planned to address these problems. The needs assessment also revealed a number of opportunities that required attention. For example, the potential inherent in Korea's recent economic transformation in industry would seem to offer future new options to the policy planners of Seoul.

The Seoul knowledge exploration. The researcher executed this PPM stage by conducting an extensive literature review and content analysis of more than twenty-five years of published research by French urbanist and geographer, Jean Gottmann.[31] This particular approach was taken because it was hypothesized that Seoul's future might benefit from a long-term strategy, one component of which would be based on developing the regional economy's service sector and services employment potential. Special attention was paid to information-age, post-industrial and transactional employment generation.[32]

The Seoul proposal development. The product of this PPM stage was a strategic-level proposal for Seoul's regional policy planners to consider. It was sketched out at a level of overview that was intended to provide food for thought, but also generalized enough to encourage the Seoul policy planners to elaborate and "Koreanize" the strategy into operational detail. The proposal was labeled the "Transactional Metropolitan Paradigm."[33]

The Seoul program design. In order to provide the clients with examples of some of the specificity required for the implementation of a transactional planning strategy, several alternative programs were introduced.[34] These programs included tactics to avoid creation of new manufacturing jobs in Seoul, initiatives to develop clusters of transactional and services employment and office centers, the integration of Seoul's new and developing subway system into this strategy, the creative and widespread use of high-rise buildings for living and for work, emphasis on compact spatial patterns for such development, complementary residential area locations, capitalizing on Seoul's primacy and not dismantling its transactional potential, minimizing private automobile ownership, promotion of amenities and services for transactional transients, and so on. These are illustrative of possible actions for the ultimate tactical programming by Seoul-region planning staff.

The Seoul program implementation and transfer. The basic notion proposed here was to execute the strategy's programs from the principle that planning and development "risks are greatest by starting too big, not too small." Thus, implementation included piloting, testing and experimenting Seoul's transactional metropolitan strategy initially in the central business district and at selected subway crossroads in the suburbs. With the ultimate establishment of a demonstrated transactional employment base, it was suggested that lower-level information-oriented services be diffused systematically down Korea's urban hierarchy to medium and smaller cities throughout the country. This and other planned pilot-to-demonstration-to-full implementation experimental sequencings followed from the PPM propositions described early in the chapter.

The Seoul program evaluation. The major emphasis in this PPM stage was to stress the identification and use of measurement criteria upon which monitoring and assessment of the planned programs of the transactional metropolitan strategy could take place and be effective.

Numerous nominal-scaled transactional indicators were proposed to measure progress toward the planning targets that will be set for Seoul and its region. Since these early and relatively primitive efforts at suggesting measures for transactional urbanization were made, Nagashima has demonstated the use of analogous, but more effective criteria in measuring urbanization in Japan's Tokaido Megalopolis.[35]

The evaluation design also included the recommendation to reform the Korea census especially as applied to the region of Seoul, so as to have its categories and variables compatible with the regular survey of these new transactional and recent information-age dynamics and demographics. Areal units, location of census respondents, and the periodicity of transactional behavior were included in the program evaluation design.

Sri Lanka

The application of PPM in this case study represents an example of its use in doing policy analysis research. Further, this case contrasts to the Seoul situation, in that it did not seek to effect a change or impact policy. Rather, the purpose here was to use PPM to *analyze* the policies in effect in Sri Lanka and their relationship to that country's recent pattern of urbanization. PPM was selected as the analysis method. It was used because, as a policy and planning tool, it was seen to have the elements needed to analyze policy and planning processes. Thus, this is an example of applied, rather than action research.

The Sri Lanka initial mandate. The sponsor for this research was the U.S. Fulbright-Hays Program. The principal client was the researcher. The PPM mandate was secured by means of the approval of the applied-research proposal. The purpose of the research was: (a) to identify Sri Lanka's government policies on urbanization and counter-urbanization, and (b) to determine the role that these policies had in producing Sri Lanka's pattern of urbanization. Sri Lanka has maintained a long-term balance between urban and rural population that has been stable for more than a generation. For three decades or so Sri Lanka has had approximately 80 percent of its population living in the countryside and approximately 20 percent of its population living in urban areas. Its largest city region, Colombo, over most of that period has maintained its proportionate share of the urban population (i.e., around 20 percent).

The Sri Lanka problem exploration. By means of exploratory interviews, field observation and survey of records and documentary evidence, the historical and geographical patterns of Sri Lanka's urbanization and urban development were assessed. The major learning was that no single, explicit policy of urbanization or counter-urbanization produced Sri Lanka's stable urban-rural balance. Instead, the exploratory research demonstrated that the pattern was more a function of individual, segmented sector-by-sector policies, rather than a holistic, integrated, coordinated and intentional outcome of an urbanization policy. This researcher has labeled this "a case of policy serendipity."[36]

The Sri Lanka knowledge exploration. Having acquired some clarity into the roots of the country's urban pattern, a series of depth interviews was conducted with selected experts in Sri Lanka's public policy-making and its urban development. These included government officials from the cabinet level downwards, researchers and academics, and private voluntary organization leaders. They were probed to elicit their informed and experienced views on the role of past sector and development policies in the countryside and for the cities.[37] Also, these experts were interviewed for their perceptions of likely future patterns of urbanization in the next generation of Sri Lanka's development.

The Sri Lanka proposal development stage. The main result of this stage of the application of PPM as a tool of policy analysis was to reveal that two schools of informed thought prevail on Sri Lanka's future urban-rural balance. One school says that little additional urbanization will occur; the other forecasts that forces already are in motion that will operate to enhance the attractiveness of metropolitan Colombo and medium-sized cities and therefore increased rural-to-Colombo and other urban-area migration can be expected. Such a significant shift could have profound effects on Sri Lanka's stable urban-rural balance. For example, if successful, government policies for the promotion of foreign investment in Colombo-area free trade zones might well produce sufficient new jobs to stimulate greater in-migration to the Colombo region. Each school supported its views with evidence and sound argumentation.

The Sri Lanka program design. Following the PPM proposition of selecting an alternative program option from the several sketch-proposed futures of the previous stage, the Urban Development Authority of Sri Lanka, among other policy agencies, was scrutinized for its role and planned impact on Colombo's future development. In fact, its future plans and current programs would suggest that, indeed, the Colombo region will grow as a whole, but the spatial distribution of that growth is likely and is intended to be deconcentrated (i.e., in the new capital area of Sri Jayawardenapura) rather than having further population growth densely clustered in the center city of Colombo. In addition, planned and expected growth in the country's small towns and medium-sized cities was seen as operating to: (a) mute possible migration to metropolitan Colombo, (b) increase urbanization nationwide, but principally in the smaller urban centers,[38] and (c) have such small urban centers develop in the Dry Zone and Mahaweli Ganga development area in direct response to massive colonization and resettlement programs.

The Sri Lanka program implementation and transfer. The PPM principle of starting small and experimenting before expanding a new program was found to be a long-practiced approach of Ranasinghe Premadasa, the Minister of Local Government, Housing and Construction, and the Prime Minister of Sri Lanka. In many development projects, he would direct that an initial pilot effort be established and, depending on its results and popular reception, the effort would be expanded or not. Examples include housing projects and village reawakening schemes.

The Sri Lanka program evaluation. The government's Ministry of Plan Implementation tracks policies and programs. It monitors the progress of the government's "Lead Projects," as in the case of the Accelerated Mahaweli Program, the Urban Development Authority, the Greater Colombo Economic Commission, the Integrated Rural Development Program, and the Export Development Board. The Ministry's Annual *Performance* Reports serve the effective evaluation function of bringing public attention to high priority national development planning policies.

Summary

To conclude, the Program Planning Model has been introduced here as an example of a useful and widely applicable qualitative planning tool. To demonstrate its utility, two cases in Asian urban development planning were selected. The Seoul, South Korea case study suggested PPM's strength as an action research method and policy planning device. The Sri Lanka case documented PPM's role as an analysis of policy tool and as an example of applied research.

END NOTES

[1]Mathew B. Miles and Michael A. Huberman. *Qualitative Data Analysis: A Sourcebook of New Methods* (Beverly Hills: Sage Publications, 1984), p. 21.

[2]*Ibid.*, pp. 10-11.

[3]Douglas B. Lee, Jr., "Requiem for Large-Scale Models," *J. of the American Institute of Planners*, Vol. 39, No. 3 (May 1973), pp. 163-178.

[4]Pablo Gonzales. *The Fallacy of Social Science Research: A Critical Examination and New Qualitative Model* (New York: Pergamon Press, 1981).

[5]Peter A. Clark. *Action Research and Organizational Change* (London: Harper & Row Publishers, 1972), p. 23.

[6]*Ibid.*, pp. 8-24.

[7]Warren G. Bennis, Kenneth Benne, Robert Chin and Kenneth E. Corey (eds.). *The Planning of Change*, 3rd ed. (New York: Holt, Rinehart and Winston, 1976). Chapter 7 of this book is recommended because it documents both Delbecq's 1971 "Program Planning Model (PPM)," and G. K. Jayaram's "Open Systems Planning" which emphasizes the importance of the organization's external environment and long-range planning as a way to be directive and responsive to change.

[8]Andrew L. Delbecq and Peter K. Mills, "Managerial Practices That Enhance Innovation," *Organizational Dynamics* (Summer 1985), pp. 24-34.

[9]Andre L. Delbecq, Andrew H. Van de Ven, and David H. Gustafson. *Group Techniques for Program Planning: A Guide to Nominal Group and Delphi Processes* (Middleton, Wisconsin: Green Briar Press, 1986).

[10]Andrew H. Van de Ven and Richard Koenig, Jr., "A Process Model for Program Planning and Evaluation," *J. of Economics and Business*, Vol. 28, No. 3 (1976), pp. 161-170.

[11]Andre L. Delbecq, "Relating Need Assessment to Implementation Strategies: An Organizational Perspective." Paper delivered at the Second National Conference on Need Assessment in Health and Human Services, Louisville, Kentucky, March 29, 1978, 19 pp.

[12]Kenneth E. Corey. *Neighborhood Grantsmanship: An Approach for Grassroots Self-Reliance in the 1980's* (Cincinnati: Community Human and Resources Training, Inc., 1979).

[13]Andre L. Delbecq and Sandra L. Gill, "Political Decision-Making and Program Management," *Translating Evaluation into Policy*, Robert F. Rich (ed.) (Beverly Hills, California: Sage Publications, 1979), pp. 23-44.

92

[14]Andrew H. Van de Ven, "Problem Solving, Planning and Innovation. Part I. Test of the Program Planning Model," *Human Relations*, Vol. 33, No. 10 (1980), pp. 711-740.

[15]Andrew H. Van de Ven, "Problem Solving, Planning and Innovation. Part II. Speculations for Theory and Practice," *Human Relations*, Vol. 33, No. 11 (1980), pp. 757-779.

[16]Delbecq, Footnote 9.

[17]Delbecq and Gill, Footnote 13.

[18]Delbecq, Van de Ven and Gustafson, Footnote 9.

[19]*Ibid.*

[20]Norman J. Kiritz, "Program Planning and Proposal Writing," expanded version, *The Grantsmanship Center News*, Vol. 5, No. 3 (May/June 1979), pp. 33-79.

[21]Delbecq, Van de Ven and Gustafson, Footnote 9.

[22]Corey, Footnote 12.

[23]Richard Beckhard and Rueben T. Harris. *Organizational Transition: Managing Complex Change* (Reading, Massachusetts: Addison-Wesley Publishing Company, 1977).

[24]John Mordechai Gottman and Robert Earl Clasen. *Evaluation in Education: A Practitioner's Guide* (Itasca, Illinois: F. E. Peacock Publishers, 1972).

[25]Delbecq, Footnote 11.

[26]Gottman and Clasen, Footnote 24.

[27]Nathan Caplan, et al. *The Use of Social Science Knowledge in Policy Decisions at the National Level* (Ann Arbor: Institute for Social Research, The University of Michigan, 1975).

[28]Van de Ven, Footnote 14.

[29]Andre L. Delbecq, "The Hospital Trustee: An Organizational Perspective," *Education of a Hospital Trustee: Changing Roles for Changing Times*, Lewis E. Weeks, (ed.) (Battle Creek, Michigan: The W. K. Kellogg Foundation, 1977), pp. 52-60.

[30]Kenneth E. Corey, "Transactional Forces and the Metropolis," *Ekistics*, 297 (Nov./Dec. 1982), pp. 416-423.

[31]Jean Gottman. *The Coming of the Transactional City* (College Park, Maryland: Institute for Urban Studies, University of Maryland, 1983).

[32]Kenneth E. Corey, "The Status of the Transactional Metropolitan Paradigm," in *The Future of Winter Cities* (Beverly Hills, California: Sage Publications, 1986).

[33]Gottman, pp. xvi-xvii.

[34]Kenneth E. Corey, "The Status of the Transactional Metropolitan Paradigm: An Application to Planning the Metropolitan Region of Seoul, Korea," pp. 39-49 in *Proceedings of the Fourth Annual Applied Geography Conference*, B. Epstein and J. Frazier (eds.) (Binghamton: State University of New York, 1981).

[35]Catharine Nagashima, "The Tokaido Megalopolis," *Ekistics* 289 (July/Aug. 1981), pp. 280-301.

[36]Kenneth E. Corey, "Deconcentrated Urbanization in Sri Lanka: A Case of Policy Serendipity." Urban Studies Working Paper No. 1 (College Park: Institute for Urban Studies, University of Maryland, November, 1984).

[37]Dayalal Abeysekera. *Urbanization and the Growth of Small Towns in Sri Lanka, 1901-71*. Paper No. 67 (Honolulu: East-West Center, 1980).

[38]M. W. J. G. Mendis. *Urbanization and Urban Development in Sri Lanka* (Colombo: USAID Office of Housing and Urban Development, 1982).

9

The Gemeinschaft/Gesellschaft Approach: A Conceptual Framework for Planning and Designing Arab Towns

Frank J. Costa and Allen G. Noble

Urbanization and economic development are closely related phenomena. As a society changes from one that is primarily rural to one primarily urban, its economic structure necessarily changes. The social organization of a society also is deeply affected by this change. Primary and kinship relations characterize the rural society, while secondary and instrumental relationships are a feature of urban society.

Saudi Arabia in recent decades has evolved very rapidly from a traditional and pastoral society into one which is highly modernized and urbanized. This paper is concerned with the effects of such tremendous change on the built-form of Saudi Arabian settlements.

The Traditional Form of Arab Towns: Categories of Urban Space

The traditional form of the Arab town was dictated by both environment and the religion of its inhabitants. The hot and arid climatic conditions prevailing in the Arabian peninsula impose a certain introverted form on the town and its constituent structures. Arab towns are built close to the ground with few high buildings. Most structures are grouped together to provide shade and create cooler micro-climates. Few, if any, setbacks exist from the building line and the building entry usually is immediately adjacent to the street. The relationship between houses creates a distinctive urban form, an almost continuous low-rise and high-density settlement. The street pattern of this settlement is highly irregular, made up of many narrow, winding and dead-end streets. The introverted character of the dwelling is reinforced by religious concerns which stress the privacy of the family setting and the seclusion of the female members of the family.[1] The traditional Arab town is a unique physical phenomenon molded by the physical and religious environments that surround it.

Private space in Islamic societies is safe and secure. Public space, on the other hand, is viewed as completely unsafe and must be eschewed by females. The "social invention" of what can be called semi-private space is an attempt to create a protected area outside the dwelling unit itself within which kin-like responsibilities (and freedoms) govern.[2]

At the town or city level, the traditional foci of the entire settlement are the Friday mosque, market, and the major government building (Figure 9.1). The interlocking and organized character of the urban form created by these foci and their ancillary activities have been described by Spreiregan:

> In the center stands a mosque, the spiritual and intellectual center of the city — its brain and heart. Nearby is the palace of the ruler, so the center is a place of decision as well. Then, near the mosque, one finds candle and perfume makers who supply the mosque with some of its ceremonial requisites. As a center of learning the mosque is bordered by the university which includes an ample library. Merchants of fine leathers, papers, and cloths supply the materials for binding the books. This center of finery supplies goods for clothing as well as for the mosque and its library, and the cloth merchants require a sheltered enclosure, a roofed hall, which can be locked. Consequently, the quarter for carpenters, locksmiths, and metalsmiths lies alongside. Taking a few more steps we are at the city gates, where we find saddlemakers and hostels for travelers. Thus, the component parts of the organized Arab city are located as logically as the organs of the human body. Their dimensions and distances are also largely determined by the mathematics of pedestrian circulation.[3]

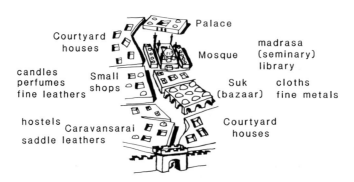

Fig. 9.1 Morphological elements of the Arab city center (after Spreiregan).

The city center and the myriad of activities that take place there constitute the environment for public life. Thus, these areas are the public spaces of the town. The disparate populations of the town's neighborhoods come together and mingle freely in these public spaces.

Major concentrations of public facilities exist at both the neighborhood level and at the town level. The semi-private character of the neighborhood results from the extension of the private domestic environment into its immediate surroundings. Family life, in the traditional sense, revolves around religious observance and domestic routine. Both of these requirements are satisfied through the neighborhood market and the neighborhood mosque, both of which serve local needs. Neighborhoods possess a high degree of ethnic and religious homogeneity. In fact, ethnic and religious segregation into identifiable districts is a long-standing morphological feature of the Arab town.[4] Thus, the neighborhood in an Arab town is highly autonomous. Its streets, markets and other public areas possess the character of semi-private space. Extended families, kinship groups and related individuals move about the neighborhood freely, but the outsider is immediately recognized and frequently made to feel as an intruder.

Neighborhoods are often the physical locus for a larger kinship group of which the family is a part. Thus, the female members of the family can move more freely within the confines of the neighborhood. The semi-private character of the neighborhood provides a release from domestic confinement while still maintaining the envelope of privacy which is so important in Islamic religious and cultural life (Figure 9.2).

Courtyard Houses: The Domain of Private Space

If a public character is evident at the town center and a semi-private character envelops the neighborhood or local district, complete privacy is the outstanding virtue of the individual house. Here privacy is sought from both the natural and human worlds beyond. Consequently, dwellings have few outside openings. Where they do exist, screening is usually provided to divert direct sunlight and prevent viewing from the outside. A typical house site in many of the older neighborhoods measures only about twelve meters by twelve meters. The house is usually no higher than two stories and without any setbacks. Walls rise directly at the property line and abut the walls of adjacent structures. Interior spaces are frequently large and high ceilinged, connected with the outside through upper level vents and wind channels to permit the heated air of the interior to rise and flow outward. Outside exposures are provided through interior courtyards or by screened exterior windows. Orientation of building openings is away from the sun and toward the north and west whenever possible.

Much of the character of the traditional Arab town derives from the design of the individual houses, especially the layout and plan of the structure. Over thousands of years, the residents of the Middle East have come to recognize the suitability of houses built around interior courtyards (Figure 9.3). In such dwellings the courtyard not only provides a focal point for the inhabitants, but also aids in the cooling of

M - Maidan
Mo - Neighborhood mosque
S - Neighborhood suk

Fig. 9.2 Interior courtyards provide open private space, while the massing of buildings creates open, semi-private areas in the neighborhood (drawing by M. Margaret Geib).

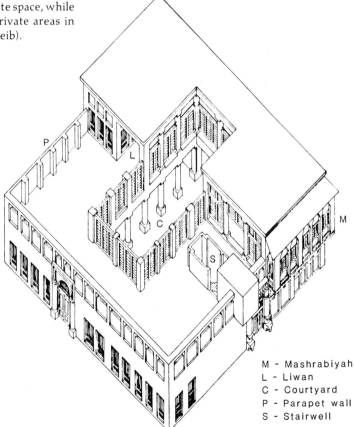

M - Mashrabiyah
L - Liwan
C - Courtyard
P - Parapet wall
S - Stairwell

Fig. 9.3 Isometric view of a traditional courtyard house (from a house in Al-Khobar).

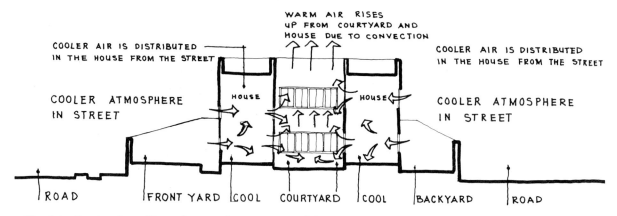

Fig. 9.4 Sectional profile explaining the convectional function of the courtyard.

the dwelling (Figure 9.4). The most common form of courtyard house, e.g., the centrally-positioned, interior court, is surrounded on all sides by the living space of the dwelling.

Less commonly encountered are houses in which the courtyard is not centrally positioned. In such houses the plan of the covered space may be L-shaped with the courtyard occupying one corner of the structure, or it may be U-shaped, surrounding the courtyard on only three sides. Finally, a related, but quite unusual, courtyard house has had a much more limited use. In this house the courtyard is divided into two parts (Figure 9.5). These two parts can be made to correspond to the public and private entrances for the dwelling, thus preserving the important dichotomy between family life and public entertaining within the same structure.

Modern Urban and Building Forms

Figure 9.6 shows a typical new subdivision of the type being widely proposed today for modern Arab cities. The subdivision illustrates several significant changes over the traditional form of the Arab town as described earlier.

Rectangular grid street systems have replaced the intricate curvilinear and irregular pattern of the older towns. No longer does the street benefit from the passive shading that was an inherent characteristic of the old towns. Uniform parcels contain detached dwellings with sideyards and front yards. Thus the climatic benefits of attached dwellings are lost.

Beyond the loss of physical enclosure with its cooler micro-climate, there is the additional loss of privacy within the dwelling. This is especially true when buildings of different heights are built adjacent to each other. Because of the hot climate, the orientation of structures without interior courts must be outward; thus new dwellings have lost their introverted character and are exposed to public view, as well as to direct sunlight and consequent heating.

The other significant change that occurs within the new built-form of the Arab city is that semi-private space is largely eliminated. In earlier periods, the physically defined and separated character of the urban neighborhood allowed its open areas to become semi-private spaces. These conditions no longer exist with grid street patterns and outward-oriented structures. Thus, an important element in the social and cultural life of the community has been significantly altered. A traditional building approach harmonizing with the culture of the people has been replaced by foreign-designed techniques with only tenuous links to Arabic society.

Finally, the new urban forms increasingly employed in Arab cities are wasteful of limited land resources. This is especially apparent in several of the rapidly expanding conurbations of Saudi Arabia. For example, the Dammam-Al Khobar metropolitan area along the Arabian Gulf is rapidly eating up the remaining arable land of the Qatif oasis.[5]

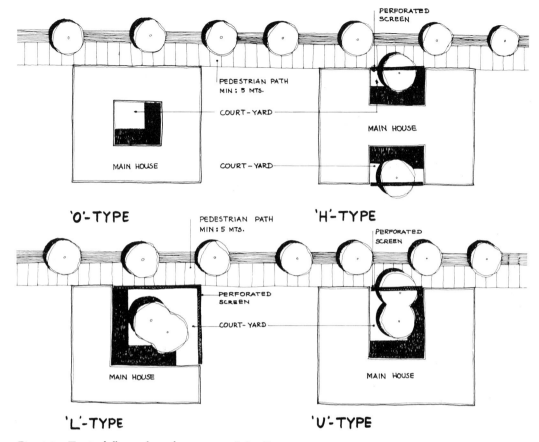

Fig. 9.5   Typical floor plans for proposed dwellings.

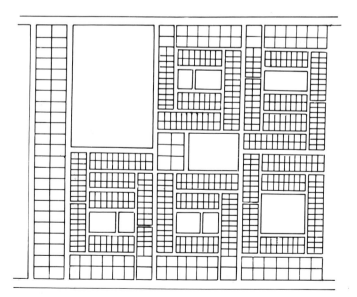

Fig. 9.6   Layout of a modern subdivision following Western planning practices.

Traditional urban design solutions in the Arab town were the product of a long period of experimentation, in which the primary concerns were to mitigate the rigors of a hot and arid climate and to foster a built-form which provided an adequate physical environment for domestic and social life, with its attendant requirements of religious observance.

The nearly complete abandonment of traditional form in the on-rush of modernization has not provided the urban resident with a satisfactory alternative. The circumstances in which Westernized urban design solutions became dominant had much to do with rapid urbanization. The older towns grew slowly and the required new sections were carefully added to the existing town. But modern Arab cities are literally exploding with growth. Under these pressures, traditional methods of construction have proven inadequate and newer methods, techniques and designs have not been modified to approximate traditional forms.

The scale of the problem of rapid urban development must not be underestimated. Vigier and Serageldin have shown that recent urban growth in the Arab world is occurring much more rapidly than it did earlier in the West.[6] In fact, this is exactly the dilemma of depending upon Western planning solutions. Western technology permits the laying out of entire sections of a city quite rapidly, and the building, in a very short span of time, of numerous multi-unit residential buildings to house large numbers of urban migrants. Unfortunately, the cost of such projects is enormous and the inhabitants are rarely psychologically comfortable in these dwellings. Belkacem refers to the "hundreds of people . . . crowded into gigantic dormitory towns, often created without the necessary infrastructure, which leaves them empty of life and soul and constitutes a living example of the most degraded form of habitat that modern architecture has ever produced."[7]

The inadequacy, or actual failure, of Western planning approaches in many Arab cities is producing a strong negative reaction from many architects and urban designers. Some of this reaction has been rooted in an almost irrational fear of any challenge to, or modification of, traditional life, and some stems from an unwillingness to accept ideas, techniques or methods not originating within the area and culture. A much larger group, however, consists of individuals who do not reject Western technology or practice out of hand, but who have come to recognize that these features and approaches must be applied to the Arab city in such a way that the underlying fabric of Islamic culture is not torn asunder in the process. Even in Western societies, planning methods have often produced unfortunate results because culture and societal patterns have not been adequately considered.

Gemeinschaft/Gesellschaft Space: Combining Traditional Form and Modern Building Techniques

What is needed are techniques which reconcile Western planning practices, on the one hand, with the Islamic culture of Arab cities, on the other. This chapter addresses only one aspect of this problem, that of devising modern subdivision and building codes.

The Arab town should be developed in such a way that certain important physical features are retained. These include:

1. the complete privacy of the individual dwelling;
2. the creation of small and intimate neighborhood-based public spaces, within which social mixing can occur without concern for possible violations of family privacy or religious observance principles;
3. the creation of clusters of commercial, governmental and manufacturing activities in which the requirements of modern economic life are met; and
4. the creation of a densely compact and low-rise overall development character for the settlement through which climatic and family privacy objectives can be achieved.

The creation of a hierarchy of urban spaces from the intimate and completely private space of the dwelling to the totally public space of the town center is the most important underlying principle for the proposed building regulations. In effect, we are proposing the creation of a dual or even a tripartite network of urban spaces.

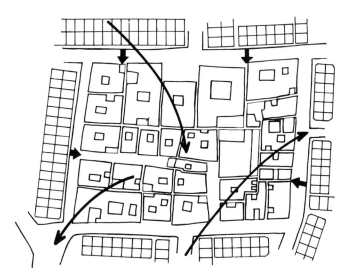

Fig. 9.7   Gemeinschaft/Gesellschaft spatial relationships. The short arrows indicate the traditional relationships and the longer, arching arrows portray the less structured associations of Gesellschaft society.

The physical character of these spaces must be appropriate for their intended activities. The semi-private space of the neighborhood would fit the well-known Western concept of "gemeinschaft" space, while the public space of the town center or other economic activity clusters of the town would be akin to "gesellschaft" space. The concept of the "gemeinschaft/gesellschaft" continuum is rooted in nineteenth century European social theory as an explanation of the transition then occurring from rural- and small-town-based society to urban society.[8] In many respects this is the same process which is taking place today in the Arab Islamic world.

Gemeinschaft society is organized around the family or kin group, within which roles and responsibilities are defined by traditional authority and social relations are instinctive and habitual. Cooperation is guided by custom. In *gesellschaft* society, social and economic relationships are based upon contractual obligations. The major groups that influence the individual are no longer kin, but professional peers. Family associations are secondary. Social relations are based upon rationality and efficiency, not tradition.

Human society needs aspects of both gemeinschaft and gesellschaft social organization for its development and continuation. Western planners have tried for decades to propose solutions to the dilemma of creating settlement forms in which both kinds of relationships co-exist. The need for the dual set of relationships is especially great in the Arab town where custom and religion isolate the family and kin group units from social intrusion. The neighborhood unit concept developed by American planners can provide an instructive model for planners and designers of modern Arab towns. The neighborhood unit is the focus of gemeinschaft relationships. Gesellschaft activities occur elsewhere. Schematically, this bifurcation of space can be depicted as shown in Figure 9.7.

A Comprehensive Land Development and Building Code

Keeping this duality in mind, the specifics of a model land development or subdivision and building code can be elaborated, which will reconcile traditional and innovative approaches. Certain basic objectives to be attained by such a model code include:

1. Creating internal and external spaces for contemporary use and for the mental and physical health of the residents.

2. Respecting the basic Islamic principles for family privacy from both external sound and vision.

3. Recognizing climatic conditions and the use of passive heating and cooling systems as well as natural ventilation.

4. Minimizing energy use for air conditioning and transportation.

5. Fostering simplicity, economy and concentration of development.

6. Recognizing the interrelationship, but separate character, of movement systems. Neighborhood or residential areas should have a pedestrian movement system, while the citywide movement system should be vehicular.

7. Providing the opportunity for a healthy social environment that encourages religious, cultural, educational, physical and recreational activities at both the neighborhood and city levels.

8. Controlling land uses through zoning, suitable subdivision, relative densities and restricted building heights.

9. Creating a hierarchy of spaces for human life ranging from the completely private space of the private dwelling through the semi-private space of the residential district or neighborhood to the public space of the city center.

As a means of illustrating the utility of the proposed code, its application for subdivision control is outlined below. The following are basic points which highlight many of the differences between the proposed code and most existing codes in Arab towns.

1. No land will be subdivided for building without permission from the responsible body (municipality or public body) authorized to provide the preliminary permit.

2. A complete preliminary project, including project objectives and detailed urban design for the project area, must be submitted for approval from the appropriate authority.

3. The preliminary project should include land subdivisions, location of major buildings and their use, the population density, major roads, entrances to lots, pedestrian walkways, in addition to areas for facilities required by the municipality, such as schools, mosques and shopping facilities.

4. Contour lines and their relationship to buildings must be shown on a separate drawing.

5. The project submission should also include typical elevations and cross-sections.

6. The project submission should specify the number of residential units, population density, and percentage of built-up area.

7. No land should be subdivided until permission from the authority is granted and the project approved.

Conclusion

Geographers and planners in the Arab world are coming to realize that the solution to the many problems associated with their rapidly growing urban areas must be found in a synthesis of Western building technology and traditional Islamic concepts of urban life. In the past, the temptation was to simply import Western technology and to introduce basic Western concepts such as urban renewal, subdivision planning, garden cities and new towns. None of these approaches has solved the problem. Indeed, in many instances they have aggravated the situation or created a range of new difficulties.

The adoption of a uniform subdivision and building code, as proposed in this chapter, will make possible the orderly development of rapidly growing Arab cities and, at the same time, will preserve the important Islamic traditions of the society within which such development is taking place.

END NOTES

[1]M. M. Abdel Aziz Noor, "Factors Underlying Traditional Islamic Urban Design," *Planning Outlook*, Vol. 24, No 1 (1981), pp. 29-30.

[2]Janet Abu-Lughod, "Contemporary Relevance of Islamic Urban Principles." Paper given at 1st International Symposium on Islamic Architecture and Urbanism, Dammam, Saudi Arabia, January, 1980, pp. 7-8.

[3]Paul Spreiregan, *The Architecture of Towns and Cities* (New York: McGraw Hill Book Company, 1965), p. 121.

[4]Xavier de Planhol, *The World of Islam* (Ithaca, New York: Cornell University Press, 1959), pp. 9-14.

[5]A. F. Moustapha and F. J. Costa, "Al Jarudiyah: A Model for Low Rise/High Density Development in Saudi Arabia," *Ekistics*, 287 (Mar.-April 1981), pp. 100-101.

[6]Francois Vigier and Mona Serageldin, "Urban Needs for Modernizing Societies: New Directions in Planning," in Serageldin, Ismail and Samir El-Sadek (eds.), *The Arab City: Its Character and Islamic Cultural Heritage* (Riyadh, Saudi Arabia: Arab Urban Development Institute, 1982), pp. 13-21.

[7]Youssef Belkacem, "Bioclimatic Patterns and Human aspects of Urban Form in the Islamic City," in Serageldin, Ismail and Samir El-Sadek (eds.), *The Arab City: Its Character and Islamic Cultural Heritage* (Riyadh, Saudi Arabia: Arab Urban Development Institute, 1982), p. 10.

[8]Ferdinand Tonnies, *Community and Society* (East Lansing, Michigan: Michigan State University Press, 1957).

10

Development by Negotiation: Chinese Territory and the Development of Hong Kong and Macau

Bruce Taylor

Introduction

Although Asia taken as a whole is not one of the most highly urbanized continents, the large cities of East and Southeast Asia have shown tremendous population growth in recent years. With this rapid growth has come unchecked physical expansion, and many Asian cities are facing problems traceable to urban sprawl that are familiar to American planners — traffic congestion, inadequate infrastructure on the urban fringe, and encroachment of urbanization onto agricultural land are only three from the familiar litany. The situation is made more complex in many cities because, as in America, the central city has little if any control over the territory outside its highly-circumscribed borders. Development on the fringe then goes completely unregulated, or is controlled by ineffective and perhaps disinterested provincial officials or in some cases by fragmented local governments.

One response by planners in a number of Asian cities has been to make the attempt to extend their planning authority over broad areas outside the city boundaries. Allowing them to do so lets them consider city and surrounding hinterland as constituent parts of an integrated "city-region" for which a unified development plan can be produced, creating a situation where the phased decentralization of people and jobs into the countryside can be substituted for hit-or-miss scatteration.[1] An excellent example appears in Indonesia, where the "Jabotabek" planning region encompasses not only the Jakarta agglomeration but the nearby cities of Bogor, Tangerang, and Bekasi together with a good deal of rural territory.[2] A similar approach is used in such disparate Asian cities as Shanghai, Seoul, and Manila.

The focus of this paper is on two Asian cities where planners are not able to extend the territory under their jurisdiction. They are the British colony of Hong Kong and the nearby Portuguese-administered enclave of Macau, both confined within borders established by treaty between China and the colonizing power in the last century. Both cities suffer from most of the same ills resulting from overcrowding that plague their counterparts elsewhere in Asia. But unlike in any other Asian city, with the exception of the city-state of Singapore, planners in Hong Kong and Macau do not have even the theoretical option of extending their ability to control urban growth over a large expanse of countryside. One consequence is that urban population densities in both cities are among the highest in the world, a situation which is only partly alleviated by active (albeit geographically limited) programs of decentralization pursued over the past 15 years, notably by Hong Kong.

Though officials in Hong Kong and Macau have direct control over only a very small territory, there are numerous chances for them to make use of the land and resources of the People's Republic of China in providing for the needs of the people in their own enclaves. Doing so requires negotiation on a case-by-case basis with local, provincial, and sometimes national officials in China. Under Deng Xiaoping and his associates, China has opened its doors much more widely to the outside world, and nowhere is this more evident than at the borders with Hong Kong and Macau. The trickle of travelers over Hong Kong's Lo Wu bridge and through Macau's Barrier Gate ten years ago has mushroomed into a flood, and if anything the two-way flow of goods between the enclaves and China has grown even more rapidly. All evidence indicates that despite China's oft-stated opposition to "colonialism," the chances are better now than at any time in the past thirty-five years that its officials will agree to actively collaborate in developing its resources for the partial benefit of residents in Hong Kong and Macau. Similarly, as a result of the Sino-British agreement on Hong Kong's future, under which Hong Kong will revert to Chinese sovereignty in

1997, it would appear at first glance that colonial officials there would be equally willing to engage in cooperative efforts with China.

We can envision, then, a process which we might term "development by negotiation" operating in Hong Kong and Macau, as a substitute for the expansion of territory under the direct jurisdiction of the two colonial administrations. Through a process of bargaining involving Chinese officials at different levels of government, their Hong Kong and Macau counterparts, and private interests based in the two enclaves, agreements are reached which allow for the use of China's territory and resources principally to meet needs expressed by the people of Hong Kong and Macau. The intention of this paper is to examine the extent to which Hong Kong and Macau have benefited from this process of "development by negotiation," focusing on five areas where such collaboration across political boundaries exists or has been proposed, and from these examples to draw conclusions as to what factors (notably political ones) have promoted or inhibited the process. First, though, it is necessary to discuss the Chinese government's own plans for the development of its territory near the Hong Kong and Macau borders, as these will have a significant bearing on the probability of successful "development by negotiation."

The Special Economic Zones

Perhaps no other action has been more symbolic of the opening of China to the outside world than the creation in 1979 of Special Economic Zones (SEZs) at four locations in Guangdong and Fujian Provinces. The SEZ concept was not new, as similar "export processing zones" or "free trade zones" are seen in many countries.[3] What *is* new is the application of the concept in a country which is avowedly socialist — suggesting that, at least in this case, the strict application of Marxist/Leninist doctrine has been subordinated to China's pursuit of modernization. Kwok and Fong list several objectives which the SEZs are intended to accomplish:

a) allowing China to gain experience in the application of modern technology and management techniques;

b) increasing foreign exchange earnings through the production of commodities for export;

c) creating jobs for Chinese workers, with enhanced possibilities for on-the-job training;

d) setting up a "laboratory" environment where the possibilities for coexistence of market-directed and centrally-planned economies might be carefully examined;

e) enhancing China's socialist modernization program.[4]

To this list might be added the objective of satisfying a rapidly increasing domestic demand for consumer goods without increasing China's foreign trade deficit. This last objective has attained prominence recently as the income of some entrepreneurial workers and peasants has risen sharply.

Two of the four Special Economic Zones, Shenzhen and Zhuhai, are located adjacent to Hong Kong and Macau, respectively (see Figure 10.1). (The other two are at Shantou in Guangdong Province and Xiamen in Fujian Province.) Both the Shenzhen and Zhuhai SEZs were carved from rural territory with no large settlements and little pre-existing industry of any sort. Their development into modern industrial, residential, and commercial complexes thus has required vast expenditures on the development of basic infrastructure, including such fundamental requisites for modern industrial cities as paved highways, ports that can handle ocean-going shipping, and networks for supplying electricity and water to factories or housing developments.[5] The central Chinese government has supplied some of the needed funds, while the SEZ administrators have made strenuous efforts to attract the balance from elsewhere, including Hong Kong and Macau.

Shenzhen is by far the largest of the SEZs, encompassing 327.5 square kilometers just north of the border with Hong Kong (Figure 10.1). The area was a remote rural part of Bao'an *xian* (county) before the creation of the SEZ in 1979, with no settlement larger than 20,000 residents. Through 1984 Shenzhen's administrators were reported to have spent 3.5 billion yuan (US$1.12 billion) on infrastructure development.[6] The need to spend such vast sums is due to Shenzhen's large size, its great east-west extent, and the primitive state of its pre-existing facilities. The plan for Shenzhen reserves the eastern

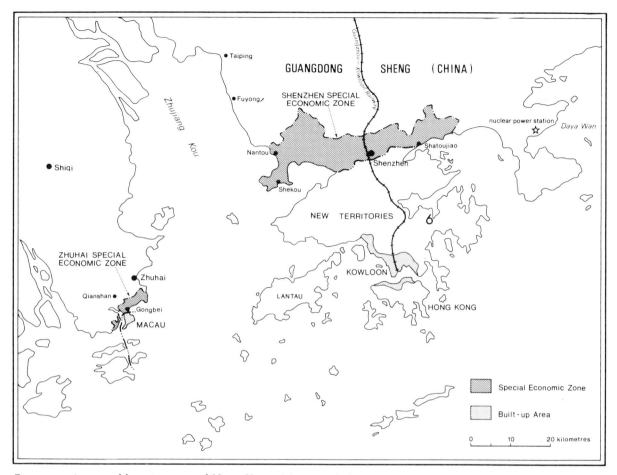

Fig. 10.1 A general location map of Hong Kong, Macau and their adjacent areas.

third of the zone, which is hilly, for mostly recreational uses. The central portion is designated for commercial/residential growth and light industry, while in the west the heavy industrial areas, the port, and perhaps an onshore support base for South China Sea oil exploration are to be developed.[7]

Zhuhai SEZ is very much smaller than Shenzhen; its 15.2 square kilometers of territory make it about the same size as neighboring Macau. Like Shenzhen, it was a rural area before 1979, and like Shenzhen its administrators have spent freely on infrastructure projects (some 400 million yuan [US$128 million] through 1984).[8] The plan for Zhuhai places special emphasis on tourist development, but also reserves some area for light industry. Industrial growth has been hampered in Zhuhai because of inadequate road transport links to other parts of China and port facilities with limited capacity, though projects to remedy both deficiencies are now under way.

Facilitating the development of Hong Kong and Macau is not one of the intended purposes of the two Special Economic Zones. However, it is obvious that as China develops the areas along the Hong Kong and Macau borders into modern industrial districts, the two enclaves are increasingly likely to be able to benefit from activities carried out by Chinese administrators in China's territory. Beyond this, the Chinese themselves recognize that under some circumstances, an investment in facilities serving the needs of Hong Kong and Macau residents pays dividends to China and to the SEZs. An example is when tourists from Hong Kong and Macau contribute, through their expenditures on food, lodging, admissions, and travel, to China's foreign exchange earnings.

Thus the development of Special Economic Zones enhances the opportunity for Hong Kong and Macau residents to benefit from "development by negotiation." In the following sections we take a closer look at the status and achievements of "development by negotiation" in several fields where collaboration between Hong Kong or Macau and China exists or has been proposed. Most of these projects involve the two Special Economic Zones although some also involve territory beyond their borders. As will become evident, there is a good deal of variability in the progress made to date on the different matters at hand. It is the reasons for this uneven level of achievement which especially interest us in this paper. Some thoughts on the subject appear in the final sections.

Basic Infrastructure

In the last section we noted the vast effort that has gone into building up the infrastructure of the Shenzhen and Zhuhai SEZs. Inevitably some of these facilities will be interconnected with the existing infrastructure networks in Hong Kong and Macau. In theory, this works to the benefit of all parties involved. For the enclaves, China can serve as a supplier of reserve capacity (say, of water supplies) in times of severe need. From China's standpoint, the cost of an infrastructure project which provides some benefits to Hong Kong and Macau can be shared with the governments of one or both of the enclaves.

With their own reservoir capacity limited and with desalination a very expensive alternative, both Hong Kong and Macau have concluded that obtaining water from China is a necessity. It is no accident that long-standing agreements govern the supply of water from China to both territories. In Hong Kong's case, arrangements to import water from China date back to 1960, long before any thought was given to urbanization in Shenzhen. The amount of water supplied by China has expanded gradually from an initial 23 million cubic meters to an estimated 325 million cubic meters in 1985, the latter representing more than half of Hong Kong's total water consumption in that year. To assure adequate supplies in the future, Hong Kong signed in 1984 a 15-year agreement with China under which as much as 620 million cubic meters of water annually could flow to the territory by 1995. Hong Kong will spend close to HK$2 billion (US$256 million) on pumping stations and pipeline improvements to handle this increased supply.

A second area where close cooperation between Hong Kong, Macau, and China has occurred is in the integration of the regional electric power grid. Macau's government-owned electric company took the lead in purchasing electricity from China by signing an agreement in 1980 with Guangdong Province. An interconnection between the two power networks was finished in 1984, and is credited with rescuing Macau residents from the periodic summer blackouts they had endured up to that time. Hong Kong's electricity grid is also interconnected with China's, though the situation in Hong Kong is the reverse of Macau's since Hong Kong is a net seller, not a buyer, of electricity. Chinese officials believe that by 1988, with the completion of new coal-fired generating stations, it will no longer be necessary to buy electricity from Hong Kong.

The most significant cooperative development in this area, however, is the forthcoming 1800-megawatt nuclear power station at Daya Bay, east of Shenzhen. This project, the first of its kind in China, is a joint venture between the Guangdong Nuclear Investment Company, a Chinese company, and the Hong Kong Nuclear Investment Company, a subsidiary of the territory's China Light and Power Company. Under an agreement signed in early 1985, about two-thirds of the output from the Daya Bay plant will be transmitted to Hong Kong when the plant is commissioned in the early- to mid-1990s.[9] The Hong Kong company views the project as a preferable alternative to building new coal-fired stations in Hong Kong, which would require extensive site development and stringent environmental controls. For China, of course, the acquisition of French and British nuclear technology represents, at least in the none-too-critical eyes of the Chinese leadership, a substantial coup for the nation's modernization program.

Among the other examples of cooperative infrastructure development that might be cited, the use by Macau of landfill from China in reclaiming land from the sea merits special mention. Macau has only minuscule land reserves of its own, and reclamation is the easiest way for the Portuguese enclave to form new sites for the building of factories or housing. The landfill which goes into the reclamations must, however, come from Zhuhai as Macau has almost no sites from which earth can be taken. This means that the tacit approval of China is needed before any reclamation project can begin in Macau. At the time of writing a contract was under negotiation between the Macau government and a China-controlled trading company in Macau over an extensive reclamation project planned for the northeast of peninsular Macau, which is intended for use as an industrial area.

There are, of course, some instances where negotiations between Hong Kong or Macau and China over a proposed infrastructure project have not producted results — as with the aborted plan to open landfill sites in Shenzhen to dispose of solid waste emanating from Hong Kong. Nor has the bargaining always been trouble-free: talks on the Daya Bay nuclear plant almost collapsed in 1985 over matters of cost and financing, even after approval in principle had been reached by the companies involved. However, on balance there have been more examples of cooperation across political boundaries on matters pertaining to basic infrastructure than in any other field, and the agreements hammered out among the three governments have resulted in substantial demonstrable benefits to the people of Hong Kong and Macau. They illustrate perhaps better than any other examples can the potential which is inherent in "development by negotiation."

Recreation and Tourism

Among the most pressing needs of Hong Kong and Macau residents is better access to open space and recreational facilities. In the congested urban areas of Hong Kong and Macau open space is necessarily limited to small parcels. Outside the urban areas more land is available, and in Hong Kong nearly 40 percent of the territory's rural land — largely the undevelopable hillsides — is designated as parkland. Despite these best efforts, facilities in Hong Kong alone cannot meet the rapidly-growing demand for leisure opportunities spawned by increasing affluence among a growing population.

The potential benefits from developing tourist resorts and recreational facilities in China catering to the Hong Kong and Macau markets were recognized early on by officials in the Shenzhen and Zhuhai SEZs. Several advantages were gained from an emphasis on tourist-related development in the early stages of growth. First, when compared to industrial development, recreational development was less costly and demanded a smaller immediate investment in supporting infrastructure. Second, resort hotels or amusement parks were less risky propositions for foreign investors than were most types of industrial plants. Establishing a track record of profitable partnerships with foreigners in tourist-related enterprises would help in overcoming any apprehension felt by investors concerning the untried SEZ investment climate. Finally, of course, visitors from Hong Kong and Macau contributed immediately through their expenditures to China's earnings of foreign exchange.[10]

In these early stages, tourist development in the two SEZs focused on so-called "holiday camps," such as the Xili Reservoir Holiday Camp in Shenzhen, which offered facilities for picnicking, swimming, and active recreation largely for short-term visitors. These were criticized as being unimaginative and duplicative of each other, and the large developments planned for some sites have been scaled down. Planners in Shenzhen now intend to locate recreational facilities at sites near reservoirs and beaches, complemented by shopping centers in Shenzhen town and at the nearby border crossing point of Luohu (spelled Lo Wu in Hong Kong). All of these will be aimed mostly at residents of Hong Kong, though Shenzhen is also becoming popular with domestic tourists from other parts of China. Zhuhai, on the other hand, is making a concerted effort to attract international tourists, aided by Macau's travel industry which plays a significant role in the Portuguese enclave's economy. Package tours combining a stay in Macau with a visit to scenic points in Zhuhai and the surrounding districts are heavily promoted by Macau hoteliers and tour operators.

A prerequisite for the success of these Chinese recreational developments is relatively unhindered access to them by visitors from Hong Kong and Macau, and here great improvements are visible on both sides of the borders. In China, new paved highways reach some of the more remote and scenic areas in and near the SEZs. New piers at Shekou (Figure 10.1) in Shenzhen and at Jiuzhou in Zhuhai have opened up possibilities for direct ferry links to Hong Kong and Macau; indeed, private ferry operators in Hong Kong now run fast hoverferry services to both SEZs. In Hong Kong, access to China was vastly enhanced by the completion in 1983 of electrification and double tracking on the railway line running to the border (Figure 10.1). The railway's capacity for China-bound traffic has more than doubled since that work was finished. Vehicular access has not been neglected, either, with a second border crossing at Shatoujiao finished in 1985 and a third scheduled to open in 1987. It is now possible to ride scheduled buses linking Kowloon and Shenzhen, and numerous charter operators maintain fleets of tourist coaches licensed for both Hong Kong and China.

These improvements in internal transport facilities unfortunately are not complemented by improvements at the border crossing checkpoints. The majority of China-bound passengers from Hong Kong pass through the rail crossing at Lo Wu, where stories of overcrowding and delay have attained the status of local legends — especially on weekends and holidays when many residents pay extended visits to their relatives in China. Visitors to recreational sites in Shenzhen, especially day trippers, are seriously deterred by the prospect of long delays. Part of the problem is created by inadequate physical facilities on both sides of the border to handle the crowds of travelers (a point which applies equally well to the checkpoint at Gongbei, between Macau and Zhuhai). Both Hong Kong and Shenzhen are constructing new immigration and customs terminals to alleviate overcrowding, which may promise some relief by 1987 if enough personnel are available to man the counters in the new facilities.

However, limited physical facilities represents only one aspect of the border crossing problem — an equally serious deterrent is the need for recreational visitors to China to pass through four rigorous immigration and customs checks (two each way). The content of immigration and customs regulations which are applied at the borders is, of course, not determined with reference to recreational travelers alone, and the needs of the tourist industry in China are an insignificant point when such regulations are framed (especially in Hong Kong). Much more critical in the eyes of Hong Kong's policy-makers is the need to control illegal immigration from China, while in China's eyes the problem of smuggling currency, illegally-imported consumer goods, or other contraband through the SEZs into the remainder of China has taken on special significance. There is no indication from any government in the region that it is prepared to bend its rules for the sake of promoting cross-border tourism. Nor is it likely that collaborative talks will bring fruitful results soon, as Hong Kong, Macau, and China each for their very different own reasons have an interest in maintaining a high level of border security.

When compared to the pace of cooperative infrastructure development, cooperation in developing opportunities for cross-border recreational and tourist movement appears both slow and fragmentary. A good deal of progress has been made in building the transport links and physical facilities. Yet this alone is inadequate in the absence of policy changes in the field of immigration and customs control which would facilitate the freer movement of travelers to and from recreational sites in China. It is owing to such basically non-negotiable matters of general public policy that "development by negotiation" begins to founder as a means of obtaining much-needed facilities for the people of Hong Kong and Macau. This point also pertains to other areas of potential cooperation, as is seen later in this paper.

Housing

The tremendous growth experienced in Hong Kong and Macau owing to legal and illegal immigration from China has resulted in a serious shortage of affordable housing in both territories. Hong Kong has attempted to overcome this problem by a massive program of public housing construction, which between 1954 and 1982 produced nearly 500,000 units of low-cost housing sheltering more than two million people.[11] Nevertheless, many residents of Hong Kong (and Macau, with no comparable program of its own) suffer unhealthy and sometimes unsafe living conditions in squatter areas or in private tenements built to low standards.

Sites that are suitable for modern high-rise public housing developments are hard to come by in Hong Kong and Macau, which slows considerably the progress of construction. Typically land must be reclaimed from the sea or hillsides leveled before a new project can go ahead, and the time lag between the start of site formation works and occupancy of the completed units can cover several years. Because of this, some housing planners in Hong Kong and Macau might cast their eyes on the readily available land in the Special Economic Zones and wonder whether housing projects located in China could help in alleviating the pressure on the existing housing stock in the two enclaves.

The Chinese have harbored similar thoughts from time to time, and in both Shenzhen and Zhuhai housing projects have sprung up which are marketed primarily in Hong Kong and Macau. However, none yet are intended to serve the same working-class mass market which is served by Hong Kong's public housing projects. Three target groups from Hong Kong and Macau have been identified by developers working in the two SEZs, but two of these — the resident managers of foreign enterprises and the buyers of vacation/retirement properties — are numerically insignificant. Managers and technical personnel involved in running SEZ factories have moved to Shenzhen, especially, in limited numbers — thus avoiding the time-consuming border crossing formalities noted in the last section. But the Chinese appear to have overestimated the size of this market, creating a glut of residences far too expensive for most local workers which have had to be sold at a steep discount from their original prices.[12]

A third class of potential buyers — daily commuters to Hong Kong and Macau from China — has received a good deal more attention. Because of lower labor costs and land prices in the two SEZs, the cost per square foot of comparable housing is lower than in the European enclaves. Private developers who have attempted to tap this market think that buyers can be attracted into housing projects in China by the low prices, the chance to live in a more spacious unit, or the ability to own a residence in China when finances permitted only renting at home. The most ambitious project of this sort was the plan — now stillborn — of Hong Kong's Hopewell Group to turn a 3,000 hectare site in central Shenzhen into a commercial/residential complex capable of housing 300,000 people, mostly from Hong Kong. This is more than the projected populations of Tai Po or Fanling, two of the medium-sized new towns designated by the Hong Kong government.

To date the progress of developments of this nature has been disappointing. An obvious explanation for the Shenzhen/Hong Kong case is that Shenzhen is far removed from the industrial jobs in Hong Kong, which remain mostly in the main urban area despite government attempts to promote the movement of industry to the new towns. The reluctance of Hong Kong's industrialists to decentralize their operations has hurt developments in Hong Kong as well as in China: Tuen Mun and Yuen Long new towns in the northwest New Territories, for instance, are viewed by many residents as being remote and inaccessible, and hence less desirable as living environments. These problems would be compounded for projects in Shenzhen by delays in crossing the border, and by the overloading of vehicular crossing checkpoints connecting the SEZ with Hong Kong.

There is no sign that either the Hong Kong or Macau government is considering sites in China for the location of new public housing. In Hong Kong's case, it is felt that enough land is available in the new towns until at least 1991, after which additional land can be reclaimed (see the later discussion of Hong Kong's long-term planning). Thus if "development by negotiation" is to meet any of the housing needs faced by residents of the two enclaves, the negotiators are likely to be from the private sector, and they will need to be aided by a sharp increase in the number of job opportunities available within a short distance of the Chinese border. The latter, however, is a prospect that appears especially dim.

Air Transportation

Hong Kong is well supplied with the facilities for handling cargo, passengers, and telecommunications that it must have in order to carry on its extensive *entrepot* trade. Hong Kong's container port, for instance, is the third largest in the world measured in terms of containers shipped, and an expansion program to increase its capacity even further is underway. Both China and Macau rely on Hong Kong's port facilities in conducting their own external trade. In the short run, there is no need for Hong Kong to attempt to make use of Chinese territory in bolstering its position as the region's hub of trade and communications.

Within the next ten years, though, the eventual need for expanding Hong Kong's airport capacity must be faced. The present airport at Kai Tak is expected to reach saturation by 1993. It is a single-runway facility built on reclaimed land, with the runway and paralleling taxiway projecting into Hong Kong harbor. Its location in the heart of Kowloon, with consequent noise problems, means that the addition of a second runway is out of the question. A plan to solve both the capacity and noise problems by constructing a replacement airport off the northern coast of Lantau Island (see Figure 10.1) remains indefinitely shelved, as the Hong Kong government feels it cannot afford such an expensive project while it is still recovering from a period of deficit spending.

A modern international airport is especially demanding of the one resource — land — which is in shortest supply in Hong Kong. Hence it is not surprising that proposals have circulated since 1980 to build an airport in Shenzhen which would serve both Hong Kong and China. The Chinese central government has given approval in principle for the construction of an international airport to serve Shenzhen at a site just outside the SEZ, on the Zhujiang Kou (Pearl River Estuary) coastal plain between Fuyong and Nantou (see Figure 10.1). The initial phase of construction, optimistically slated for completion in 1988, would provide runway and terminal facilities to handle Boeing 737s or similar aircraft. Future expansion over a 15-20 year period would allow the airport to accommodate jumbo jets and serve more than 20 million passengers annually.[13]

The main purpose of this ambitious airport project is, of course, to link the SEZ with the other major population centers of China via scheduled air services, which it does not have at present. It is evident, though, that Hong Kong-bound flights could also touch down at Shenzhen, making it in effect Hong Kong's second airport. If Shenzhen's airport is to fulfill this role, careful attention must be given from the earliest planning stages to the possibilities for cooperation in the areas of landing rights, air traffic control, and immigration/customs proceedings. This would require a continuous dialogue between aviation and immigration officials in Hong Kong and their counterparts in Shenzhen.

To date there is no evidence that any talks concerned with collaboration in these areas have taken place. The view of Hong Kong officials is that the Shenzhen airport is "an internal matter" for the Chinese authorities. This is in spite of the quite obvious effects on air traffic control at Kai Tak which another international airport within 50 kilometers might be expected to have. It is possible that Hong Kong's planners think that the distance between the proposed site and the Hong Kong frontier (to say nothing of the built-up area) would render Shenzhen's airport a very unattractive destination for Hong Kong-bound flights. Certainly this would be the view taken by an airline "exiled" to Shenzhen as a consequence of any cooperative arrangements between the two governments. However, it is equally possible that the prospects for negotiating acceptable air service agreements involving the two airports are viewed as very dim by aviation authorities in Hong Kong, perhaps bearing in mind the complex discussions between Britain and China over control of Hong Kong's own landing rights during the recent negotiations on Hong Kong's political future. We return to this subject in a later section.

On the other side of the Pearl River Estuary the situation is a bit different. Macau has no airport of its own, and most visitors to Macau reach the territory by sea from Hong Kong. A feasibility study for the development of an airport on reclaimed land between Macau's offshore islands of Taipa and Coloane was finished in 1983. As with other projects in Macau requiring reclamation, approval from China would be required for construction to go ahead. It now appears that Macau's project will be shelved in favor of a proposal by the Zhuhai authorities to build a "medium-size international airport" at a site about ten kilometers southwest of the SEZ (due west of peninsular Macau). Details of the project remain sketchy, but it is thought that the Zhuhai airport would serve both the SEZ and Macau, with passengers to either territory having to pass through only one immigration/customs checkpoint.

If the Zhuhai airport goes ahead on this basis, it will mean that Macau and Zhuhai have reached a level of cooperation in the development of air transport services that appears unlikely to be equaled on the eastern side of the estuary. It is too early yet to be sure of the outcome of this or any of the various other proposals for airport construction mentioned here. But it is certain that over the longer term at least part of the air travel needs of Hong Kong and Macau residents will be met by facilities located in China, regardless of the degree of cooperation given by Hong Kong and Macau officials in the planning of those facilities.

Long-Term Planning Programs

To conclude our examination of specific areas where "development by negotiation" has had an impact, we turn to the nature of the long-term planning programs adopted by Hong Kong, Macau, and the two Special Economic Zones. Creating the ideal state of mutually beneficial symbiosis between China and the two European enclaves requires that both sides take note of the potential benefits of cooperation across the region's borders in drawing up their long-term development plans. On the Chinese side, the planners must maintain sufficient flexibility in administering their policies so that proposals for cooperative development made by the governments of Hong Kong or Macau, or by private interests based there, might receive a suitable hearing. In Hong Kong and Macau, planners must not consider the future growth of the two territories in total isolation from their surroundings, but instead should make a point of examining how the pattern of planned growth they propose might best be integrated with the rapid expansion taking place to the north of their borders.

Looking at the Chinese side first, there is strong evidence that proposed development projects emanating from Hong Kong and Macau are given serious consideration, particularly when the party from outside proposes the injection of additional development capital into the SEZs. Shenzhen's draft master development plan, prepared in late 1981, has been altered several times in order to accommodate projects suggested by foreign investors.[14] Examples include the Hopewell Group's proposed major housing development, noted earlier, and an express highway linking Hong Kong and Guangzhou backed by the same company. In other cases the planners in Shenzhen have turned over the responsibility for preparing detailed layouts for large-scale development projects to the foreign investors involved, willingly accepting the risk that adjacent tracts might be totally uncoordinated with each other or duplicate each other's facilities.

It would appear that, far from being inflexible, the Shenzhen authorities may be overly accommodating to outside interests, at the expense of attaining a coordinated internal growth pattern within the SEZ. Politically, of course, it would be very difficult for Shenzhen officials to reject a project where a heavy investment in, say, infrastructure was assumed by a foreign investor.

The same conclusion applies with even greater force to the smaller Zhuhai SEZ, where the authorities have given virtually free rein to foreign investors in directing the planning for some of the zone's most ambitious development projects — including a deep-water port and a "science park" intended to lure technologically-advanced industry. In both Zhuhai and Shenzhen long-range planning programs would not seem to create any institutional barriers to "development by negotiation" intended to serve the needs of Hong Kong and Macau residents, as long as the SEZ administrators were convinced that a project bestowed direct economic benefits on their region or promoted in the longer run the modernization of China.

The situation in the two enclaves is quite different. Planners in Macau appear to be less hesitant than those in Hong Kong in coordinating their programs for developing major facilities with the Chinese (e.g., the airport projects mentioned in the last section). Several reasons might be cited for this, including the need to import landfill from China noted earlier and the desire by Macau to obtain a measure of independence from Hong Kong in respect to its trade and its vital tourist traffic — collaborating with China to do so should that be the best or easiest way. However, Macau's stance also reflects the governing style typical of its Portuguese administrators, who are known to consistently seek accommodation with China on major political issues affecting the territory. Often this is done through consultation with China's unofficial but very powerful representatives in Macau, who operate through banks and major trading companies.

Despite this it is easy to overstate the extent of cooperation between Macau and China on planning matters. A comprehensive plan for the entire territory of Macau — its first — currently is being prepared by a European consulting team. The plan's provisions are shrouded in secrecy, but it is known that Zhuhai officials have not been consulted at any point in its development. Proposals by Zhuhai for new bridges linking peninsular Macau with the Chinese mainland have not been accepted by the Macau government.

The case of Hong Kong is more complex. Until the 1980s Hong Kong had no comprehensive plan guiding development throughout the territory; instead, its officials made do with a series of small-scale plans for areas where development pressures were most intense (including the seven designated new towns) coupled with a vague overall policy guideline encouraging the decentralization of people and job opportunities away from the urban area.[15] The completion in 1984 of Hong Kong's first truly comprehensive plan, the so-called "Territorial Development Strategy (TDS), has heralded a significant change. In preparing the TDS, the government first commissioned five "subregional studies" from consulting firms, each intended to examine in depth the size and scale of future development that could feasibly be carried out in one part of Hong Kong. Government planners then combined the recommendations from the five studies into a single comprehensive development strategy, using a complex method of comparative evaluation relying heavily on mathematical optimizing techniques. The findings suggest a sharp departure in the future from Hong Kong's recent policy favoring decentralization. Although the new towns will continue to grow, further expansion of the main urban area is also recommended, to house about 310,000 people in its initial stages.[16]

The TDS pays close attention to the prospects for integrating the more rural New Territories (outside the new towns) with the main urban area of Hong Kong. Indeed, the subregional studies were intended to examine how urban growth could best be extended into less urbanized territory while still meeting other social, environmental, and financial objectives. The attempt to integrate Hong Kong's urban area with its surroundings ends at the Chinese border, however, with the single exception that cross-border traffic movements are accounted for in the transport element of the TDS. At no time do the planners suggest that Chinese territory might be used for housing, for the relocation of the airport, or for recreational purposes, despite the moves in these directions by other parties which were noted earlier in this paper.

We can advance several explanations for the failure of Hong Kong's planners to consider the prospects for benefiting from "development by negotiation" during the preparation of the TDS. One plausible explanation notes that contrary to most public opinion, Hong Kong has more than adequate reserves of developable land assuming that today's prevailing levels of density continue into the future. Thus unlike Macau, Hong Kong can accommodate as many as 3.3 million extra people and 1.2 million more jobs beyond the expected 1990 totals without immediate reliance on China.[17] A related point is that the volume of cross-border travel to facilities in Shenzhen would remain small when compared to the volume of internal travel in Hong Kong no matter how great the extent of "development by negotiation." Naturally, Hong Kong's planners view the internal travel as their main interest.

As in Macau, though, the attitude of Hong Kong's planners towards cooperation with China would appear to depend partly on political circumstances. During the negotiations between Britain and China over Hong Kong's future which concluded in 1984, the issue of land policies during the transition period leading to China's takeover in 1997 was one of the most contentious ones laid on the bargaining table. The resolution of the issue impinged directly on the Hong Kong government's longer-term planning strategy: if the granting of land leases were restricted in any way, then the planners' ability to govern the evolution of Hong Kong's spatial structure would be directly affected. The eventual Joint Declaration agreed to by the two sides did in fact impose restrictions: the present (British) Hong Kong government is limited to offering no more than 50 hectares yearly for lease until 1997, excluding land used for public housing, and it must set aside part of the income it receives from land leases for use by the post-1997 "Special Administrative Region" government.[18] It is notable that these are the only points in the Joint Declaration where the present government is bound to take any action which might affect its current policies.

Certainly the framers of the Territorial Development Strategy may have been aware of these matters. Their considering of Hong Kong's future growth in isolation from China can be interpreted in this light as a way of preserving for the Hong Kong government as much autonomy in carrying out its favored development programs as is possible under the restrictions set in the Joint Declaration. "Development by negotiation," requiring as it does the use of territory outside the planners' direct control, could only complicate the process of translating their vision of Hong Kong's future spatial form into tangible reality. (This theme of preserving autonomy and freedom of action reappears in the next section.)

The Politics of Negotiation and Development: An Extended Analysis

The preceding sections have touched on a wide range of matters that have been the subjects of "development by negotiation," at least on paper. It is evident that the extent to which Hong Kong and Macau residents have actually benefited from the process is very uneven. The benefits appear to be greatest in the area of basic infrastructure development and least on such matters as air transport. In this section an attempt is made to analyze why these variations have occurred, giving special attention to political issues in the region and the effects they are having on intra-regional cooperation.

A first attempt at explaining the variation in what has been achieved by "development by negotiation" might focus on the complexity of the issues raised during the bargaining process, and whether they impinge on public policy questions that transcend the matter under discussion. The greatest degree of success in integrating development across political boundaries might be expected when the issues are relatively straightforward, sharply defined, and limited to questions concerning the technical content or economic viability of the proposals. Basic infrastructure development of most sorts would fit this description. This need not mean that such negotiations are easy, as the lengthy bargaining process over the Daya Bay nuclear plant makes clear. Yet even in this complex case the discussions have centered on economic issues and not on the broader ramifications of relying on nuclear power. The politically-charged debates heard in the West over the relative merits of "hard" versus "soft" energy paths have been muted in Hong Kong, and probably invisible in China.

Greater difficulty in carrying on "development by negotiation" occurs when the bargaining process touches on matters considered to be fundamental questions of policy which are the domain of the individual governments involved. Examples from the issues discussed in this paper include the content of immigration restrictions, which affects the use of Chinese territory for housing and recreation; the location of industrial employment, which again affects housing and also is an element of longer-range planning; and the right to allocate facilities at a territory's airports, which affects the coordination of air services. The issue of air transport planning, in fact, raises a third and even more complex problem: some issues transgress into the murky waters of international relations. Conceivably as many as eight administrations — China, Britain, Portugal, Hong Kong, Macau, Shenzhen, Zhuhai, and Guangdong Province — could have a stake in air service agreements affecting the region, and with so many governments involved any attempt to renegotiate the bilateral and international agreements under which air services are regulated presents almost insuperable obstacles.

Thus we might wish to place issues on a continuum of organizational and political complexity, with the least complex and least politically contentious issues presenting the best opportunities for benefiting from "development by negotiation." This explanation is intuitively satisfying, but it does not go far enough in accounting for attitudes which are evident in the region. It does not, for instance, explain why there seems to be greater resistance towards initiating proposals for collaboration among administrators in the two enclaves, especially Hong Kong, than there is among the Chinese. To understand this situation, another element must be introduced into the picture: the importance of political autonomy in the affairs of the region, and particularly in events which have occurred in Hong Kong since the signing of the Sino-British Joint Declaration outlining its future.

Successive Chinese governments since the Qing dynasty have regarded Hong Kong and Macau as Chinese territory and the Chinese "compatriots" living there as Chinese nationals. The People's Republic has tolerated the autonomous administration of the two enclaves by Britain and Portugal because of their undoubted value in such tasks as promoting China's exports and serving as listening posts for monitoring developments abroad. For their part the two European nations have maintained an anachronistic colonial presence in Hong Kong and Macau partially at the request of the Chinese inhabitants, who value the freedoms which they enjoy under the colonial administration.

The approaching expiry of the New Territories lease forced Britain's hand and led to the opening of negotiations with China over Hong Kong's future. From the start it was evident that Hong Kong's residents wished to preserve the territory's way of life, based on the capitalist system, but equally evident was China's insistence that sovereignty over Hong Kong was non-negotiable. The impasse which resulted led to a severe crisis of confidence which affected local property and financial markets. Only with the development of the so-called "one country, two systems" principle was this impasse resolved. China agreed in writing that the future administration of Hong Kong would enjoy "a high degree of autonomy"[19] in order to reassure Hong Kong residents that the territory's way of life and the freedoms enjoyed by its residents would remain the same for 50 years after 1997. Among the most important assurances were that local executive, legislative, and judicial power would remain independent of Beijing, except for matters of defense and foreign affairs.

Subsequent events have shown, though, that many Hong Kong residents harbor considerable doubt about the willingness of either the Chinese or the British government to implement the promise of "a high degree of autonomy." The Chinese have been accused of meddling in affairs of local administation when they question the merit of political reforms introducing a higher degree of direct public participation in the governance of Hong Kong. For their part, the British are sometimes seen, rightly or wrongly, as masters of a lame-duck administration which is unwilling to stand up to Chinese pressure. Both Britain and China have denied these accusations strongly, but it is unlikely that they purposefully will do anything which could be viewed as compromising the independence of Hong Kong's present or future administrations.

Viewed in this light, the asserting by Hong Kong and Macau of a measure of independence from China in terms of, say, their long-term planning programs represents one confirmation of the administrative autonomy promised them by the Chinese leadership. The reluctance to undertake "development by negotiation" except in cases where issues can be viewed mostly in a technical or economic light (as in matters related to basic infrastructue) is due to a reluctance to yield partial control over the course of the future development of their territories, as a consequence of making use of land and resources which are under the control of another government.

We now can reinterpret our earlier explanation of variation in the benefits conferred by "development by negotiation" through introducing the added factor of political autonomy. Those areas where the benefits have been greatest are not only the ones where the issues are most straightforward and least overtly political: they also are ones where the autonomy of the region's governments — meaning their policy-making power — is least likely to be threatened by the implementation of cooperative agreements reached through the negotiation process. Those areas where there has been least progress, such as over air services, are ones where the potential for diminution of autonomy and freedom of action under the terms of any cooperative agreement would be most serious. Despite the benefits that might be gained through cooperation, the decision-makers in power may feel that the price paid in terms of lost autonomy is too steep. Those who would object are, of course, the ones for whom autonomy is most important — symbolically, at least, if not practically — as the consequences of even a perceived loss in policy-making power would be severe. At present, these are the government officials of Hong Kong, with Macau's leaders likely to follow suit after negotiations on its future commencing in 1986 reach their conclusion.

Conclusion

The preceding section would indicate that political considerations will limit the scale of "development by negotiation" to a moderate level, and its scope to specific areas where questions over political autonomy are unlikely to raise their head. Thus there is unlikely to ever be the same sort of integrated development planning in the Pearl River Delta planning region as is envisaged for many other Asian capitals. Planners in the other cities have tried to erase the boundaries which separate for planning purposes the city from the countryside with the stroke of a pen. But in the Pearl River Delta political boundaries retain a symbolic significance which transcends their physical importance, and will certainly continue to do so even after Hong Kong and Macau become administratively part of China.

It remains to be seen whether further political developments in the run-up until 1997 will result in a climate where "development by negotiation" can flourish, creating significant benefits in many fields for the residents of Hong Kong and Macau. At the moment, though, the most likely prognosis is for a pattern of urbanization in the region marked by fragmentation, with perhaps some sporadic attempts at coordinating the region's continued development — through negotiation or otherwise.

END NOTES

[1]Michael Pacione, (ed.) *Problems and Planning in Third World Cities* (London: Croom Helm, 1981); Yue-Man Yeung, The Great Cities of Eastern Asia: Growing Pains and Policy Options, *Chinese University of Hong Kong, Department of Geography, Occasional Paper No. 69*, Hong Kong, 1985.

[2]M. Specter, "A Sprawling, Thirsty Giant," *Far Eastern Economic Review*, Vol. 123, No. 73, March 29, 1984, pp. 23-28.

[3]K. Y. Wong and David K. Y. Chu, "Export Processing Zones and Special Economic Zones as Generators of Economic Development: The Asian Experience," *Geografiska Annaler*, Vol. 66B, 1984, pp. 1-16.

[4]R. Y. W. Kwok and P. K. W. Fong, "The Economic and Social Impact of Shenzhen Special Economic Zone Development: A Planning Analysis," discussion paper prepared for conference *Resources and Development of the Pearl River Delta*, Hong Kong, 1983, p. 2.

[5]Yen-Tak Ng and David K. Y. Chu, "The Geographical Endowment of China's Special Economic Zones," pp. 40-56 in *Modernization in China: The Case of the Shenzhen Special Economic Zone*, K. Y. Wong and David K. Y. Chu (eds.) (Hong Kong: Oxford University Press, 1985).

[6]Lawrence MacDonald, "Export Gloom in Shenzhen," *South China Morning Post*, November 4, 1985.

[7]Anthony G. O. Yeh. "Physical Planning," pp. 108-130 in *Modernization in China*, footnote 5.

[8]*An Open Coastal City — Zhuhai* (Zhuhai: Office of the Administration of Zhuhai Special Economic Zone, 1984), p. 15.

[9]Albert Chan and C. K. Lau, "Signing Marks a Nuclear Milestone," *South China Morning Post*, January 18, 1985.

[10]M. K. Lee Fong, "Tourism: A Critical Review," pp. 79-90 in *Modernization in China*, footnote 5.

[11]E. G. Pryor. *Housing in Hong Kong*, 2nd ed. (Hong Kong: Oxford University Press, 1983); Y. M. Yeung and D. W. Drakakis-Smith, "Public Housing in the City-States of Hong Kong and Singapore," pp. 217-238 in *Urban Planning Practice in Developing Counties*, John L. Taylor and David G. Williams (eds) (Oxford: Pergamon Press, 1982).

[12]David K. Y. Chu, "Population Growth and Related Issues," pp. 131-139 in *Modernization in China*, footnote 5, reference on p. 137.

[13]Albert Chan, "Shumchun Airport Set for Takeoff," *South China Morning Post*, February 10, 1985.

[14]Yeh, footnote 7, pp. 123-124.

[15]See M. Roger Bristow, *Land-Use Planning in Hong Kong* (Hong Kong: Oxford University Press, 1984) for a detailed history of Hong Kong's efforts in planning.

[16]E. G. Pryor, "An Overview of Territorial Development Strategy Studies in Hong Kong," *Planning and Development*, Vol. 1, No. 1, 1985, pp. 8-20, reference on p. 18.

[17]Pryor, footnote 16, p. 16.

[18]*A Draft Agreement between the Government of the United Kingdom of Great Britain and Northern Ireland and the Government of the People's Republic of China on the Future of Hong Kong* (Hong Kong: Government Printer, 1984), Annex III.

[19]*A Draft Agreement . . .*, footnote 18, p. 11.

11

Regional Sex-Ratio Variation of Indian Cities

Ashok K. Dutt, Charles B. Monroe and Bilkis Banu

Introduction

The sex ratio, the ratio of males to females, is an important element of a country's demographic structure and relates to its socio-economic, cultural and physical character.[1] Analysis of the spatial variation of the sex ratio is an important area of study for sociologists, geographers and planners. While sociologists are concerned with the delinquent behavior of single males in the cities, geographers are interested in establishing causal relationships for the inter- and intra-city variation of sex-ratios. Planners, on one hand, secure more housing in the cities to enable male migrants to house their families and, on the other hand, discourage rural to urban migration by creating more work opportunities in the villages. This paper examines the variation of sex ratio in the largest cities of India in order to establish national and regional patterns.

India has more males than females according to national data.[2] This is partly due to more male births;[3] however, the high mortality rate of females between the ages of 15 and 44 appears to be a more significant factor.[4] Other cultural and demographic factors are also related to the sex ratio.[5] The predominance of males is more evident in the large cities.[6] This is the result of large numbers of males immigrating from rural to urban areas, particularly to the cities of north India.

This study focuses on the differential sex ratio in the Class I cities of India, those with a population of 100,000 or more (Fig. 11.1). By analyzing its variation, this study intends to show a regional pattern in the sex ratio.

The study has four major objectives:

1. To describe the overall pattern of the sex ratio among the Class I (population greater than 100,000) cities.
2. To identify regions with similar sex ratio structures and examine differences between regions concerning sex composition.
3. To trace the relationship between the sex ratio and other demographic variables, e.g., male and female population growth rate, percentage of literates to total population, and percentage of Christian population.
4. To determine whether there is a relationship between sex ratio and city size.

A regional study based on Indian cities is quite appropriate. With the exception of the northeast region, cities are distributed equitably across the country. Mills and Becker have pointed out that India has the most dispersed distribution of city sizes of any country in the world.[7] Even the four largest cities (Calcutta, Bombay, Delhi and Madras) are located in four different regions of the country.

Non-agricultural, principally urban, occupations employed only 9 percent of females in 1971 compared to 91 percent of males. Therefore, employment possibilities for females in urban areas are lower. Most females in urban areas are employed in traditional (agriculture and handicraft oriented) and semi-traditional occupations. Only 20 percent of the female workers in the non-agricultural sector in 1971 were employed in the "modern" sector, whereas 13 percent were in "traditional" and 67 percent in "mixed" sectors.[8]

In urban areas the potential for employment is in modern and mixed sectors, and most males obtain these positions. In 1971, only 12 percent of the total urban employment was traditional. Of the entire

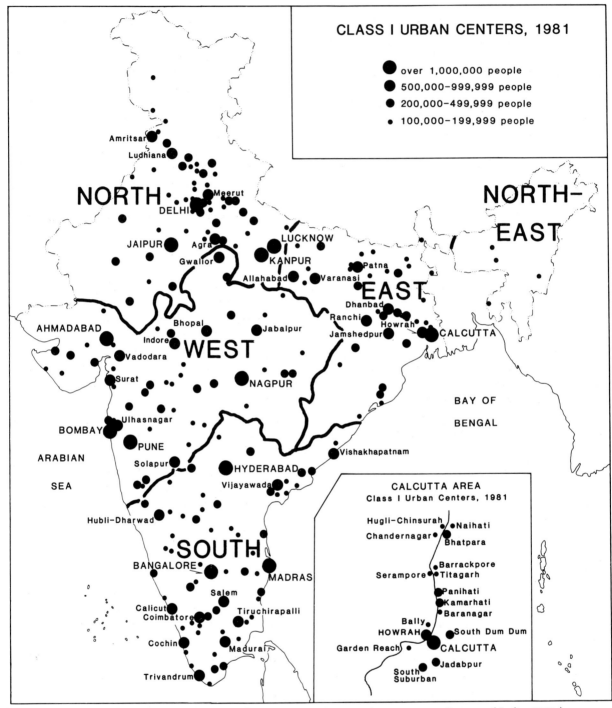

Fig. 11.1   Class I cities in India divided into four size groups, 1981. (Data source: Census of India, 1981.)

modern sector, only 8 percent of the positions were held by females, whereas in the mixed sector, 24 percent were filled by females. Thus, males dominate the employment structure of urban areas.[9]

Dutt, Monroe and Vakamudi analyzed 57 districts of India with 32 percent or more people living in urban areas.[10] They used 1981 census data and determined that the proportion of female agricultural laborers in the urban districts to total female agricultural laborers in the country was 50 percent higher than the proportion of male agricultural laborers in the urban districts to total male agricultural laborers in the country. This study also found that the proportion of female marginal workers in the urban districts to total female marginal workers in the country was 8 times higher than the ratio of male marginal workers in the urban districts to total male marginal workers in the country. Both proportions indicate that a large number of females in urban areas are employed in the traditional sector or are employed as part-time marginal laborers. However, the proportion of male manufacturing and service (M/S) workers of the urban districts to total male M/S workers of the country was 2.5 times higher than the female M/S workers of the urban districts to total female M/S workers of the country. This finding further corroborates the conclusions of Mitra et al. that females are employed in much lower proportions than are males in the more attractive manufacturing and service sector.

Methodology and Data Sources

This paper examines the spatial variation of the sex ratio in large Indian cities as it relates to several demographic variables, including growth rate of the male and female population, literacy rate, and percentage of Christian population. The 1981 census data are used to show a general pattern of sex composition in cities to develop a regional pattern of the sex ratio. Spatial variation in urban sex composition by regions provides, with the help of maps, a general background of the regionally differentiated national pattern. Analysis of the results by Pearson's correlation and multiple regression will help identify regions based on sex structure. These analytic methods have been adopted to determine the association between sex ratio and demographic variables.

Class I cities, as determined by the 1981 census of India, are the basic units of the study. Five regions — North, South, East, West and Northeast — based on India's Planning Commission, are used to characterize the spatial pattern of the sex structure (Fig. 11.2).

Sex ratio (females per 1,000 males) is the dependent variable in the analysis. Six demographic variables have been selected as independent factors, based on their expected relationship to the dependent variable and the availability of data. Data on sex ratio and most independent variables are obtained from the 1981 census of India. Because data on Christian population are not available for 1981, this variable has been taken from the census of 1971.

Data Analysis

The analysis of sex structure by region is carried out, in part, through use of Pearson correlation. The method is used to show the statistical relationship between sex ratio and the independent variables for the 216 Class I cities to identify sex ratio differences from one region to another in relation to population growth, number of males and females, literacy rate for males and females, and percentage of Christian population. This method gives the degree of association for each variable with the sex ratio.

At the national level, the sex ratio is highly correlated with population growth rate, literacy rate of males and females, and the percentage of Christian population in the Class I cities (Table 11.1). The negative relationship between the sex ratio and population growth rate in the cities suggests that a higher growth rate will be associated with a lower sex ratio. On the other hand, because sex ratio is positively correlated with literacy rate and percentage of Christian population, any increase of these variables relates to an increase in the sex ratio in the Class I cities. Table 11.1 also illustrates that the sex ratio is inversely related to the number of males and females in the population.

In addition to the initial findings for all Class I cities, the Pearson correlation values also indicate a regional pattern to sex structure in India (Table 11.1). This regional variation can be discussed in two ways: North versus South and East versus West.

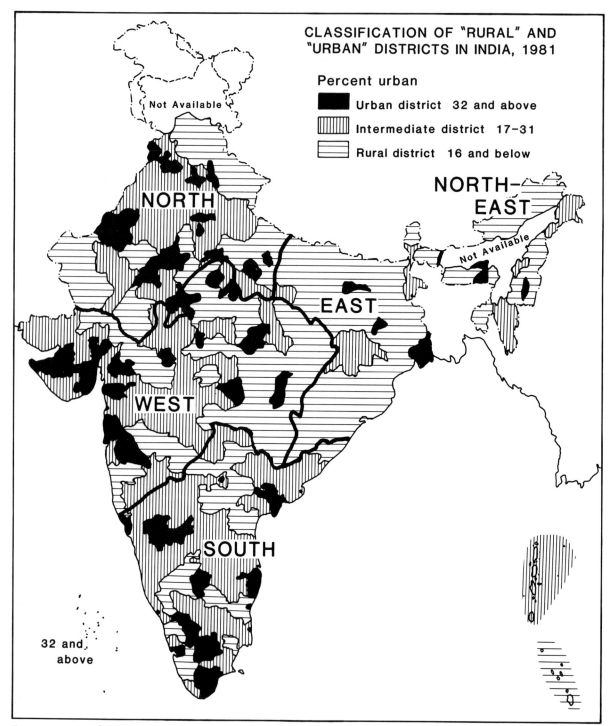

CLASSIFICATION OF "RURAL" AND
"URBAN" DISTRICTS IN INDIA, 1981

Percent urban

Urban district 32 and above

Intermediate district 17–31

Rural district 16 and below

NORTH

NORTH–
EAST

EAST

WEST

SOUTH

Not Available

Not Available

32 and
above

Fig. 11.2   Classification of rural, semi-urban and urban districts in India, 1981, by regions. (Data source: Census of India, 1981.)

TABLE 11.1

Pearson's Correlation Between Sex Ratio and Demographic Characteristics for the Cities in the Five Regions of India, 1981

Dependent Variable: Sex Ratio = Number of Female Per 1000 Male

INDEPENDENT VARIABLES	NATIONAL		NORTH		SOUTH		EAST		WEST		NORTH-EAST	
	Pearson Correlation	Signifi-cance	Pearson Correlation	Signifi-cance	Pearson Correlation	Signifi-cance	Pearson Correlation	Signifi-cance	Pearson Correlation	Signifi-cance	Pearson Correlation	Signifi-cance
Population Male	-.1970	.002**	-.2359	.043***	-.2267	.035***	-.1794	.131***	-.3249	.009**	-.8311	.185
Population Female	-.1741	.005**	-.2239	.052***	-.2119	.045***	-.1717	.142***	-.3156	.011**	-.7110	.241
Growth Rate 1971-81	-.4518	.000*	-.1097	.215***	-.6869	.000*	-.5671	.000*	-.3645	.004**	.1689	.440
Literacy Rate of Male	.3047	.000*	-.1893	.089***	.3802	.001*	.3312	.017**	.1504	.141***	.7802	.215
Literacy Rate of Female	.2719	.000*	-.2234	.052***	.4760	.000*	.3222	.020**	-.2115	.064***	.0614	.486
Christianity	.3193	.000*	-.1316	.172***	.3627	.001*	-.1087	.249***	-.2975	.015**	.5562	.312

* Highly Significant   (P < .001)
** Significant   (P ≤ .05)
*** Not Significant   (P > .05)

North-South Regional Pattern of Sex Ratio

Figure 11.3C clearly shows the North-South regional distinction in terms of sex structure of cities. Sex ratios in the North are lower than those of the South. The average sex ratio in the South is about 955 as opposed to only 854 in the North. All 10 cities with a sex ratio over 1,000, i.e., more females than males, are located in the South.[11]

The reasons for a high sex ratio in the South can be attributed to several factors. Sex ratio in the South has a strong inverse correlation with growth rate and a positive correlation with literacy rate of both males and females and Christianity (Table 11.1). The high literacy rate[12] and higher percentage of Christians of the South appear to influence a more balanced sex structure in the South (Figures 11.3B and 11.4B). As with all Class I cities, the sex ratio in the South is inversely related to the growth rate.

As opposed to the South, the sex ratio in the North shows a very insignificant relationship with demographic variables (Table 11.1). Thus, other factors might be responsible for a low sex ratio in the cities of the North.

Previous studies on sex disparity of Indian cities reveal that male-dominated immigration[13] and religious rigidity were the primary factors responsible for the low sex ratio in the North. In North, East, and West India, Hindus and Moslems tend to keep their women in villages, while males migrate to cities. The men visit their families in the villages only once or twice a year.

This may also be explained by other socio-economic factors of India. Northern cities generally lack employment opportunities, and female migrants find it difficult to find employment. This lowers female migration in the North when compared to the South where employment opportunities are greater. Other studies on sex disparity show similar results. The social and religious laxity, higher employment opportunity, and higher literacy rate (Figure 11.4A) positively influence the sex ratio in the South.

East-West Regional Pattern of Sex Ratio

A similar pattern of contrast can be observed in the variation of urban sex ratios between the East and West regions of India (Figures 11.3, 11.4 and 11.5). The degree of variation between the East and West is not as great as between North and South. The average sex ratio in the East is 837 compared to 888 in the West (Figure 11.3C). Of the five regions of India, the East has the lowest sex ratio.

Except for population growth rate, the Pearson correlation does not reveal any highly significant relationships between the sex ratio and the demographic variables in these regions. Growth rate is negatively correlated with the sex ratio, and in the East, this correlation is more significant when compared to the West (Table 11.1).

The East shows .a more significant positive association between the sex ratio and male-female literacy rate (Table 11.1). This indicates that as the literacy rate increases, so does the sex ratio. In addition, the West shows a more significant relation between sex ratio and male-female population and the percentage of Christian population (Fig. 11.3).

Of all the regions, the East has the greatest rural "push" factor in operation because it has: a) the highest density of population, particularly in the rural areas, b) the most aggravated form of landlessness within the agricultural community, c) a low per capita income in general, and d) a limited application of green revolution techniques in farming. The unemployed and marginally employed males of the rural areas naturally look to the cities, mainly the large ones, for elusive employment. They are "pushed" to the cities, where most end up with full or partial employment in the informal or 'mixed' sector at low wages. Thus, the condition for single male migration to cities is deeply entrenched in the East.

A relatively high sex ratio in the West compared to that of the East relates to the "male selective" out-migration. In the states of Rajasthan and Gujarat in the West, the sex ratio is over 900, a more balanced sex structure compared to the states of Maharashtra and Madhya Pradesh. Large out-migration of the male population from the cities of Rajasthan and Gujarat has occurred towards other parts of India as well as out of the country. The tradition of trading and business activities of Marwari merchants of Rajasthan produced large migrations to different parts of India, where they established new businesses. Such highly "male selective" out-migration from the West has been encouraged by the business attraction in Bombay as well as the cities of Africa, the United Kingdom, and the West Indies.[14]

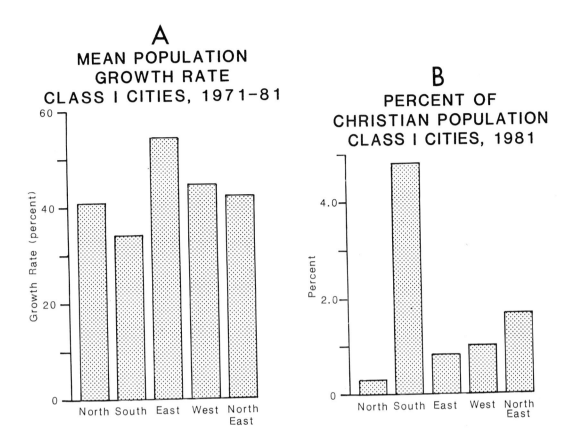

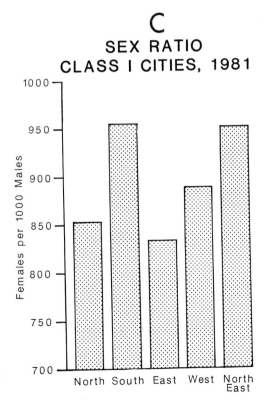

Fig. 11.3   Demographic characteristics of India by regions, 1981.

124

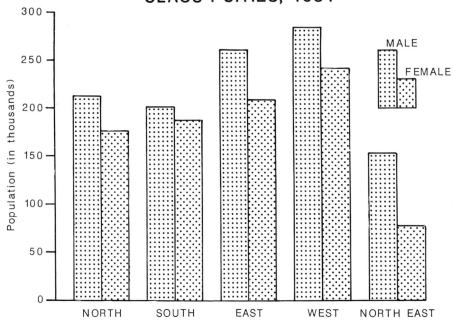

A MEAN NUMBER MALE AND FEMALE POPULATION
CLASS I CITIES, 1981

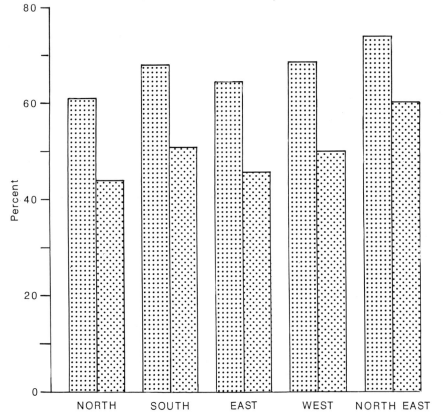

B MEAN MALE AND FEMALE LITERATES
CLASS I CITIES, 1981

Fig. 11.4   Mean population (A) and mean literates (B). Male-Female composition of
Class I cities by regions, 1981. (Data source: Census of India, 1981.)

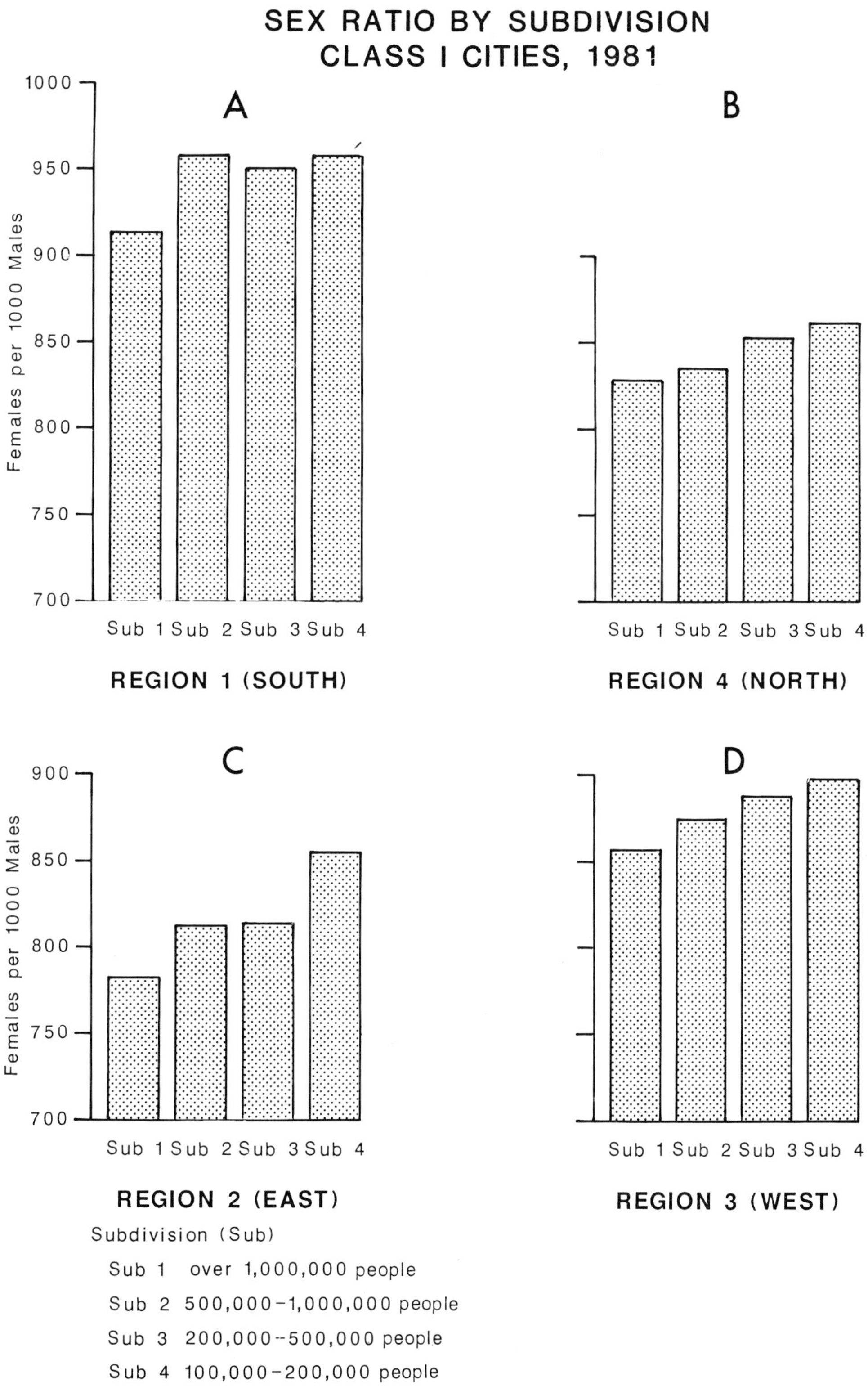

SEX RATIO BY SUBDIVISION
CLASS I CITIES, 1981

Fig. 11.5   Sex ratio by subdivisions and regions of Class I cities, 1981.
(Data source: Census of India, 1981.)

Multiple Regression Analysis

Multiple regression is used to analyze the relationship between the sex structure of the cities and selected demographic variables. Although the relationship between the dependent variable, sex ratio, and the independent variables has been examined both on national and regional levels, results show less significant trends for the regions.

Using the 216 Class I cities in India, the stepwise regression procedure shows four variables to be significant at the .05 probability level (Table 11.2). The most important variable is the 1971 to 1981 growth rate of the cities, followed by the percentage Christian population, male population in 1981, and male literacy rate in 1981. Whereas the Christian and male literacy variables are directly related to the dependent variable, the growth rate and male population are inversely related. The four variables together account for approximately 34 percent of the variation in sex ratio for the 216 Class I cities.

Regional analyses examining the relationship between sex ratio and the demographic variables show large variation in results by region (Fig. 11.4). In the cities in the South, the population growth rates for 1961 to 1971 and from 1971 to 1981 are both significant and produce a 60 percent level of explanation for the sex ratio. In the North, no variables are related to the sex ratio at the .05 probability level.

Only the 1971 to 1981 population growth rate is significantly related to sex ratio in the regression for the cities of East India. The level of explanation is approximately 32 percent. In West India, both the 1961 to 1971 population growth rate and the 1981 male population are inversely related to the sex·ratio at a significant level. However, the degree of explanation is only 28 percent.

The multiple regression points out that the most recent population growth rate (1971 to 1981) of the largest Indian cities is significantly related to the male-female ratio both nationally and for the South and East regions. If cities were growing at a higher rate during the preceding decade (1971 to 1981), a large percentage of the migrants were single males who have not had the opportunity to advance economically. The higher housing costs of the city have limited their ability to bring their families from the villages. Moreover, many recent low-income migrants also take a longer time to overcome the traditions associated with *purdah* or the seclusion of females. Migration of the female member of the family to the city requires a considerable change in traditional attitudes, which only occurs over time.

Relationship Between City Size and Sex Ratio

Apart from the correlation and regression, an analysis of sex ratio data and size of cities reveals other important features. There is a considerable variation found in sex ratio in relation to city size (Fig. 11.5). The largest cities show a lower sex ratio when compared to smaller cities.

Such variation of sex ratio can be attributed to many factors. (1) Large cities attract more people from secondary cities and rural areas. A heavy flow of rural-to-urban migration (especially to the large metropolitan areas) has been a significant characteristic of the Indian urbanization.[15] (2) This migration has resulted in a housing shortage which forces the migrants to leave their families behind.[16] This results in a great disparity in the male-female ratio in large towns, e.g., Calcutta has only 783 females for 1,000 males, Bombay 773, and Delhi 808.[17]

Another study on the sex variation of Uttar Pradesh concluded that: (1) there is an inverse relationship between the sex ratio and degree of industrialization (percent of workers in tertiary and secondary activities) and (2) there is a positive correlation between sex ratio and an increase in the primary (agriculture) workforce.[18]

Conclusion

The overall assessment of demographic variables and their association with sex ratio leads to the conclusion that the size of population, literacy rate, religious composition, and overall growth rate of the city population are the chief determinants of this ratio in the cities of India.

Sex ratio differences in the cities of India are a national phenomenon, and cultural and economic reasons accentuate the differences. Hindus and Moslems, who account for about 95 percent of India's population, have developed a *purdah* or female seclusion system with regionally varied intensity. In

127

TABLE 11.2

Multiple Regression Between Sex Ratio and Selected Independent Variables

(significant variables only)

Dependent variable: Sex Ratio = Number of Females Per 1000 Males

Independent Variables	National (R^2 = .34)		South (R^2 = .60)		East (R^2 = .32)		West (R^2 = .20)	
	(a)	(b)	(a)	(b)	(a)	(b)	(a)	(b)
Population Growth Rate (1971-81)	-	.000	-	.000	-	.000		
Percentage Christian Population (1971)	+	.000						
Male Population (1981)	-	.000					-	.000
Male Literacy Rate (1981)	+	.002						
Population Growth Rate (1961-71)			-	.000			-	.000

a Direction of Relationships: (-) inverse, (+) direct

b Level of significance

Note: No variables related to sex ratio at .05 for the North and North-East regions.

Source: 1971 and 1981 Census of India and authors' calculations.

general, the system has discouraged women from migrating to urban areas where they are more exposed to and have to interact with men on many occasions. In the villages, because of detached houses, the availability of more open space and established patterns of separate male/female activities, women can adhere to their traditional purdah. Hence, the movement of females to urban areas means a significant break in the age-old attitude toward mixing between the sexes. As purdah is less rigorous in the South, southern women moving to urban areas are not as inhibited by its requirements. Christians in general do not practice purdah because of an increased Western cultural influence. Therefore, cities with a larger proportion of Christians tend to have a more balanced male/female ratio.

In general, Indian cities have a larger percentage of males than females and the percentage increases as the population increases. The larger the city, the greater the housing shortage and more opportunities for violation of purdah. As a result, female migration with husbands to these cities is discouraged.

Many male migrants to the city move from the ancestral villages thinking that they are leaving only temporarily. For them, breaking the ties with the village for the first few years of a move seems unthinkable. Leaving his woman in the village gives the male the mental satisfaction that he has not

MODEL SHOWING DETERMINANTS OF THE SEX RATIO OF CLASS I CITIES OF INDIA

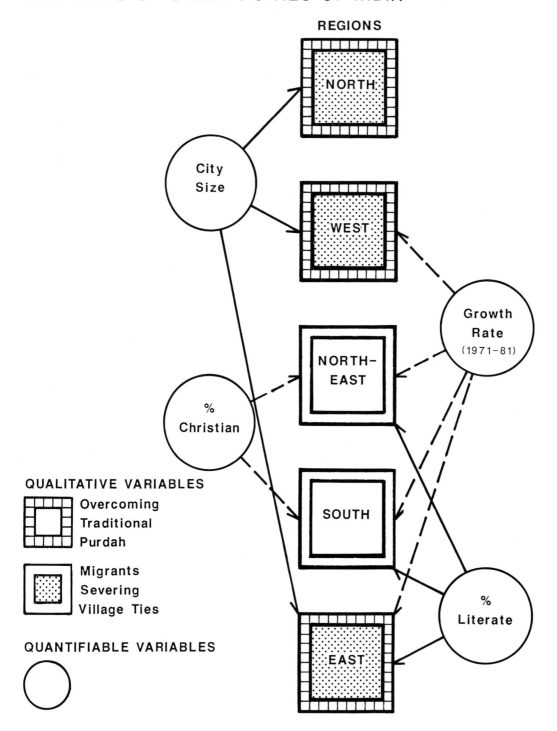

Fig. 11.6 A descriptive model showing determinants of the sex ratio of India's Class I cities.

broken the tie. When the male, after spending some time in the city, is mentally prepared to bring his wife and children from the village, he is confronted with the much higher cost of urban housing. For this reason, a large number of them are unable to bring their families, even after they have overcome the cultural barrier.

In summation, the determinants of the male-female sex ratio variation can be represented by a descriptive model (Fig. 11.6) which indicates that four quantifiable and two qualitative variables are chiefly responsible for regional changes in the male-female ratio of the Indian cities. The larger size of the city accounts for the greater male dominance in North, East and West regions, the historic Northern India. Greater percentages of Christian population in the cities affect the South and Northeast regions by bringing about a greater balance of the male-female ratio. Compared to other regions of India, these two regions have a much greater proportion of their city population as Christians.

A larger number of male migrants are entering the cities of all regions except the North because of higher growth rate of the cities. Higher or lower literacy rates influence the cities of the Northeast, East and South regions in polarizing or balancing the sex differences. A recent rural migrant to a city has a hard time in severing the tie with his village. This non-quantifiable, psychological phenomenon is operative in all five regions, which discourages the migrant from bringing his family from the village to the city. As purdah is more prevalent in the Moslem-influenced, historic Northern India, the North, East and West regions are most affected. In those regions, male-dominated migration is a usual feature of the villages and this traditional attitude, which cannot be quantified for our analysis, affects the male-female ratio.

END NOTES

[1]P. B. Desai, *Size and Sex Composition in India* (Bombay: Asia Publishing House, 1969); Amrit Lal, "Age and Sex Structure in India," *Geographical Review of India*, Vol. 24 (March 1962), pp. 7-29; and B. D. Miller, *The Endangered Sex: Neglect of Female Children in Rural North India* (Ithaca, NY: Cornell University Press, 1981).

[2]Census of India, *Provisional Population Totals: Rural-Urban Distribution, Part 2*, 1981.

[3]J. C. Sen, "The Sex Composition of Indian Towns with 20,000-50,000 Inhabitants, 1961," *The Indian Geographical Journal*, Vol. 38 (1963), pp. 90-99.

[4]Sen, footnote 3; and Amrit Lal, footnote 1.

[5]Miller, footnote 1.

[6]Amrit Lal, footnote 1; Desai, footnote 1; and F. Z. Siddique, "Regional Analysis of the Sex Structure of the Population of Uttar Pradesh," *National Geographical Journal of India*, Vol. 28 (May-June 1982), pp. 74-85.

[7]E. S. Mill, *Studies in Indian Urban Development* (New York: Oxford University Press, 1986).

[8]A. Mitra, et al., *The Status of Women: Shifts in Occupational Participation, 1961-71* (New Delhi: Abhinar Publications, 1980).

[9]Mitra, footnote 8.

[10]A. K. Dutt, C. B. Monroe and R. Vakamudi, "Rural-Urban Correlates for Indian Urbanization," *The Geographical Review*, Vol. 76, No. 2 (1986), pp. 173-183.

[11]*Census of India*, footnote 2.

[12]Amrit Lal, footnote 1; and Sen, footnote 3.

[13]Siddique, footnote 6; Amrit Lal, footnote 1; and Sen, footnote 3.

[14]Sen, footnote 3.

[15]Qazi Ahmad, *Indian Cities: Characteristics and Correlates* (Chicago: The University of Chicago, Department of Geography, 1965); and R. W. Bradnock, "India's Cities: Hope for the Future?", *Geography*, Vol. 66, Part 3, pp. 208-220.

[16]A. K. Dutt, et al. *India in Maps* (Dubuque, Iowa: Kendall-Hunt Publishing Company, 1976); and A. K. Dutt and M. Margaret Geib, *Fully Annotated Atlas of South Asia* (Boulder, Colorado: Westview Press, 1987), pp. 126-127.

[17]*Census of India*, footnote 2.

[18]Siddique, footnote 6.

12

Slums of Urban India

Sudesh Nangia

Though substandard living areas have posed problems in the Presidency towns of Calcutta, Bombay and Madras since the early 20th century, slums in India have attracted general attention only since the 1950s with the passage of the first slum legislation in 1956. Originally enacted for Delhi, the act was extended to other Union Territories of India with the main objective of improvement and clearance of slum areas and protection of tenants in such areas from eviction and exploitation.[1]

In determining whether a building is unfit for human habitation according to the act, consideration is given to its condition in respect to repair, stability, natural light and air, water supply, drainage and sanitary conveniences, freedom from dampness and facilities for storage, preparation and cooking of food and for the disposal of waste water.

This definition lays emphasis on the physical aspects of a slum. It refers to the structural quality, availability of basic services and the quality of its environment. The building referred to may be an authorized or unauthorized (squatter) structure. The act, however, does not make mention of the ownership of land or structure and the legality and illegality of structures. The main objectives behind enactment of this act are to:

- improve the living conditions of slum dwellers, either by clearing or by environmental improvement;
- protect the interests of the residents so long as the slums last or until they are improved;
- provide necessary infrastructure to the slum dwellers and recover its cost from the owner;
- provide compensation to slum dwellers in the event their properties are completely taken over by the state (equivalent to 60 times the monthly rent);
- provide for demolition of buildings in the event repairs are not sufficient to make them reasonably habitable; and
- undertake redevelopment of slum areas wherever feasible in the public interest or to permit owners of slums to undertake such redevelopment in accordance with approved plans.[2]

Estimates of Slum Population

Any attempt to estimate slum population is beset by two problems: 1) varying definitions of slum areas in different states, and 2) the unavailability of comprehensive data. The database is thus quite weak. There are no systematic time-series data on slum population in India. Only after the nationwide sample survey of slums, produced by the National Sample Survey Organization (NSSO) in 1976-77 and published in 1980, did a tentative estimate of slum population in class I cities (above 1 lakh, i.e., 100,000, in 1971) become available.

Another set of data on slum population released in 1981 was computed by the National Building Organization of the Ministry of Works and Housing. These estimates were based on the data provided by states for securing funds for improvement of slum areas under the Environmental Improvement Scheme. The Town and Country Planning Organization has based its own estimates of slum population in states on data provided by the states and Union Territories for the implementation of a 20 point program for the weaker sections by the government of India.

Other estimates are based on materials produced in 1972 by the Planning Commission working group who prepared 'low estimates' presuming that 20 percent of the country's urban population lives in slums and squatter settlements and will continue to live so. It also released 'high estimates,' presuming that in the future 25 percent of the urban population of India will be living in slums and squatter settlements.[3] According to these estimates, of a total of 162 million people living in urban areas in 1981, at least 32 million lived in slums and squatter settlements (Table 12.1). This population is likely to rise to at least 38 million by 1985, 45 million by 1991, and 62 million by the year 2000, according to the low estimates placed by the task force set up by the Planning Commission. The high estimates place the figures at 47, 56, and 78 million, respectively.

The proportion of slum populations shows a wide variation throughout the country, from 7.27 percent in Kerala to 37.04 percent in West Bengal (Table 12.2). The states with high concentrations, i.e., above 30 percent, are West Bengal, Bihar, Uttar Pradesh, Delhi, Andhra Pradesh and Orissa. These states occupy the major part of the middle Ganga Valley, lower Ganga Valley and the eastern coastal areas (Fig. 12.1). Medium concentrations, i.e., between 20 to 30 percent slum population, occur in Maharashtra, Punjab and Rajasthan, all in the western and northwestern areas of the country. Low concentrations of

TABLE 12.1

Slum Population in India
1981 - 2000 A.D.

(Population in million)

Year	Urban Population	Percentage slum Population	
		Low* Estimates	High** Estimates
1981	162	32 (20%)	40 (24.7%)
1985	188	38 (20.2%)	47 (25%)
1990	225	45 (20%)	56 (24.9%)
2000	310	62 (20%)	78 (25.2%)

Source: Task Force on 'Planning for Urban Development' Estimates.

* All India low estimate: assuming 20% of additional urban population will be in slums, squatter settlements etc.

** High estimates: assuming 25% of additional urban population will be in slums, squatter settlements etc.

TABLE 12.2

Slum Population in Selected States of India, 1981

(Population in '000)

	State/Union Territory	Total Population	Total Urban Population	Urban Pop. as % Total Pop.	% living in slums
	India	**658,141**	**156,189**	**23.73**	**20.00**
1.	Andhra Pradesh	53,593	12,458	23.25	34.77
2.	Assam	---	1,326	---	17.90
3.	Bihar	68,823	8,699	12.46	36.70
4.	Gujarat	33,961	10,556	31.08	16.20
5.	Haryana	12,851	2,822	21.96	14.69
6.	Karnataka	37,043	10,711	28.91	9.28
7.	Kerala	25,403	4,771	18.78	7.27
8.	Madhya Pradesh	52,138	10,589	20.31	18.5
9.	Maharashtra	62,715	21,967	35.03	29.70
10.	Orissa	26,272	3,106	11.82	30.45
11.	Punjab	16,669	4,620	27.72	27.80
12.	Rajasthan	34,109	7.140	10.93	23.50
13.	Tamilnadu	48,297	15,928	32.98	16.80
14.	Uttar Pradesh	110,886	19,973	18.01	32.76
15.	West Bengal	54,485	14,433	26.49	37.04
16.	Delhi	6,196	5.714	92.94	30.19

Sources:

i. National Building Organization, Ministry of Works and Housing Estimates, 1983.

ii. Census of India, Paper 2 of 1981 -- Provisional Population Totals, p. 26.

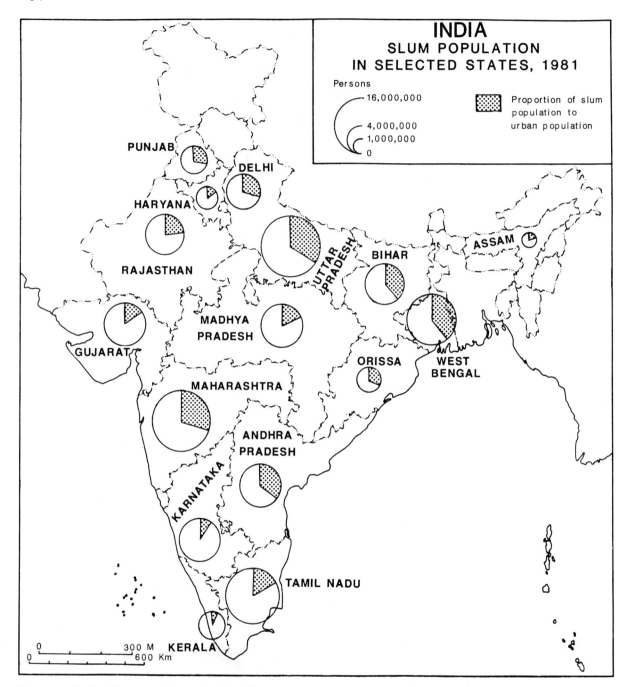

Fig. 12.1   India: Slum population in selected states.

slum population, i.e., below 20 percent, exist in Tamilnadu, Karnataka, Kerala, Madhya Pradesh, Gujarat and Haryana.

This concentration of slum population can be related both to the degree of urbanization and to industrialization and can be placed into four groups. First are those states with a low degree of urbanization and a low slum population such as Rajasthan, Kerala and Haryana. These states are primarily agricultural and thus their populations have a rural orientation.

Second are states with a low urbanization and high slum population, including Uttar Pradesh, Bihar and Orissa. These states suffer from a high density of population on agricultural land. The "push" factor operating in rural areas releases population to urban centers, which may or may not be sufficiently developed to absorb additional migrants. Lack of building activity and consequent unavailability of housing results in a concentration of poor migrants in slums or squatter settlements.

The third combination is that of high urbanization and high slum population, as in the states of Maharashtra, West Bengal and the Union Territory of Delhi. These are the most developed areas of India and hence attract a large number of rural-urban migrants. This is sometimes referred to as the "pull" factor. The migrants, coming from rural and poor urban families, tend to concentrate in squatters quarters and slums.

A final combination is that of high urbanization and low slum population and is found in Tamilnadu and Gujarat. These states exhibit a balanced regional development.

From the estimates of the National Building Organization, it appears that as the population of the urban centers increases, the percentage of slum dwellers increases. Hence, towns with a population of less than one lakh (100,000) have only 10.66 percent of their population living in slums, while cities with a population between one and three lakhs have 18.12 percent of their population living in slums. The percentage of slum population increases to 19.56 in cities with population size varying between three and ten lakhs, and further increases to 30.78 percent in cities with population size above one million.

The Planning Commission estimates that the twelve metropolitan cities of India combined have 33 to 38 percent of their population living in slums and squatter settlements. The figures range from 15 percent for Pune to 45 percent for Delhi (Fig. 12.2). Metropolitan Delhi is followed by Bombay and Kanpur (40% each), Calcutta (35%), and Madras and Nagpur (30% each). House building activity in the metropolitan cities has not kept pace with the expansion of urbanization, industrialization and tertiary activities. Land values and rental values having gone up, the rural-poor migrants have to squat on public or private lands or squeeze into existing slums.

Salient Features of Slums

The density of slum population is higher in small cities than in large cities (Table 12.3). For instance, cities with a population size of 1 to 3 hundred thousand show a density of 151 persons per acre; 300,000 to 1 million, 111 persons per acre; and for one million and above, 97 persons per acre of slum land.

Among the metropolitan cities, Kanpur has the maximum density of slum population (484 persons per acre) followed by Delhi (225) and Hyderabad (210). The low density metropolitan centers are Bombay and Bangalore, having 40 and 48 persons per acre, respectively. Thus, as is clear from the figures in the metropolitan cities, density is not positively related to the size of the city.

Average household size, like density, is higher in small cities than in large ones. In cities with a population size of less than one million, average household size is 4.8 persons, while in cities above one million, the size drops to 4.6 persons per household.

In cities below one million population, more than 50 percent of the houses in slums are owned by the inhabitants. In million plus population cities, the percentage drops to 42.5. Houses which are neither owned nor rented account for less than 9 percent in all cities, regardless of size. Monthly rent of structure varies from Rs. 15 to Rs. 18 (Table 12.4).

In cities with less than one million people, 55 to 60 percent of the houses have *kacha* (uncemented) walls, 8 to 9 percent have *semi-pucca* walls, and 32 to 37 percent have *pucca* (cemented) walls. In million plus population cities, 33 percent of the houses have kacha walls, 17 percent have semi-pucca walls, and almost 50 percent of the structures have pucca walls. Nearly 52 percent of the structures in cities of all sizes have semi-pucca roofs. As the city size increases, the percentage of structures with kacha roofs decreases and those with pucca roofs tend to increase.

The slums are the major deprivation spots within the cities (Table 12.5). Nearly 90 percent of the structures in all size classes of cities do not have separate latrines. Only 44.8 percent of the population in small cities, i.e., 1-3 hundred thousand population, 51.5 percent of population in medium-sized cities, i.e., 300,000 to 1 million, and 81.9 percent of the population in large-sized cities, i.e., one million and above have access to public latrine facilities. An underground sewerage system exits only for 3.9 percent, 10.5 percent, and 44.8 percent of the population in small, medium and large-sized cities, respectively. Besides,

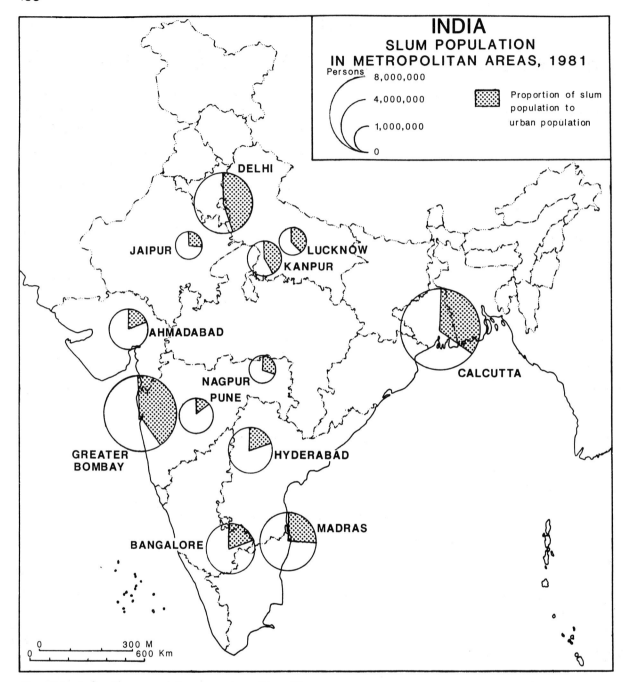

Fig. 12.2   India: Slum population in metropolitan cities.

46.3 percent of the slum population in small cities, 48.6 percent in the medium cities and 34.7 percent in the large cities is exposed to flooding during the monsoon period.

However, the slum areas have comparatively better access to electricity, roads, drinking water and garbage disposal systems. More than 80 percent of the population living in slums has access to electricity. Classified by size of city, 78.1 percent of the slum population in small cities, 85.4 percent in medium cities and 91.6 percent in large cities is accessible by approach roads other than kacha (unpaved) roads. Nearly 80 percent of the population in small and medium cities and 93.5 percent in large cities has access to a tap or tubewell as a source of drinking water, although these are often community or neighborhood facilities.

TABLE 12.3

Density of population and average household size in slum areas

City or City group (1971)	Average number per acre of land	Persons per household
100,000 to 300,000	151	4.8
300,000 to 1 million	111	4.8
One million plus (declared slums)	97	4.6
Calcutta	88	3.7
Bombay	40	4.5
Delhi	255	4.7
Madras	190	5.0
Bangalore	48	5.6
Hyderabad	210	5.1
Ahmedabad	73	6.1
Kanpur	484	4.0

Source: NSSO, SARVEKASHANA, Vol. III, April 1980.

Obtained from Shelter for the urban poor and slum improvement IV,

Planning Commission, Govt. of India, New Delhi, Sept. 1983, Table 2.13, pp. 41.

Similarly, as the city size increases, the facilities for garbage disposal also increase. Thus, while 75.7 percent of the slum population is benefitted by garbage disposal facilities in small cities, 89.9 percent is benefitted in large cities.

Slum Improvement Strategies

Awareness of the need to improve slum living conditions may be traced back to 1930 when, under the Municipal and Corporation Acts, landlords were required to make improvements in slum areas. If they failed to do so, the local bodies reserved the right to implement the necessary improvements and to realize the cost of improvements from the landlords. Initially, these improvements were in the form of street-lighting, handpumps, and so forth. This went on until the end of the pre-Independence period.

Slums again received attention in 1956 when the slum area legislation (Improvement and Clearance Act) was passed. Accordingly, the slum clearance and improvement scheme provided for the acquisition of slums, rehousing of families with low incomes, i.e., earning less than Rs. 350 month, improvement of environmental conditions, and construction of night shelters. Under this scheme, a *pucca* tenement of 16.66 sq. meters of floor area, two rooms, a bath and a latrine, with a cost varying from Rs. 2700 to Rs. 4000, was also to be provided to each family. The amount for such construction was raised in 1971, varying from Rs. 5380 to Rs. 7000. As a result of the implementation of this scheme, nearly 89,000

TABLE 12.4

Some characteristics of slum dwellers 1976-77 (31 NSS Round)

Characteristics	City Groups		
	Small Size (100,000 - 300,000)	Medium Size (300,000 - 1 million)	Large Size (over 1 million)
Percent house owned	54.12	50.74	42.47
House neither owned nor rented	8.61	6.20	8.88
Rented House	37.27	43.06	48.65
Average monthly rent in Rupees	15.11	18.22	17.92
Walls percent Katcha	59.38	54.76	33.18
Walls percent semi-Pucca	8.95	7.94	17.46
Walls percent Pucca	31.67	37.30	49.36
Roofs percent Katcha	37.51	30.36	23.55
Roofs percent Semi-Pucca	52.21	52.59	52.23
Roofs percent Pucca	10.28	17.05	22.22
Latrines % no separate latrines	89.96	91.22	91.80

Source: NSSO: Servekshna, Vol. III, April 1980.

Obtained from Shelter for the urban poor and slum improvement IV, Government of India, Planning Commission, New Delhi, September 1983, pp. 42.

tenements were constructed from 1956 to 1971. However, this covered only one-half percent of the total slum households in cities with populations above 100,000.

In addition to tenements, some plots, ranging in size from 92.59 sq. meters to 111.11 sq. meters, were developed with an earthern platform, a proper latrine and a platform for bathing, and leaving the rest of the structure to be raised by the slum dwellers themselves. The size of the plots in subsequent years was considerably reduced because of the large-scale, illegal transfer of plots by slum dwellers. For instance, in Delhi it was reduced to 21 sq. meters by 1970. The scheme was mainly adopted in Madras and Delhi. By 1970, Madras had provided 8,500 plots of 90 sq. meters and Delhi, 25,000 plots of 80 sq. meters and 21 sq. meters.

In April, 1972 a central scheme for environmental improvement in slum areas was introduced whereby financial assistance was granted to state governments for undertaking slum environment improvement programs in cities with population above 8 lakhs. The cities thus identified were Calcutta, Bombay, Delhi, Madras, Hyderabad, Bangalore, Ahmedabad, Kanpur, Pune, Nagpur and Lucknow. This improvement scheme made provision for water mains, sewers, stormwater drains, community baths, latrines, water taps and street lighting. It also provided for widening the existing lanes, pavement of lanes, construction of new roads, and landscaping and horticultural operations. The scheme further provided parks, playgrounds, community and welfare centers, police and fire stations, schools, hospitals, and dispensaries on a nonprofit basis.

TABLE 12.5

Infrastructure Facilities to Slum Population, 1976-77 by city group
(Percentage of population having facilities)

| | | City Groups | | |
	Facilities Provided	Small Size (100,000 - 300,000)	Medium Size (300,000 - 1 million)	Large Size (over 1 million)
1	Electricity	82.1	85.4	81.1
2	Approach Road	78.1	87.1	91.6
3	Tap/Tubewell for drinking water	79.9	79.2	93.5
4	Latrine facility	44.8	51.5	81.9
5	Underground sewerage system	3.9	10.5	44.8
6	Garbage disposal system	75.7	84.7	89.9
7	Slum areas waterlogged during monsoon	46.3	48.6	34.7
8	Some development made in slum areas during the last five years	53.9	63.9	56.2

Source: NSSO, SARVEKSHNA, Vol. III, April 1980.

Obtained from: Shelter for the Urban Poor and Slum Improvement IV, Planning Commission, Govt. of India, New Delhi, Sept. 1983, pp. 43.

This scheme also envisaged the construction of *pucca* slum dwellings, with water closets, bathrooms, water taps, either inside the premises or near the dwellings, conversion of a privy to a waterborne system with connection to the main drainage, providing smokeless *chulhas* (hearths) and sinks in the kitchen, paved courtyards, electricity, and enlarged rooms, windows and ventilators. Preference was given to slums located on public lands. Improvement of slums located on private lands was affected only in those areas where adequate legislation was in place to prevent landlords from claiming increased rent on account of improvement. In the Fifth Five-Year Plan (1974-1979), this scheme was financed as a part of the minimum needs program of the government of India and was extended to all cities with a population of 300,000 and above.[4]

In the Sixth Five-Year Plan (1980-1985), the slum improvement scheme focused on the 10 million people living below the poverty line in urban areas with populations above 100,000. The basic amenities to be provided, in addition to housing, were water supply, sanitation, drainage, sewerage, transportation and recreation. The plan provided an outlay of Rs. 1505 million in the state plans to meet these objectives,[5] to be achieved at an expenditure of Rs. 150 per person. A mid-term appraisal of the Sixth Plan indicated that 3.77 million people had been covered, between 1980-1983, leaving a balance of 6.23 million persons to be covered for the remaining two years of the plan period.[6] The states, however, speeded up their work and by April, 1984 a slum population of 7 million was covered, leaving only 3 million to be reached during 1984-1985. Under the Central Incentive Grants Scheme, the government has provided an additional sum of Rs. 150 million to the states for the improvement of urban slums and has thus raised the per capita amount to be spent to Rs. 250.[7]

The reasons for the poor performance of the scheme are many, including delays in the release of funds by state goverments; non-declaration or belated declaration of slum areas by the states, paucity of funds from the local bodies and escalation in the cost of various services since inception of the scheme.

The above account reveals that several approaches have been experimented with and are in operation to improve the housing conditions of the urban poor. Slum and squatter clearance and provision of tenements for the slum dwellers on alternate sites was tried. This project was deemed too complex and thus was only partially completed in favor of alternate strategies for the improvement of housing.

The next experiment was in the improvement of slums and squatter settlements. This called for environmental improvement of existing sites, establishment of a uniform size for existing plotted areas, and financial assistance to the dwellers for improvement of their shelter.

The comprehensive site and service program calls for the provision of basic infrastructural facilities and demarcated plots of a given plinth area to be distributed to the slum and squatter settlers whose removal from the existing site is in the public interest. Such programs are not only for rehabilitation but are also for new migrants to the cities. As the new rehabilitation sites are in proximity to the cleared sites, the work pattern of slum dwellers is not disturbed. In this entire program — whether environment improvement or slum and squatter clearance, removal and rehabilitation — the emphasis is on security of tenure to promote better construction and maintenance of tenements by the slum dwellers.

Conclusion

Since the early 20th century, there has been an awareness of the existence of slums and squatter settlements in the large cities of India. An attempt to identify slums started only with the slum areas legislation (Improvement and Clearance Act) of 1956. As yet, not all the states have completed the goal of slum identification in their cities. However, various organizations, such as the National Sample Survey, Town and Country Planning Organization, National Building Organization and the working group established by the Planning Commission, have estimated the slum population of India as 20 percent of the total urban population. This percentage is likely to go up to 25 percent by the year 2000 when the slum population will reach 78 million. The concentration of slum population is related to the degree of urbanization which indicates that construction of houses is not in proportion to the rush of migrants to the urban centers. A profile of various characteristics of slums indicates that the density of slum population and the average household size are greater in the small cities than in the large cities. Not more than 50 percent of the slum dwellers own the tenements in which they live. Almost 50 percent of the structures have either *kacha* walls or roofs. Nearly 90 percent of the structures do not have a separate latrine. Lack of underground sewerage facilities and exposure to flooding during the monsoons are almost universal. The only facilities provided on a large scale are electricity, drinking water, an access road, and garbage disposal facility under the Minimum Needs Program and Environmental Improvement of Urban Slums schemes of the central government.

Various slum improvement strategies have been introduced such as provision of built-in tenements, site and service scheme, in-site service scheme, and environment improvement program. In addition, financial assistance is provided to slum dwellers for improvement of their shelters. Per capita expenditure is earmarked for slum environment improvement by the state authorities. Despite all efforts, the problems of slums and squatters in India have been approached only marginally.

END NOTES

[1]Government of India, Ministry of Law, Justice and Company Affairs. *The Slum Areas (Improvement and Clearance) Act, 1956* (96 of 1956). As modified up to October 1, 1981, New Delhi, 1981, p. 2.

[2]Girish K. Mishra and Rakesh Gupta. *Resettlement Policies in Delhi* (New Delhi: Indian Institute of Public Administration, 1981), pp. 1-25.

[3]Government of India, Planning Commission. *Shelter for the Urban Poor and Slum Improvement IV*, New Delhi, September, 1983, pp. 11-23.

[4]Sudesh Nangia. *Innovative Approaches to Help Slum, Squatter and Rural Households Improve Their Dwellings in India.* Monograph prepared for ESCAP/UNIDO, Division of Industry, Human Settlement and Technology, Bangkok, March, 1984, pp. 7-10.

[5]Government of India, Ministry of Works and Housing. *New 20 Point Programme*, New Delhi, July 19, 1984, pp. 4-7.

[6]Dogra Bharat, "Housing the Urban Poor: Demolition by Another Name," *Business Standard* (Aug. 3 1984).

[7]"Slum Improvement Scheme Reviewed," *Employment News*, Vol. IX, No. 21, Saturday, August 25, 1984, p. 3.

13

The Morphology of a Temple Town Center: Madurai, India, 1975

Allen G. Noble, Ashok K. Dutt, and Charles B. Monroe

Madurai is one of the important pilgrimage centers of India. The city, named after the famous north Indian Hindu pilgrim site of Mathura, became the southern capital of the Pandya kingdom well before the Christian era. Ptolemy mentions it as Modoura.[1] Though for a short while (1327 to 1372) the city was subjected to the Muslim rule of the Delhi-based Tughluqs,[2] it has remained essentially a Hindu sacred place for almost 2,000 years. The great Meenakshi temple complex, built largely in the 17th century by the Hindu Nayaka kings, dominates not only the city landscape, but also the orientation and economy of the city. The goddess Meenakshi (a form of Parbati, one of the most powerful of Hindu goddesses), the namesake of the temple complex, according to Hindu mythology was the betrothed of the god, Sundareswar (a south Indian form of Siva, one of the two main gods of the religion). Their marriage was not performed, however, because her maternal uncle could not arrive on time. As a matter of fact, the union eternally awaits consummation, a fact symbolically depicted by the residence of Meenakshi and Siva in separate temples within the complex.[3] Pilgrims come to the temple complex from the entire Indian subcontinent, and especially from the densely populated plains of Tamilnadu, to worship at the twin shrines of Meenakshi and Sundareswar. Such a large influx of visitors is reflected in certain of the activities carried on in the central business district area of Madurai which surrounds the temple complex.

Structure of the City

Though the original settlement on the south bank of the river Vaigai existed as early as the first century,[4] the present city traces its establishment to the Vijayanagara Empire (about 1450). The city began to assume its present form only in the following century under the Nayaka kings (Fig. 13.1). At this time extensive double walls were constructed to enclose the city which had grown up with the Meenakshi temple at its center. The present pattern of streets reflects the location not only of these walls but earlier ones as well, giving the inner city a series of concentric streets (Fig. 13.2). The outer-most set (the Veli streets), constructed in the second quarter of the 19th century with the demolition of the last and largest series of walls and moats, is taken in this study as the boundary of the city center. The present-day city of Madurai extends well beyond these streets through the establishment of residential extensions and the location of large mills and factories with associated worker residences.

Madurai has also spread across the river Vaigai. Initially, this was a result of the establishment of the British Civil Station in the 19th century. In the British view, the wide but easily bridged river provided a desirable boundary between the native Madurai settlement and the largely European station. The sparsely settled land of the Civil Station provided ample room for large bungalows set in spacious, walled compounds. The population density in the Civil Station remains much lower than south of the river, streets are often tree lined and there is far less congestion. Public, administrative and recreational facilities characterize the Civil Station. Among the more important are the women's college, the government hospital, the American college, the Collector's Office, the medical school, the old race course, the English club, Lady Doak College, the Cosmopolitan Club, the government tourist bungalow, the Pandian Hotel and the Gandhi museum.

Thus, in its layout, Madurai follows closely the pattern of many other Indian cities — a crowded, congested indigenous city, coupled with a much more open, essentially European-created, administrative center.[5] Adhering to the traditional Indian city model described by Dutt,[6] the city center is not only the main activity place of the people from within and outside the city, but also has a much higher density of population compared to the peripheral area. Commodity sale and related retail trades comprise the main

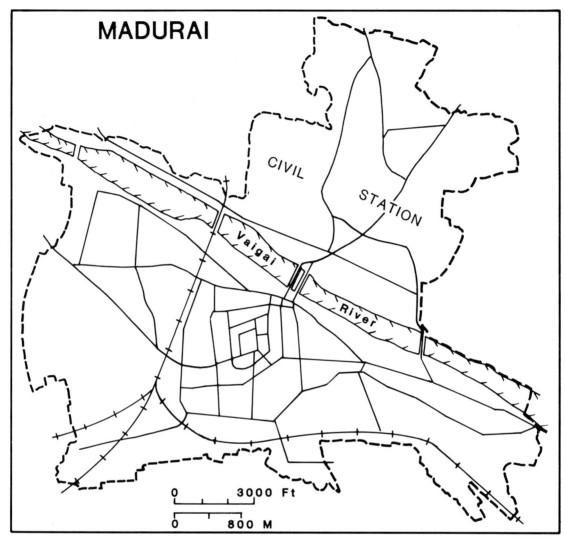

Fig. 13.1   General map of Madurai, India.

activities of the center. The intersection immediately to the south of the Meenakshi Temple is the focal point of activity. Throughout the city center are the houses of the wealthy merchants, who often live in dwellings above or behind their shops.

What sets Madurai apart from most other traditional Indian cities is the importance of the Meenakshi Temple. The temple directly affects the composition and location of business activities in central Madurai. Within the temple precincts are a number of small scale vendors who offer a range of goods consumed in various ceremonies, or which are left at the numerous shrines of the temple as offerings to the gods. Additionally, some vendors, especially flower sellers, congregate along the outside of the temple compound wall. The items which all these vendors sell are referred to as "archana goods" (offerings for the gods). One can also find astrologers and fortune tellers along the temple compound wall. None of these individuals, who often occupy shifting locations, has been included in the survey of city center activities discussed below. Our attention has been focused on "permanent" activities, in fixed locations outside the temple.

Madurai center is not only a central place that serves the city and city region, but it also caters to the retail, wholesale and service activities of the temple and its pilgrims. Thus the center has generated an activity pattern related both to the temple and to the traditional city.

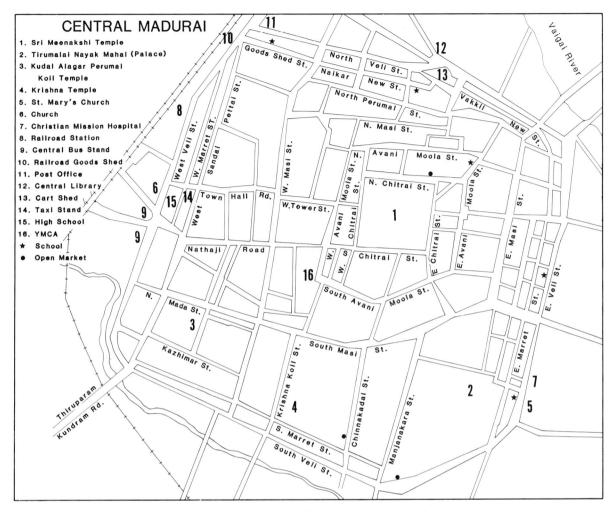

Fig. 13.2 Madurai: Concentric street patterns and public administrative facilities.

Methodology

A property-by-property census was taken in 1975 for the area within the limits of the former wall, i.e., the area designated as the city center in this study. The 62 types of commercial service and other activities identified by this survey were reduced to 14 categories in order to highlight the influence of the temple on the activity pattern of the city (Table 13.1). Each category of activity was then plotted on dot maps. The patterns of distribution are described and explained in the following sections. The discussion, however, does not shed much light on the tendency of some businesses to cluster. To investigate this aspect, two qualitative indices are calculated for each business activity: the areal mean or geographic centroid, and the standard distance or index of dispersion about the centroid. For each business activity the individual establishments were placed on an X-Y grid system and horizontal (X) and vertical (Y) coordinates measured (Table 13.2). Both indices were calculated using these coordinate pairs (X,Y).

The areal mean was determined in each activity using the following formula:

$$\overline{X} = \sum_{i=1}^{N} X_i / N \qquad\qquad \overline{Y} = \sum_{i=1}^{N} Y_i / N$$

Xi = horizontal coordinate value for ith establishment
Yi = vertical coordinate value for the ith establishment
N = the number of establishments

146

TABLE 13.1

Census of Commercial Properties, Madurai Center, 1975

		Number	% of Total
Temple Oriented Businesses		33	2.4
Archana Goods	5		
Coconut Shops	2		
Fruit Stalls	14		
Flower Stalls	12		
Travel Oriented Businesses		122	8.7
Travel Agencies	23		
Lodges	42		
Choultries	2		
Khadi Crafts Stores	2		
Jewellers and Goldsmiths	53		
Vehicle Oriented Businesses		81	5.8
Lorry Sheds	8		
Auto Repair Works	33		
Auto Spare Parts Stores	40		
Wholesale or Bulk Businesses		74	5.3
Grain Stores	40		
Fertilizer Stores	6		
Gunny Bag Stores	3		
Coconut Mandis	2		
Fruit Godowns	7		
Grocery Mandis	16		
Construction Materials Businesses		80	5.7
Timber Stores	14		
Tile Stores	3		
Glass and Mirror Stores	2		
Paint Shops	22		
Electrical Shops	15		
Hardware Stores	24		
Food Oriented Businesses		164	11.7
Groceries	82		
Super Markets	3		
Bakeries	24		
Sweet Stalls	32		
Four Mills	6		
Oil Mills	4		
Vegetable Stalls	13		

	Number	% of Total
Restaurants	110	7.9
Utensil and Household Goods Suppliers	36	2.6
Plastic Goods 7		
Aluminum Vessels 10		
Tin Ware 17		
Coir Stores 2		
Clothing Oriented Businesses	184	13.2
Textile and Clothing 141		
Footware Stores 17		
Tailor Shops 18		
Dry Cleaners 8		
Medical Oriented Activities	76	5.4
Clinics 61		
Chemists (Drug Stores) 13		
Country Drugs 2		
Offices and Office Related Activities	74	5.3
Offices 19		
Banks 16		
Typists 3		
Stationery Stores 36		
Economy Related Activites	73	5.2
Pawn Shops 31		
Fancy Goods 10		
Perfumeries 2		
Hair Salons 5		
Photo Studios 9		
Optical Goods 9		
Watch Repair Shops 7		
Miscellaneous Activities	288	20.6
Theaters 5		
Printing 10		
Leather Goods 3		
Umbrella Shops 2		
Service Establishments 206		
General Stores 62		
Vacant Premises	4	0.3
TOTAL PROPERTIES	1398	100.1

Source: Field Survey, 1975

TABLE 13.2

Number, distance and mean distance (centroid) of business activities, Madurai Center, 1975

		N	**X**	**Y**	**STD**
1	Construction Materials Stores	3	2175	1354	5.12
2	Gunny Bag Stores	3	2717	1145	7.45
3	Coconut Mandis	2	2619	1197	10.12
4	Country Drugs	2	2590	1087	13.04
5	Khadi Crafts Stores	2	2115	1131	15.53
6	Choultries	2	2064	1204	18.82
7	Archana Goods	5	2580	1084	22.06
8	Fruit Godowns	7	2644	1248	22.76
9	Coconut Shops	2	2613	1073	26.08
10	Umbrella Shop	2	2517	1098	28.28
11	Coir Stores	2	2601	1143	30.10
12	Super Markets	3	2623	913	34.88
13	Typists	3	2623	1036	41.69
14	Glass/Mirror Stores	2	2634	1050	47.21
15	Optical Goods	9	2185	1105	55.78
16	Jewelry Stores	53	2377	956	67.57
17	Vacant Premises	4	2322	1342	71.08
18	Leather Goods	3	2370	1037	72.26
19	Vegetable Stalls	13	2474	1188	74.52
20	Plastic Goods	7	2514	1107	87.32
21	Lorry Sheds	8	2432	691	90.29
22	Aluminum Vessels	10	2471	1053	93.64
23	Oil Mills	4	2607	1094	113.30
24	Fruit Stalls	14	2533	1164	113.54
25	Fancy Goods	10	2202	1104	120.55
26	Auto Spare Parts Store	40	2378	1321	136.42
27	Hair Salons	5	2527	1250	142.87
28	Chemists (Drug Stores)	13	2453	1256	145.13
29	Flour Mills	6	2165	982	151.34

		N	**X**	**Y**	**STD**
30	Pawn Shops	31	2250	910	158.55
31	Grocery Mandis	16	2597	1001	173.44
32	Dry Cleaners	8	2288	1040	190.10
33	Fertilizer Stores	6	2665	987	198.99
34	Printing Stores	10	2390	1118	203.64
35	General Stores	62	2433	1064	205.15
36	Textiles/Clothing	141	2392	1008	210.02
37	Watch Repair Shops	7	2234	892	210.22
38	Auto Repair Works	33	2464	1258	212.98
39	Stationery Stores	36	2392	1044	220.62
40	Theaters	5	2391	1120	221.01
41	Perfumeries	2	2374	1086	225.12
42	Banks	16	2312	1158	226.80
43	Lodges	42	2220	1092	228.22
44	Photo Studios	9	2315	1016	228.73
45	Flower Stalls	12	2406	1004	230.87
46	Paint Shops	21	2305	973	230.87
47	Travel Agencies	23	2308	1131	233.24
48	Electrical Shops	15	2349	1129	237.46
49	Restaurants	110	2350	1038	245.04
50	Offices	19	2312	1134	248.00
51	Footware Stores	17	2358	1039	249.06
52	Hardware Stores	24	2426	980	251.76
53	Bakeries	24	2319	1114	252.02
54	Grain Stores	40	2576	959	259.33
55	Service Establishments	206	2341	1019	260.47
56	Sweet Stalls	32	2286	1108	262.88
57	Grocery Stores	82	2449	1037	263.42
58	Tailor Shops	18	2318	964	266.47
59	Tin Ware	17	2344	984	272.16
60	Clinics	61	2415	1024	278.96
61	Timber Stores	14	2251	1070	281.49
62	Residential Locations	560	2327	1012	289.90

150

The mean coordinates (X,Y) can be plotted on the grid (map) to represent the spatial location of the geographic centroid for the set of establishments. This point does not necessarily represent the location where most establishments are found, however. It merely represents the geographic center, or center of gravity, for the spatial distribution (Fig. 13.3).

The standard distance or index of dispersion is calculated using the areal mean, as follows:

$$SD = \sqrt{\left[\sum_{I=1}^{N}(X_I-\overline{X})+\Sigma(Y_I-\overline{Y})\right]/N}$$

Standard distance values represent the relative deviation of the individual establishments of a particular activity from its geographic centroid. The index value is relative to the scale of the coordinate system but is uniform for all the activities mapped in Madurai.

When the standard distance has a relatively small value, the establishments will cluster close to the geographic centroid, whereas a large dispersion value will be produced when the establishments show much variability about the centroid. In this manner, the standard distance index indicates how accurate

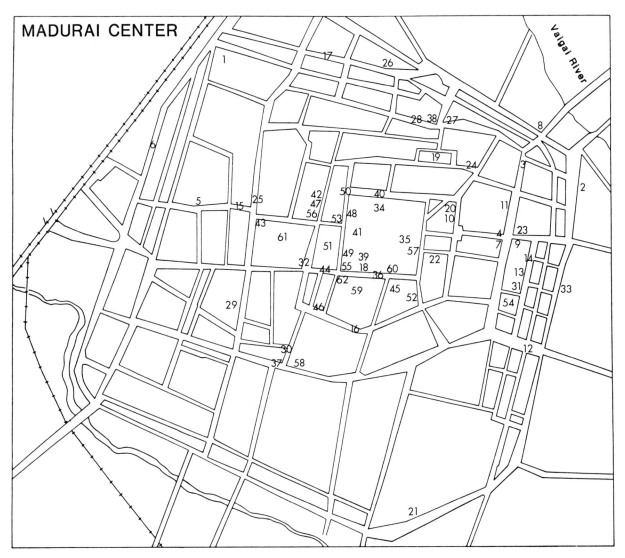

Fig. 13.3   Madurai: Centroids of businesses.

the centroid is in representing the location pattern of the establishments. The lower the value, the more accurate the mean summarizes the geographic pattern. Clustering tendencies and patterns are discussed in the final section of the chapter

Temple-Oriented Business

Certain facilities and locations within the center act as magnets for particular kinds of commercial activity (Fig. 13.2). The Meenakshi Temple is the most obvious such facility. Because of the large number of visitors to the temple, a number of shops, in addition to the vendors inside and along the walls of the temple, offer archana goods, i.e., fruits, flowers and coconuts, all of which are used as religious offerings (Fig. 13.4).

The main entrance of the temple is to the east, opposite Swami Sannathi Street, and it is along this street that activities of this category are clustered. Some flower stalls also occur in other parts of the center, especially along Nathaji Road, which connects the central bus stand with the temple and is a principal route for pilgrims (Fig. 13.5). Other religious centers and the hospital do not affect the location of flower stalls. Two flower stalls near the southern edge of the center are in proximity to one of the open markets where fruits, vegetables, fresh meat, grains and other items are sold. This proximity may explain the occurrence of the flower stalls, enabling shoppers to buy flowers at the same time food and other household items are purchased at the neighboring market.

The largest concentration of fruit stalls lies only two blocks away from the temple entrance in the northeast corner of the center, where 10 such premises occur in a single block. Such a location is midway between the temple and the river Vaigai and is explained by the practice of the large number of pilgrims who take a ritual dip in the river to cleanse themselves before making offerings at the temple. The pilgrims offer fruits including coconuts to temple gods. A part of the offering called *prasad* is supposedly touched by these gods and is, therefore, considered sacred. Subsequently, *prasad* is brought home to be

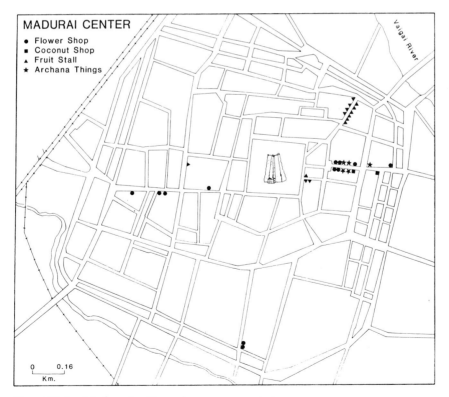

Fig. 13.4 Madurai: Temple-oriented businesses.

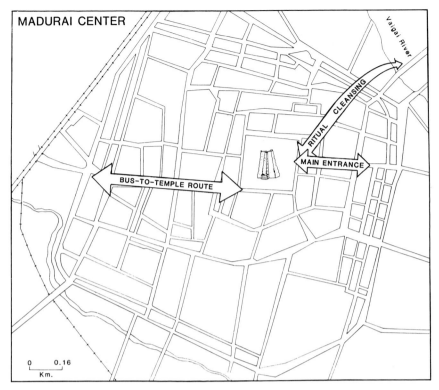

Fig. 13.5 Dynamics of temple-
oriented business locations.

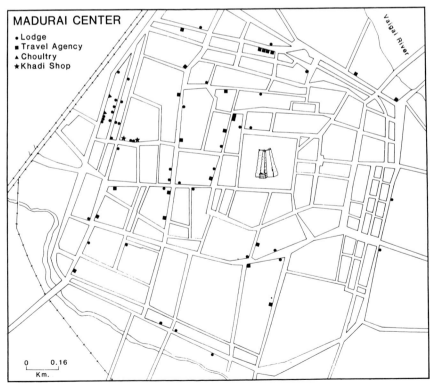

Fig. 13.6 Madurai: Travel-
oriented businesses.

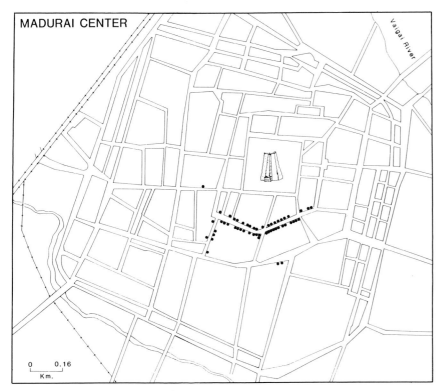

Fig. 13.7 Madurai: Jewelry shops
and goldsmiths.

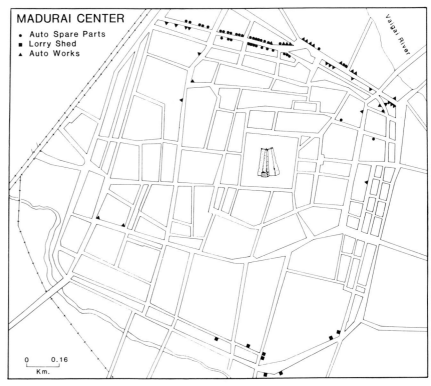

Fig. 13.8 Madurai: Vehicle-
oriented businesses.

shared by family members. The archana goods and flowers are used in the process of worship, and parts of the flower touched by the gods are also considered sacred and are brought home.

Shops selling archana goods, coconuts, fruit or flowers account for only 2.4 percent of all stores in the center. The number would be significantly greater if the temple vendors had been included, however. They were excluded because they were not permanently structured establishments.

Travel Oriented Businesses

The location of travel agencies is given in Figure 13.6. The pattern appears to have little direct relationship to the location of travel facilities, such as the railway station or the central bus station (Fig. 13.2). Perhaps this is not surprising, since the services of travel agencies are used mostly by local residents planning travel out of Madurai. At the same time, few travel agencies are situated in the eastern part of the center furthest away from the travel facilities.

Lodges and *choultries* are generally distributed in the zone between the railway station and the temple, the natural route followed by the many tourists who arrive by rail (Fig. 13.6). Lodges are small, modest hotels with only the most spartan furnishings, but possessing simple facilities for food preparation. Choultries are even more basic, consisting usually of completely unfurnished rooms where groups of pilgrims can spread mats for sleeping. Western-style hotels in Madurai are limited to the civil station, north of the river.

The two *khadi* goods (native handicrafts) stores lie along Town Hall Road, equally distant from the central bus stand and the railway station, and on the route from them to the temple (Fig. 13.6). These shops frequently are patronized by pilgrims wanting a souvenir of their trip. A location between the travel facilities and the temple seems logical.

Jewelry is another item frequently purchased by pilgrims, or by others in association with religious celebrations. Hence, important pilgrimage temples in India often attract concentrations of goldsmiths and jewelers. In Madurai the shops of these craftsmen show a very strong concentration on South Avani Moola Street (Fig. 13.7). Perhaps the desirability of comparison shopping for items which are of relatively high value for pilgrims with uniformly low incomes encourages the great degree of concentration which these shops demonstrate.

Taken together, travel-oriented businesses make up almost nine percent of the total of all activities found in the Madurai center. Jewelry shops, choultries and khadi stores are highly clustered, but clustering of travel agencies and lodges is less evident.

Vehicle-Oriented Businesses

Businesses oriented to vehicles show a peripheral locational pattern (Fig. 13.8). In part this is because of the larger space required for repairing vehicles and in part because the narrow and indirect streets in the inner areas of the center discourage passage of motor vehicles. Taken together, vehicle-oriented businesses account for just over six percent of all businesses.

Lorry sheds, for the repair of buses and trucks, cluster in the southeastern corner of the center, whereas automobile repair shops occupy the northern fringes. In the latter case, location may be influenced by the higher income residential properties concentrated in the civil station across the river, since higher income families are most apt to own automobiles.

The location of stores selling auto spare parts correlates closely with that of the auto repair shops upon which they depend. There may also be correspondence in the southwestern part of the center where two repair shops and a parts store are close neighbors. Spare parts for lorries are purchased in the auto spare parts stores or they come from outside the center.

No independent gasoline service stations occur in Madurai center, although a few repair facilities sell gasoline. The independent gasoline service stations in Madurai are all located out of the center on the main roads leading into and out of town.

Wholesale or Bulk-Item Businesses

Like the businesses discussed in the previous section, grain stores have peripheral locations (Fig. 13.9). Two distinct clusters can be identified — one occurs in the same area as the lorry sheds, perhaps because of the need for larger premises and ease of accessibility when handling bulk goods. A larger and more concentrated group lies in the northeastern corner of the center. This area is clearly a center for wholesaling activities with fertilizer stores, coconut mandis, fruit godowns, and grocery mandis also concentrated in the area, but each activity is segregated in distinct subdistricts (Fig. 13.10). Also located in the northeast are stores supplying gunny bags. Clearly their location is governed by the presence of businesses handling bulk items.

Construction Materials Businesses

Another group of businesses which frequently deal in bulk commodities are those supplying various construction materials. A high degree of concentration characterizes timber and lumber stores. Two quite distinct clusters exist at opposite sides of the center (Fig. 13.11). In one instance, proximity to the railway may explain the locational pattern and, in the other, nearness to lorry sheds, and hence a different mode of transport, may offer a locational clue.

A strong tendency to cluster also is evident in the case of tile stores and is somewhat less conspicuous with glass and mirror stores. The other types of stores selling construction materials — paint, electrical, and hardware stores — are scattered throughout the center with little evidence of concentration. However, hardware stores are lacking throughout the northwestern quadrant of the center, but no reason is readily apparent.

Food-Oriented Businesses

Food-oriented businesses are numerous (about 12% of all businesses) and show no consistent pattern of distribution or clustering. Grocery stores, which make up about half of this category, are widely scattered but with two areas of above average concentration, one to the northeast and the other to the southwest (Fig. 13.12). The pattern of retail grocery stores helps explain the concentration of grocery godowns in these two directions.

Only three supermarkets serve Madurai and tnese are all close together in the eastern side of the center. Generally speaking, supermarkets are larger than grocery stores and carry a much wider line of goods. They also serve a larger market area than do most grocery stores.

Bakeries and sweet stalls, in contrast to supermarkets, are small-scale operations and sell only perishable products. Hence, there are many more of each of these kinds of stores than supermarkets in Madurai. Furthermore, both types of stores have a scattered locational pattern. A tendency toward a number of small clusters is more evident with sweet stalls than with bakeries.

Two food items which require some processing before sale are cooking oil and flour (Fig. 13.13). Four establishments crush oil seeds and sell the resulting cooking oil on the premises. These small oil mills occur in two pairs, both located on the eastern side of the center. Flour mills are more diffused, but only on the western side of the center. No correlation exists between flour mills (Fig. 13.13) and grain dealers (Fig. 13.9).

Finally, vegetable stalls have a high degree of propinquity, all but one being located along North Avani Moola Street (Fig. 13.13). These stalls are close to the main central market on North Chitrai Street (Fig. 13.2). The other, larger and hence more specialized, vegetable market is in the south of the center on Chinnakadai Street and because of its size may have a negative effect on the location of small individual vegetable stalls in the immediate area (compare Figs. 13.2 and 13.9).

Restaurants

Restaurants are ubiquitous in the Madurai center (Fig. 13.14). Only textile and clothing shops and service establishments exist in greater numbers (see Table 13.1). Furthermore, although several examples may be cited where two restaurants are adjacent to one another, larger clusters are completely

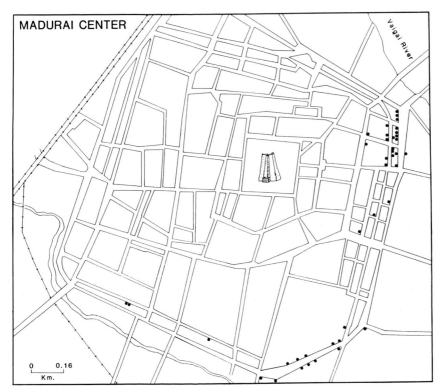

Fig. 13.9   Madurai: Grain stores.

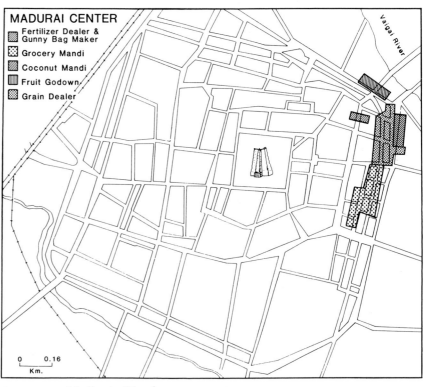

Fig. 13.10   Madurai: Warehouse districts.

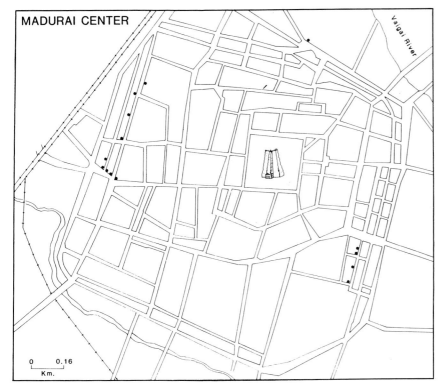

Fig. 13.11 Madurai: Timber and
lumber stores.

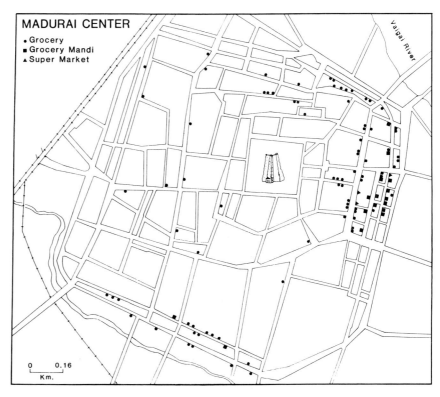

Fig. 13.12 Madurai: Grocery
stores, super markets and grocery
godowns.

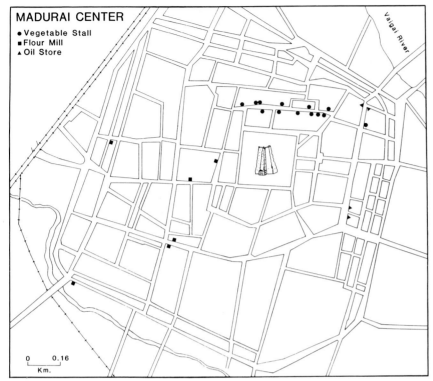

Fig. 13.13   Madurai: Flour mills, oil
stores and vegetable stalls.

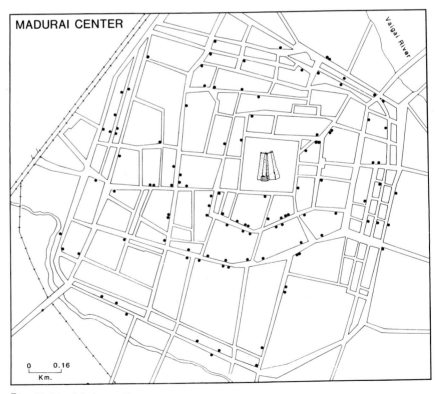

Fig. 13.14   Madurai: Restaurants.

lacking. Facilities, such as the railway station and the bus stand do not appear to attract restaurants as is true in other cultures and towns.

Utensil and Household Goods Suppliers

In contrast to restaurants, stores which supply cooking utensils and related items are all more or less clustered (Fig. 13.15). Plastic goods stores occur to the east of the Meenakshi Temple and their location correlates closely with temple-oriented businesses (Fig. 13.4). Perhaps the reason is that many of these stores sell inexpensive souvenirs purchased by temple visitors, as well as plastic household utensils. The major cluster of stores selling aluminum and other vessels is to the southeast of the temple, although a few such stores have opened elsewhere. Tinware stores occur in two clusters; one on Chinnakadai Street in the south is quite concentrated, with eleven stores in a single block. The other grouping, in the northern part of the center, is much more diffused and contains only six stores. Because of low numbers, little can be said about the location of *coir* shops except that they are near one another and not far from the coconut mandis.

Clothing-Oriented Businesses

Textile and clothing stores are more numerous than other kinds of stores in the Madurai center, except for service establishments. Included within this classification are shops selling yard goods, as well as those which offer ready-made clothing. Despite being widely distributed across the entire center, a tendency to cluster to the east and south of the Meenakshi Temple is evident. In contrast, footwear stores are scattered throughout the center with no apparent clustering. Tailor shops and dry cleaning establishments are also widely diffused.

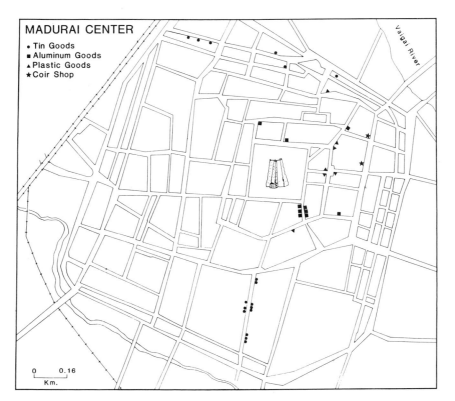

Fig. 13.15 Madurai: Utensil and household goods suppliers.

Medical-Oriented Properties

Medical clinics are located so as to serve the entire center with a minimum of travel by patrons, although an above-average concentration of these clinics occupies the entire eastern side of the center. The two premises where country drugs (homeopathic and aurovedic medicines) are dispensed are close to one another, to the east of the temple. Their location in close proximity to archana goods stores and other temple-oriented businesses may indicate a clientele of rural dwelling pilgrims. Close by, but a little further east, is the smaller of two groupings of chemists (pharmacists). The larger concentration is in the northern part of the center.

Offices and Office-Related Activities

The three public typists in Madurai all have offices on the eastern side of the center. Public typists not only prepare various legal forms and official documents for customers, they also read and prepare letters for those who are illiterate. Often in other Indian cities their offices will be found in proximity to governmental premises such as customs houses, freight depots, and registration offices. In Madurai the rationale for typist locations is not clear.

The pattern of general office locations is dispersed. Included within this classification are advocates' offices as well as a wide variety of business offices. Madurai is not a city of great commercial activity, other than that of commodity trade and retail services. Madurai does not possess a clearly identifiable financial district, although four of the 16 banks in the center are situated across the street from the railway station. This probably indicates that the banks serve the surrounding region as well as the city of Madurai. Stationery and paper products stores do show a tendency to cluster along East Avani Moola Street, where 13 stores, or 36 percent of such stores can be found. Elsewhere, stationery stores are widely dispersed (Fig. 13.16).

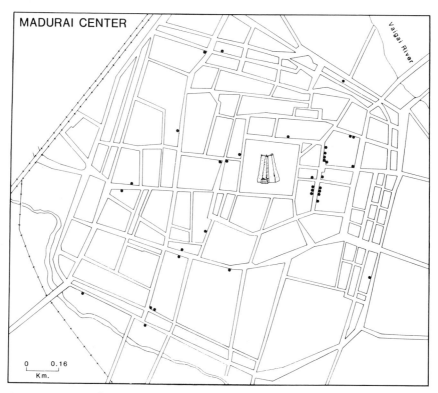

Fig. 13.16 Madurai: Stationery and paper products stores.

Economy Related Activities

This rubric incorporates a number of disparate activities all of which flourish or fail as a result of general economic influences. Pawn shops obviously reflect at least temporary economic misfortune, whereas the other types of shops are a reflection of affluence in varying degrees. The southern and southwestern sections of the center account for most of the pawn shops (Fig. 13.17). West Avani Moola Street and its southern continuation, Krishna Koil Street, have no fewer than 15 pawn shops, almost half the entire number in the center. Little can be said about the locational characteristics of watch repair shops, perfumeries, and hair salons except that in the case of the latter a concentration in the northeastern quadrant of the center is evident. This may result from proximity to the most affluent residential areas of the city which are to the north across the river. Three types of businesses show somewhat similar tendencies to cluster west of the temple (Fig. 13.18). Nine of the ten stores dealing in fancy goods (gifts, toys, baskets, decorations) lie along Town Hall Road and its extension, W. Tower Street. In the same area, but not as concentrated on these particular streets, are photography studios and optical goods stores. That eye glasses remain a luxury item in India is a strong comment on the continuing state of underdevelopment.

Miscellaneous Activities

Finally, certain kinds of commercial activities do not lend themselves to incorporation along with others under any convenient heading. These establishments, which include cinemas, printing shops, leather goods stores and umbrella shops, have been grouped under a miscellaneous heading. The small number of shops for most of these activities precludes a discussion of locational pattern.

Also included within this general category are service establishments (petty stores) and general stores. In the case of the former, these are tiny premises that handle a limited range of convenience and impulse goods such as *pan* (bettle nut), *bidis* (low quality, handmade cigarettes), regular cigarettes, and cold drinks. Petty stores are the most numerous kind of store in Madurai center and are widely and, on the whole, evenly distributed throughout.

General stores comprise two types of establishment. On the one hand are those businesses which offer a widely varying line of goods, so that placing them in a particular category is difficult and would be misleading. The other type of store included under this heading is that which the enumerator could not place within a particular category either because shops were closed and shuttered at the time of the survey or which carried items not readily identifiable.

Patterns of Clustering

The spatial pattern of the retail and service activities in the central area of the city is guided by: (a) historical evolution, (b) transport and accessibility pattern, (c) physical site factors, and d) functional characteristics of the urban area. In the case of Madurai, the historic position of the city wall has determined the location of the city's central area; the river delimited the extent of the central area towards the north; and the siting of the temple, which attracts pilgrims from all over the country, provides a functional base oriented to religion and tourism. The location of the Meenakshi temple over several centuries affected many central place activities on the main roads running around the temple in concentric parallelograms. Ultimately this area became the main concentration of the city's retail and service activities. These four factors have determined the spatial distribution of retail and service activities in Madurai. Four distinct patterns can be identified: (a) concentration in a single node or in a linear grouping, (b) multiple concentrations, (c) a ubiquitous or randomly dispersed pattern, and (d) a mixed pattern combining elements of the first three. These and the resulting variations of pattern are represented as a descriptive model in Figure 13.19.

Certain business activities tend to cluster close to each other to form specialized business areas. For example, the Madurai temple-oriented shops cluster at the northeastern side of the city (Fig. 13.4), whereas the 206 service establishments, 110 restaurants (Fig. 13.14), 82 grocery stores, 32 sweets stalls and 61 clinics are ubiquitously spread over the city because the permanent residents of the city, as well as the pilgrims visiting the city and residing at various lodges and hotels, need their services at decentralized

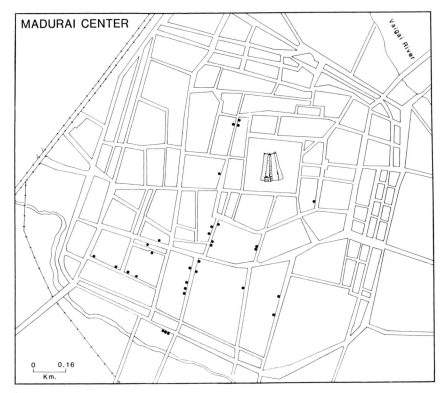

Fig. 13.17 Madurai: Pawn shops.

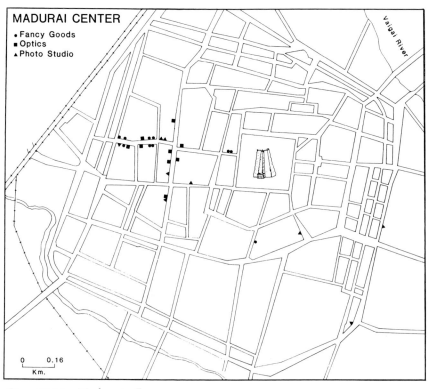

Fig. 13.18 Madurai: Economy-
related businesses.

locations. The indices of concentration indicate a tendency of greater dispersal as the number of shops and establishments increase. This is particularly evident from Pearson's correlation of coefficient value of +.36 (p=.002). However, despite this general tendency, the jewelry stores, (Fig. 13.7), vegetable stalls (Fig. 13.13), aluminum vessel shops (Fig. 13.15), and optical goods stores (Fig. 13.18), have greater concentration though their numbers are relatively larger. Conversely, perfumeries and photography studios have much greater dispersal, despite their lesser number of establishments.

There are two other types of clusterings that need explanation. One is *twin* concentration and the other is *linear*. Chemists, tin, timber and grain stores have twin concentrations (Fig. 13.9) and are at the periphery of the business area core. Their locations are attracted by the ease of accessibility of bulky goods movement. The auto works, auto spare parts, fertilizer stores and grocery warehouses are located in a linear fashion at the eastern margin of the business area (Figs. 13.8, 13.10), only a little north of the lorry sheds. The vegetable stalls, also in a linear fashion, are located only a block from the temple wall in the core of the business area (Fig. 13.13).

Centroids of Commercial Activities

Centroids of each commercial activity were located by plotting mean distance (Fig. 13.3). The attraction of the temple is so great that almost half the centroids fall within a block of the temple walls. The southeast portion of the business area has very few centroids, whereas both northeast and northwest have several centroids forming subsidiary concentrations; five centroids fall between the temple and the railroad station, forming a third subsidiary concentration. The main and subsidiary concentrations of the centroids show that the temple is the city's main business attraction and the three subsidiary concentrations are indicative of secondary level multiple nuclei within the business area.

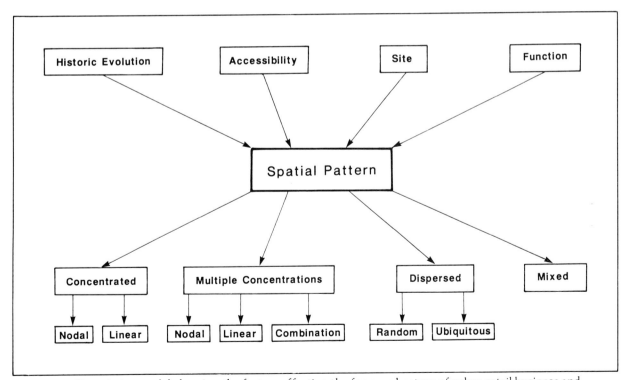

Fig. 13.19 Descriptive model showing the factors affecting the form and nature of urban retail business and service activities and the different forms of variation.

Conclusion

The commercial activities of Madurai serve both local and regional residents as well as pilgrims from a wide area. Certain activities, such as jewelry and temple-oriented shops are concentrated near the temple; but other businesses are located at the periphery of the center. Generally, the shops with larger numbers are more widely dispersed. The temple is the principal attraction of business activity though three subsidiary nuclei have developed within the Madurai center.

The attraction of the temple in locating retail activities is paramount. The location of most centroids supports this argument. The Meenakshi Temple remains the main destination of all pilgrims and, therefore, a retail or service business location near the temple or on the path of the pilgrims to and from the railroad/bus stations, or the bathing *ghat* (concrete steps descending to a water body) of the river remains the strongest locational factor.

Identification of the centroids of different retail and service activities can be used in other cities to determine whether the center of attraction is a single node, or whether multiple nodes operate. Moreover, if such identification is made temporally, shifts or trends of shifts can be recognized, which, of course, has implications for urban planning.

END NOTES

[1]B. N. Puri. *Cities of Ancient India* (Meerut, India: Meenashi Prakashan, 1966), p. 68.

[2]R.C. Mazumdar, (ed.). *The History and Culture of the Indian People: The Delhi Sultanate* (Bombay: Bharatiya Vidya Bhavan, 1960), pp. 61-89.

[3]Benjamin Walker. *The Hindu World* (New York: Frederick A. Praeger, 1968), p. 71.

[4]Attur Ramesh and Allen G. Noble, "Pattern and Process in South Indian Cities," in Allen G. Noble and Ashok K. Dutt, *Indian Urbanization and Planning* (New Delhi: Tata McGraw Hill Publishing Co., 1977), p. 45.

[5]Allen G. Noble, Ashok K. Dutt and G. Venugopal, "Variations in Noise Generation — Bangalore, India," *Geografisca Annaler* (B), (1985), 67:1, 15.

[6]Ashok K. Dutt, "Cities of South Asia," in Stanley D. Brunn and Jack F. Williams, *Cities of the World* (New York: Harper and Row, 1983), pp. 328-9 and 340-4.

Index